# THE
# MOBILE
# LEARNING
# EDGE

# THE MOBILE LEARNING EDGE

TOOLS AND TECHNOLOGIES FOR DEVELOPING YOUR TEAMS

GARY WOODILL, ED.D

*Thanks for the support, John!*
*Gary*

New York   Chicago   San Francisco   Lisbon   London   Madrid   Mexico City
Milan   New Delhi   San Juan   Seoul   Singapore   Sydney   Toronto

The *McGraw·Hill* Companies

1 2 3 4 5 6 7 8 9 10 DOC/DOC 1 9 8 7 6 5 4 3 2 1 0

ISBN 978-0-07-173676-3
MHID 0-07-173676-X

# Contents

# Introduction

The earliest humans were nomads. They used the resources found in the region in which they lived and then moved on to find new places for hunting and gathering what they needed. This changed with the introduction of agriculture and the domestication of animals. Most people became tied to the land, moving within a small geographical area as needed. With the industrial revolution, many people came to spend most of their day in a specific building—a school, a factory, a store, or an office. In short, human history is one of gradual *immobilization* of much of the population.

The digital electronics revolution has changed all that in three important ways. First, through computer networking, the *reach* of an individual has dramatically increased so that she now can connect with almost anyone around the world. Second, as she moves around the world, she can remain *connected* with family, friends, or coworkers—whomever she chooses. These changes already have had an enormous impact on the way we work, relate to others, and play, and they will continue to drive much more change in the near future. Third, *information resources* are available from anywhere at any time; there is usually no need to go to a specific location or person to find out what you need to know.

All this is contributing to changes in the way we educate and train adults. Past practices of training workers in a classroom or on the job are now supplemented by "mobile learning." An employee in training now can get the information he needs about any subject while he is on the move. He is able to change location at will while he is being trained.

This book is a starting guide for anyone in business or other organizations who wants to provide mobile learning to employees. It is not a technical book, or a "how-to" manual. It is, rather, a guide for managers and executives to help them make decisions about mobile learning. Reading it will give you insights into the issues involved and help you build a vocabulary and a set of concepts to use when you talk with the many stakeholders involved in any implementation of mobile learning in a large organization.

In the first chapter, I introduce the concept of mobile learning—its history, definitions, business drivers, business models, benefits, issues, and myths and misconceptions. The advent of mobile computing, and mobile learning in particular, has freed individuals and groups from the necessity of being confined to a specific place in order to work and learn. This momentous change was labeled "the new nomadism" by the *Economist* magazine in 2008. We see the impact that the new nomadism is having on all aspects of life, especially on learning, as we review the statistics on the use of mobile communications devices and plot their phenomenal rise in terms of technologies and applications. These changes have been taking place over a period of about 10 years, so I truly believe that mobile learning has now come of age.

In the past, distinctions between adult students and nonstudents were fairly clear. The reality today is that many full-time students are also part-time workers, and many full-time workers are also part-time students. In a recent study of workers who are also going to university, Siebert et al. (2009) found that "work-based learners learn effectively from both their community of practice in the workplace and their learning group of work-based learners within the university. . . . [A] learning group experience is valued highly by work-based students and . . . dialogue with other students in the learning group appears to make a significant contribution to enhancing their knowledge."

It is clear from the Siebert et al. study that the applications for mobile learning that are currently in use in higher education and professional schools also have utility for workplace learning. Such changes are bound to have a major impact on the formal educational system and on employee training. To understand all the factors that affect the development and provision of mobile learning, I portray mobile learning as an "ecosystem" in Chapter 2. This ecosystem is made up of various forms of mobility, hundreds of different mobile learning devices, tens of thousands of educational applications, and an infrastructure made up of networks, government regulations, and the commercial interests of various "carriers." Navigating all these are mobile learners as well as instructional designers, training executives, and instructors who support mobile learning; each group has its own needs and characteristics.

Mobile learning is *not* the same as e-learning, and in Chapter 3 I present seven principles related to learning methods that are relevant for mobile learning. These methods take into account the unique characteristics of the mobile learning ecosystem. In seeking to understand mobile learning, it is useful to apply principles taken from relevant general learning theories to mobile learning development. Mobile learning involves the senses, the surrounding context of the learner, and the network to which he is connected. From a business perspective, however, we also need to take a closer look at how mobile learning can be aligned with business objectives and strategies.

Chapters 4 to 6 present new applications of mobile learning in organizational settings. Many new uses are being invented daily as programmers and designers produce a wide variety of applications for the leading smartphone operating systems. By mid-2010, for example, over 200,000 iPhone applications ("apps") were listed on the Apple Web site. A relatively small percentage of these are "educational applications" of interest to trainers looking for inexpensive mobile training content. In Chapters 4 through 6 I also break down the uses of mobile learning into more than 50 distinct possibilities, ranging from assessments to wearable computing. I discuss these applications in terms of their general educational usefulness and their potential for application in business and training environments.

Mobile learning is relevant to managers, not just to workers. Chapter 7 reviews the various ways that management can use mobile learning, from alerts in emergencies to reporting results in a learning management system. I contrast the management of mobile learners using desktop software, with the use of mobile technologies to manage learners no matter where they are located.

Unfortunately, mobile learning (and mobile computing in general) is in a state of constant flux with new developments appearing on a weekly basis. If you plan to undertake a comprehensive strategic initiative to use mobile learning in your business, you need to develop a future-oriented strategy. This means anticipating trends and technology lifecycles, and having a sense of what might be coming in mobile learning in the next five years. This is the topic of Chapter 8 where my former colleague, David Fell, discusses the possible future(s) of mobile learning and how to construct various scenarios to plan for different contingencies. Working through the suggestions in this chapter will prepare you for unexpected developments that can change the game as well as guide you through the changes that are likely to come.

In Chapter 9, I tackle the question of how to create learning content (both learning materials and experiences) for mobile learning in businesses of various sizes. In order to design for competitive advantage, you must understand innovation processes so that the results of your work will stand the test of time when further innovations become available. There are many variables to consider and recommended processes to follow. In this chapter I go beyond applications and content to look at how to create engaging and productive mobile learning experiences.

Once a design document has been produced, there is a development process to create mobile learning content and experiences. This process follows best practices for software development and project management. There are important tools to discuss that make the job of creating content easier. However, if you don't want to create mobile learning content yourself, you can select and work with a custom content development company or convert existing materials from a variety of mobile devices.

Mobile learning can't be introduced into large enterprises on an ad hoc basis without creating a good deal of disruption. In Chapter 10, Sheryl Herle presents the process of planning, implementing, and managing an enterprise-level mobile learning network. It begins with the articulation of a vision for mobile learning and its role in the business. This means identifying all stakeholders and carrying out a comprehensive requirements analysis in order to produce an action plan. The implementation of a mobile learning plan should follow the principles of good project management. This includes being prepared to manage unexpected changes and events. Quality assurance methods and evaluations of the implementation at all stages need to be carried out. Once a system has been set up, there are the issues of control and governance of mobile learning; how is this all going to work, and who is going to be in charge of decision making?

This book also contains an appendix of resources that will help you to extend your knowledge of mobile learning. There are associations to join, blogs and Web sites to engage, conferences to attend, and publications to explore. Finally, I provide an extensive bibliography of all the references I used in this book, as well as a list of additional articles and books that will give you more depth of knowledge in this emerging field.

Because lots of changes are likely over the life cycle of this book, I will maintain a companion Web site at http://mobilelearningedge.com. Please visit this site to get frequent updates, to leave your comments, and to let me know what you see coming next in mobile learning. Mobile learning is a two-way street; I will give you my best knowledge and hope that you will respond with suggestions about what I have missed and questions that I can answer on the Web site and in the next edition of this book.

# Acknowledgments

I first started to use a mobile device for my personal learning in 1998 when I acquired my first BlackBerry. Many people have helped increase my knowledge of mobile learning along the way, too numerous to mention them all. But, some people deserve special recognition.

First, a special thank you to David Fell and Sheryl Herle for each writing a chapter in this book in their area of expertise. David Fell, the CEO of a regional high speed broadband network being built in Canada, used his newly minted MBA to offer insights into how to develop a business strategy for mobile learning. Sheryl Herle, an industry consultant with over 15 years of experience in implementation and governance of learning technologies in large enterprises, including mobile systems, grapples with the critical decisions that companies must make in order to have mobile learning work for them.

There are others in the learning and development industry who have been particularly helpful in my search for information on the direction of mobile learning. Thank you to all those who gave me permission to use images and/or case studies in this book. In particular, Robert Gadd and Katherine Guest generously supplied various kinds of materials that appear in different sections. Clark Quinn, who is writing his own book on mobile learning, offered me helpful references and advice. Frank De Stefano, Creative Director at Communica Inc. in Montreal, designed the illustrations used throughout the book.

David Metcalf and his students at the University of Central Florida have generously given me their time and PowerPoint slides on mobile learning in order to further my own education and that of others. Mary Meyers and Rob Pearson at Maritz Canada showed me some of the earliest mobile learning materials for sales training on a BlackBerry that is available. Judy Brown's mLearnopedia blog and aggregator have supplied me with lots of leads to follow in researching this book. Stephen Downes' daily newsletter on e-learning (*OLDaily*) covers mobile learning as well, and has been a steady source of new ideas and information.

For the past four years I have worked with Brandon Hall Research, where I learned a great deal from my generous colleagues, who have all been supportive of this work. In 2008, I had the opportunity to write a series of research reports on mobile learning, in which I described mobile learning as coming of age. A special thank you to Janet Clarey, who led the cultural changes at Brandon Hall Research that resulted in all of us using social media on a daily basis, including blogs, Twitter, and Facebook.

It was my Brandon Hall Research reports on mobile learning that interested Emily Carleton, the editor at McGraw-Hill who signed me up for this project and helpfully supervised its first stages. Other McGraw-Hill staff were very helpful in getting this book to final publication. Thank you to Peter McCurdy for guiding the manuscript through the various stages of development, and to Daina Penikas and Mary Therese Church for seeing the manuscript through its final production stages. Thank you to Roberta Mantus, the very capable copy editor for the book.

Finally, I would note that my wife, Karen Anderson, is a true practitioner of mobile learning, given that we have moved 11 times in our 27 year marriage. More seriously, Karen was, as usual, a constant support, my first editor, and a source of materials, in spite of the fact that during this period, she was also writing her own book on sociology. Thank you, Karen.

# The Emerging Field of Mobile Learning

I live in the country in an old house overlooking a 23 mile-long lake. Occasionally I take the train to the big city about an hour away. During this pleasant trip I'm able to enjoy a cup of tea and to work on my laptop, with satellite access to the Internet. This means I can prepare for meetings later in the day, and can look up information I need in order to have fruitful discussions with the people I'm meeting. While I'm searching for a statistic, I spot an article on a breakthrough in solar power transmission. I read it. I'm learning as the train moves.

> "All learning is mobile."
> —*Tétard et al. (2008)*

A young woman on vacation with her family in Florida goes to the Cocoa Beach pier. She watches the surfers paddling their boards out into the swells waiting for the perfect wave in order to stand up and enjoy a few seconds of freedom that comes from riding the waves. After a while, she turns her attention to the pier itself. It is made of wood and is anchored in concrete pilings that rise above the water. Curious about how and when the pier was built, she takes out her smartphone and starts its Web browser. While standing and listening to the ocean, she discovers that Cocoa Beach itself was founded by freed slaves after the American Civil War. She also learns that the pier was built in 1925.

The CEO of a large bank and the architect for its new headquarters meet at the building site to examine the progress for the planned tower. The architect, who has previously loaded "augmented reality" software into her mobile phone, points it toward the large excavation just in front of where she and her client are standing. The phone "knows" exactly where it is located and in which direction it is pointing. It takes a picture of the excavation and then superimposes, to scale, a picture of the tower as it will look when it is finished. The CEO is impressed, and more importantly, now has a very good idea of how the tower will look in relation to its surroundings.

These are just a few of the exciting ways mobile learning can improve our lives. The first phase of MOBIlearn, a European program for supporting mobile learning in the workplace that involved over 1,000 work-based learners, found that learners and their trainers used mobile technologies for all of the following activities:

- Learners communicated with peers, tutors, and assessors.
- Learners collected video, audio, and photographic evidence for their portfolios.
- Tutors and assessors assessed portfolio evidence and provided feedback.
- Learners gained access to learning content through the virtual learning environment or the Internet.
- Additional resources and instructional materials were provided through videos.
- Learners completed "written" work using Internet access for research, and they used software to type up their tasks or assignments. (Savill-Smith, 2009)

In this book, I provide over 50 different ways that learning technologies can work with "learners on the move," giving them up-to-date, personalized, and relevant information when they need it. Many people, especially in the business world, have not even heard of mobile learning. Its development over the past two decades has mostly taken place in the context of mobile teaching for K-12 schools or higher education. This book is among the very first to look at the application of mobile learning in businesses and large organizations, and to address how mobile learning can provide many businesses with a competitive edge. There are powerful business drivers pushing mobile technologies as a replacement for traditional classroom-based training in order to create a workforce that is more efficient, flexible, and informed.

## The New Nomads

For the past several hundred years most of us in Western societies have been bound to a series of places. We have a place to sleep, eat, and be with our families called home; we have a place where we go to earn money called the workplace; we have places we go to learn called schools or universities; and we have places to go for enjoyment such as movie theaters, sports centers, or "the great outdoors."

All this is changing with something that *Economist* magazine calls "the new nomadism" (*Economist*, 2008), where we are constantly on the move physically, but still also connected to our friends, families, and workplace(s). Bryan Alexander remarked on this phenomenon on college campuses as early as 2004 when he wrote: ". . . since this technology is mobile, students turn 'nomad,' carrying conversations and thinking across campus spaces, as always, but now with the ability to Google a professor's term, upload a comment to a class board, and check for updates to today's third assignment—all while striding across the quad" (Alexander, 2004). Today, we are all nomads. For many people, such as sales staff, transportation personnel, and top-tier executives, being mobile is the very essence of their work environments. And, for most of us, commuting to work is an unavoidable fact of life and takes up a significant part of the day.

What makes us successful nomads is not the fact that most of us these days are equipped, from our early teen years, with several mobile devices, but that all these devices are now connected from almost any physical place we want to be, as long as they are in range of mobile phone services. It is *mobile connectivity* that allows us to move around freely and still have all the lines of communication open wherever we might be located physically. We can become so used to being connected all the time that we become anxious if our batteries run out of power, or if we can't locate our mobile phone—a condition referred to as "nomophobia."

Relatively seamless mobile connectivity is now available on trains in Europe and North America (*Economist,* 2006), and recently became available in flight on selected airlines. In these cases it is the user's environment that is mobile and connected, allowing interaction with mobile devices such as notebook computers and smartphones.

John Traxler (2009a) has noted that "mobile technologies . . . alter the nature of work . . . especially of knowledge work." These new technologies alter the balance between the need for training and performance support, and the provision of these services through traditional means. Traxler adds that "mobile learning is emerging as an entirely new and distinct concept." Of course businesses, and even departments within a business, vary greatly in terms of their mobility needs. In some businesses, such as delivery services, workers are mostly nomadic. In other businesses, most workers are sedentary—for example, employees at a call center usually do not move around while they work. It is important, therefore, to analyze the mobility profile of your company before you undertake to deliver mobile learning in a systematic way. Even in businesses where employees stay in one place, mobile learning can be used when workers are not at their workplace. The need for speedier training is one of the main drivers for the development of mobile learning. Unlike in past decades, there are simply fewer opportunities to take time out for training. But the increased demand on workers for higher levels of performance also means that the relatively small amount of time set aside for training often takes a backseat to the need to meet production goals. Hypercompetition and the resulting demand for multitasking means that companies are often constrained to do more with fewer people. The result is less and less available time for training. In 2005, for example, it was estimated that the average number of training days completed in the United States "per person per year" was down to two days (Edwards, 2005). All this means that training often has to be done "on the fly" or outside work environments. Mobile learning provides a solution to which many companies are turning.

 ## A Brief History of Mobile Computing

The history of mobile computing is the amalgamation of three separate historical threads—the history of telecommunications, the history of radio, and the history of computing. It is not my purpose in this book to present these histories, but only to note some milestones along the way (Fig. 1.1). Technologies like the telegraph (both wired and wireless), the telephone, and radio needed to be in place before mobile communications could be developed. Like many innovations, the invention of mobile phones was a "mashup" of several separate technologies that came before.

In 1906 Lee de Forest, a radio engineer, sent a radio message to an experimental phone in a car idling on a street in New York City. In 1910, in Sweden, electrical engineer Lars Magnus Ericsson, who had retired from the telegraph and telephone business, built a telephone into his wife Hilda's car. The phone in the vehicle was connected by wires and poles to the overhead telephone lines that were spreading through the Swedish countryside. The power for the telephone was generated by cranking a handle. It wasn't a mobile phone, but it was one of the earliest examples of getting a phone out of a static location and moving around with it (Agar, 2005).

In 1946 a "mobile telephone service" was launched by AT&T in the United States using bulky radiotelephones where only one person could speak at a time. These were expensive accessories for cars, trains, and boats that only a few companies could afford. The first of these phones weighed 76 pounds and could be considered "mobile" only in the sense that they were installed in various modes of transportation and not because they were actually portable. By the early 1970s, various companies in the United States and Europe had pioneered cell phone technologies, bringing to the public true mobile phones that actually worked while their owners walked down a city street. Dr. Martin Cooper, a research scientist at Motorola, made the first "cell phone" call from a New York street in 1973 (Fig. 1.2). The first cell phone network was set up in Tokyo in 1979.

Within businesses, however, the adoption of mobile computing has been a relatively slow process. Even today, a company-provided mobile phone is often seen as a status symbol rather than a necessary business tool. Changing corporate culture isn't easy.

Commercial enterprises organized as corporations have been around for a few hundred years. Their form and processes have been described and studied in detail. Up until the end of the 1960s, people "going into business" would have been expected to start at a relatively low status position and then to work their way up through the ranks until they rose to their highest level of competence. The famous "Peter Principle" notwithstanding (i.e., that they would rise to their level of incompetence), most working people traditionally looked

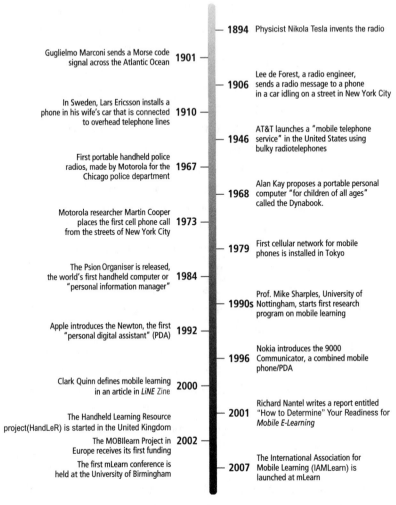

**FIGURE 1.1 Milestones in the history of mobile communications and mobile learning.**

forward to a long career working within one company or to building their own business.

What seemed to change everything was the advent of computer networking. Early computers can be seen as giant calculators, working through formulas via a set of off-on switches. But it was the development of computer networking in the early 1970s that helped push business into the constant state of flux that it is in today. The first computer networks were developed by the U.S. Department of Defense laboratories (DARPA) and a few U.S universities.

As computer networking grew and spread throughout the world, the computers themselves became smaller. In the 1960s, computers were known as

**FIGURE 1.2 Dr. Martin Cooper, speaking at a conference in Taiwan in 2007, holds an example of the first cell phone that he used to make calls in 1973. Photo by Rico Shen.**

mainframes and took up several air-conditioned rooms. The interface between computers and humans at that time was either a teletype machine, punched cards, or tape. When I was a Master's level graduate student in the 1970s, mini-computers, such as the VAX, provided computing at a much lower price. With the use of "acoustic modems" (equipped with rubber cups that fitted over the phone), I could communicate with terminals from anywhere with a telephone line. As I was completing my doctoral studies in the early 1980s, I witnessed the growth of personal computers such as the Commodore PET and the IBM PC. It was during this time that I first saw the Apple Lisa computer, which later became the Apple Macintosh. A lot has changed in a few decades.

Similarly, the history of mobile computing went through a set of stages starting with heavy metal-cased television sets with a slot for a large floppy disk, accompanied by a bulky keyboard. We used to call these computers "luggables"—the first one I owned in 1983 was a Kaypro portable computer running the CP/M operating system. A year later, in 1984, the Psion Organizer was released as the world's first handheld computer or "personal information manager." That same year, I bought one of the first laptops—a Radio Shack Model 100 with 24K of memory, and a 300-baud modem. It ran on batteries, an early example of being "untethered" to a larger computer or an electrical outlet, but its tiny LCD screen was not very useful to me while I was sitting on a beach in Southern France. Essentially, it was mostly a portable word processor and calculator, but its painfully slow modem (by today's standards) showed the power of e-mail and computer networking. In the summer of 1984 I was teaching graduate classes in education at Memorial University in Newfoundland, and was able to send the last chapter of my doctoral dissertation to the VAX computer at the University of Toronto over the phone line. At the time it was magical, even though it was so slow that I could see the individual words scrolling across the screen of the Model 100 as it communicated with the larger computer thousands of miles away.

The first educational uses of computers can be traced back to the history of "teaching machines" starting in the 1920s and "programmed instruction" methods developed in the 1950s. But true computer-based learning programs really began with the PLATO (Programmed Logic for Automated Teaching Operations) system developed for mainframe computers at the University of Illinois at Urbana-Champaign in 1960. The PLATO system featured multiple roles, including *students* who could study assigned lessons and communicate with teachers through online notes, *instructors*, who could examine student progress data, as well as communicate and take lessons themselves, and *authors*, who could do all of the above, plus create new lessons. There was also a fourth type of user, called a *multiple*, which was used for demonstrations of the PLATO system.

The 1960s saw the development of many innovations that we now take for granted. The first graphical user interface, called Sketchpad, was invented in 1963 by Ivan Sutherland, who published a description of it in his Ph.D. dissertation at MIT. In the same year, Doug Engelbart invented the computer mouse. By 1969 the first computer network was set up with funding from the U.S. military. Known as ARPAnet (ARPA stands for the Advanced Research Projects Agency), it connected four computers at the University of California, Los Angeles, (UCLA), Stanford University, the University of California, Santa Barbara, and the University of Utah.

The suitcase-based computers, with their built-in television screens, were examples of portable computers, but they still were not really mobile. The user had to carry these monsters around and then set them up on a desk or table in order to work. The computers that came next were known as laptops or notebooks because of their small size and the obvious fact that they could be operated from a lap. As laptops and notebooks were made smaller, the term subnotebook came into use to refer to the lightest and smallest among them.

Still smaller were the 1980s' programmable "pocket computers," "personal information managers," and "electronic organizers," and "personal digital assistants (PDAs)," introduced by Apple in 1992. Finally, smaller and more powerful mobile phones appeared, such as the Nokia 9000 Communicator, introduced in 1996. These were the immediate precursors of today's smartphones, and really opened up the possibilities of mobile learning.

 ## The Beginnings of Mobile Learning

The *idea* of mobile learning can be found in the science fiction of the 1960s. By 1968 computer guru Alan Kay had proposed a portable personal computer "for children of all ages" called the Dynabook. In 1972, Xerox built a prototype of Kay's vision that could store up to 500 pages, or several hours of low-quality audio.

As Marshall McLuhan once remarked, "We look at the present through a rear-view mirror. We march backwards into the future" (McLuhan and Fiore, 1967). So, it is not surprising that the first metaphor for learning with a portable computer was a book. Computers gradually got smaller in the 1980s, and Apple introduced its personal data assistant or PDA, called the Newton, in 1992, and followed up throughout the 1990s with several model upgrades. In particular, a model called the eMate 300 was a version of the Newton designed for the school market. Smaller PDAs such as the Palm Pilot, introduced in 1996, took off in terms of sales and captured the imagination of the public, including business executives.

Often it takes the introduction of a new technology to spark new thinking about innovative uses of an existing technology. It is interesting to note that a 1996 article by Harvard professor Christopher Dede (Dede, 1996) on "emerging technologies and distributed learning" in distance education makes no mention of learning with a portable or mobile device. Yet as early as 1995 articles started to appear discussing the impact of wireless and mobile technologies on classroom teaching.

Starting in the late 1990s Professor Mike Sharples of the University of Nottingham directed an active research program to investigate mobile learning (Sharples, 2000). In 2000, computer learning consultant Clark Quinn provided one of the first definitions of mobile learning, which he described as:

> . . . the intersection of mobile computing and e-Learning: accessible resources wherever you are, strong search capabilities, rich interaction, powerful support for effective learning, and performance-based assessment . . . e-learning independent of location, time and space. (Quinn, 2000)

By the early 2000s, several wireless PDAs and Bluetooth technology for wireless local area networks (LANs) were on the market, and more publications online and in print started to show up on this topic. One of the first was a report by Richard Nantel (2001) from Brandon Hall Research, titled *How to Determine Your Readiness for Mobile E-Learning*. In this report Richard described mobile e-learning as:

> . . . a new way to learn using small, portable computers such as personal digital assistants (PDAs), handheld computers, two-way messaging pagers, Internet-enabled cell phones, as well as hybrid devices that combine two or more of these devices into one. (Nantel, 2001)

Richard Nantel's document and the article by Clark Quinn were probably the first publications to talk about mobile learning for business and for use in corporate training. However, the focus of most research and publication on mobile learning has been for the K-12 school system or for use in higher education. This means that many of the examples that I use throughout this book to illustrate new ways of employing mobile learning in corporate environments come from educational contexts. This is the sector in which most of the valuable pioneering work in developing the field of mobile learning has been undertaken.

Some of the other important developments and dates in the history of mobile learning follow.

In 2001:
▶ SRI International gives over 100 "Palm Education Pioneer" grants to U.S. teachers to encourage their use in education.

In 2002:
▶ The Handheld Learning Resource project (HandLeR) at the University of Birmingham used a mobile device for children to record observations on a field trip (Sharples, 2003).

- The MOBIlearn project was first funded in Europe. Its purpose is to explore "new ways to use mobile environments to meet the needs of learners, working by themselves and with others."
- The first mLearn conference was held at the University of Birmingham.
- Teacher's in 27 schools in the UK receive PDAs for their use. (Perry, 2003)

In 2003:

- Brandon Hall Research gave the first Excellence in Learning Award to OnPoint Digital for "The FreePad Solution" a tablet-based mobile learning appliance.

In 2004:

- As the popularity of Apple's iPod media player increases, learning-on-the-go using audio podcasts gains in popularity.
- Duke University provides all incoming Freshman students with an Apple iPod with voice recording features to assist in their studies.

In 2005:

- Hot Lava Software develops and begins selling Learning Mobile Author software to corporations and educators to create their own mobile learning courseware for select PDAs and mobile computing devices.

In 2007:

- The International Association for Mobile Learning (IAMLearn) was launched at mLearn 2007 in Melbourne, Australia. Mike Sharples was elected as the founding president.

In 2009:

- The eighth mLearn conference was held in Orlando, Florida, with approximately 175 delegates in attendance (I was one of them). There were six exhibitors present, a good indication that a fledgling mobile learning industry was already starting to develop.

The introduction of a wide variety of new learning technologies has had an impact on training methods. With the rapid rise of personal computers in the late twentieth century, and the explosion of mobile phone use in the past 10 years, we've started to see a shift from the classroom model of training with an instructor at the front of the room, to a diverse mixture of approaches to learning in many different settings. Early in the development of mobile learning the emphasis was on the mobile devices themselves, but this is now being replaced by a new orientation toward understanding *learners who are connected to relevant information while they are mobile.*

The focus on what is important in mobile learning has gradually shifted over the past decade (Cook, 2008). Ten years ago mobile learning was about displaying *e-learning* on a small screen. At that time mobile learning was considered any learning that happened while someone was using a mobile device. This was followed by the view that mobile learning is any learning that happened outside a classroom-like setting. Finally, we have come to an understanding that the most important fact in mobile learning is *that the learner is both mobile and connected.* The sources of information can be in any form, from signage to interactive billboards; from mobile phones to computers embedded in our clothing. The critical factor is that a learner can be physically mobile while at the same time remaining connected to nonproximate sources of information, instruction, and data. This is in sharp contrast to the classroom model of learning, where the learner, for the most part, is *immobilized* behind a desk.

Mike Sharples (2007b) describes some of the conclusions from the final evaluation of the MOBIlearn project. "It's the learner that's mobile," he says. "Learning is interwoven with everyday life. Mobile learning can both complement and conflict with formal education." Sharples also emphasizes "the importance of context, constructed by learners through interaction."

 ## Mobile Learning Comes of Age

One of the reasons that it is hard to classify types of mobile learning is that the field is very much still in flux. The first idea that many trainers had about mobile learning was that they would primarily be able to take the content they already had developed for e-learning and put it directly onto a small screen. However, this was not very successful. Trainers soon discovered just how difficult it was to cram a computer screen worth of content onto the small screen of a mobile phone and still have it make sense to a learner. Ten years later the picture has changed significantly. In 2006, Dirk Frohberg, a researcher at the University of Zurich, suggested that "mobile learning has left the status of a newborn child" (Frohberg, 2006), because of all the things that could be done to advance learning using mobile technologies. In 2008, Sam Adkins, reviewing the rapidly growing mobile learning market, wrote, "Clearly, the 'market creation' phase for mobile learning is over" (Adkins, 2008).

All optimism aside, there's still a long way to go; we are in the early stages of development for mobile learning. There's no question that mobile learning has moved into the workplace in a big way. But this does *not* mean that there are only positive stories to be told about this experience or that everyone is using mobile learning. In a 2005 study titled "The Mobile Working Experience," IBM Europe surveyed 351 remote workers from 29 European countries (IBM, 2005). The study found:

▶ There was a rise in the number of individuals who had recently begun working in a mobile environment.
▶ Mobile workers face several difficulties in communicating and collaborating with colleagues.
▶ There is a danger that mobile workers can become disconnected from the informal networks traditionally used to share knowledge and identify opportunities within the organization.
▶ Mobile workers face many challenges in balancing the demands of work and home life.
▶ A reliable, easy-to-use technological structure was essential to the success of a mobile work environment.

The picture today is even more complex. Most people, at least in developed countries, have access to mobile devices for learning. It turns out that in the new nomadism, it is hard to tell the workers from the learners. Many full-time mobile workers are also part-time students who study at home or online. Many full-time adult students are also part-time mobile workers.

The world of work is changing. Although they are taking their time to retire, today's baby boomers are slowly moving off the stage that is the workplace and are being replaced by a new generation of workers. Members of this new generation are very different in terms of their experiences with mobile technologies. When they arrive in the workplace, their needs are also different from those of the baby boomers they replace. And, no wonder. Learning consultant Marc Prensky estimates that "the life arc of a typical 21-year-old entering the workforce today has, on average, included 5,000 hours of video game playing, exchange of 250,000 emails, instant messages, and phone text messages, 10,000 hours of cell phone use . . . to that you can add 3,500 hours of time online" (Rainie, 2006). There are five realities that we have to face with respect to this new generation of young workers:

- They are video gamers, and this gives them different expectations about how to learn, work, and pursue careers.
- They are technologically literate, but this does not necessarily make them media literate.
- They are content creators, and this shapes their notions about privacy and property.
- They are product and people rankers, and this informs their notions of propriety.
- They are multitaskers often living in a state of "continuous partial attention," and this means that the boundary between work and leisure is quite permeable. (adapted from Rainie, 2006)

These realities mean that many workplaces are going to be *disrupted* by the intervention of mobile computing and mobile learning whether or not it is in the formal plans of trainers or human resources (HR). (In Chapter 8, David Fell discusses the opportunities available to businesses resulting from the state of this fast-moving field, and he shows how to develop a future-oriented mobile learning business strategy.)

 ## Definitions of Mobile Learning

As the focus of mobile learning has shifted over the last decade, so have its formal definitions. Early definitions included any learning activity mediated by a mobile device. It was all about the technology. For example, O'Malley et al. (2003) said that mobile learning is ". . . any sort of learning that happens when the learner is not at a fixed, predetermined location, or learning that happens when the learner takes advantage of learning opportunities offered by mobile technologies." This is similar to John Traxler's (2005) definition that mobile learning is ". . . any educational provision where the sole or dominant technologies are handheld or palmtop devices." Keegan (2005) tried to define mobile learning by the size of the mobile device: "Mobile learning should be restricted to learning on devices which a lady can carry in her handbag or a gentleman can carry in his pocket." Geddes (2004) defined mobile learning as "the acquisition of *any* knowledge and skill through using mobile technology, *anywhere, anytime,* that results in an *alteration in behaviour.*"

The shift to thinking about mobile learning in terms of the learner being mobile has occurred only in the past couple of years. The emphasis has moved from a focus solely on the technology to the power of ambient and ubiquitous communications. The new focus is on learning from the learner's point of view. Mobile learning is now seen as a means of keeping people in touch with each other and with information sources, no matter where either is located, while at the same time taking the individual learner's immediate context and personal characteristics into account.

As a group of researchers in Finland note, "All learning is mobile." (Tétard and Patokorpi, 2008). The MOBIlearn project, a multiyear study of mobile learning in Europe, has this to say about mobile learning:

> . . . when considering mobility from the learner's point of view rather than the technology's, it can be argued that mobile learning goes on everywhere— for example, pupils revising for exams on the bus to school, doctors updating their medical knowledge while on hospital rounds, language students improving their language skills while travelling abroad. All these instances of formal or informal learning do not necessarily involve the use of mobile technologies, but have been taking place while people are on the move and should therefore be classified as instances of mobile learning. Moreover, mobile technologies can be used at a person's usual learning environment. In fact, there has been a substantial amount of research in recent years looking at the employment of PDAs in classrooms. By virtue of the technology's mobility, such PDA-based classroom learning has also been considered as mobile learning. (O'Malley et al., 2005)

I especially like the 2005 definition of mobile learning offered by the MOBIlearn project group, who says that mobile learning is:

> . . . any sort of learning that happens when the learner is not at a fixed, predetermined location, or learning that happens when the learner takes advantage of the learning opportunities offered by mobile technologies. (Vavoula, 2005)

In addition to formulating definitions, there have been several attempts to classify different types of mobile learning. These include classifications based on the type of technology used, type of application used, or the learning theories that are used to support a particular approach to training methods. Frohberg (2006) argues for a five-category classification scheme based on the context of learning, which he identifies as free, formalized, digital, physical, and social contexts. John Traxler came up with a similar typology in 2009:

▶ Technology-driven mobile learning
▶ Miniature but portable e-learning
▶ Connected classroom learning
▶ Informal, personalized, situated mobile learning
▶ Mobile training/performance support
▶ Remote/rural/development mobile learning  (Traxler, 2009c)

The problem with such classifications is that the categories focus on the technologies rather than on the learning itself. Thus the categories proposed by Frohberg or by Traxler cannot possibly be mutually exclusive. For example, connected classroom learning may not be mobile at all but simply refers to classrooms that are networked via the Internet. Mobile learning is, in many ways, the mirror opposite of classroom-based learning. Classifying the different types of mobile learning is difficult in light of how fast the field is changing. Later in this book I introduce over 50 distinct "uses" of mobile learning, many of which did not exist until a few years ago.

 ## Business Drivers of Mobile Learning

The use of mobile learning in large enterprises is in its infancy. In addition to the reduction of time available for training, discussed previously, there are many other business drivers that are moving it forward. These include:

▶ The widespread deployment of mobile computing means that an infrastructure for mobile learning is already in place. Among adults in industrialized countries, the use of mobile phones has become ubiquitous. This means that there is already a ready-made communications device in the pockets of most workers. Most mobile phones now have a Web browser, and the cost of mobile access to the Internet is being reduced each year.

- For many jobs, the workforce is also mobile, not fixed to a specific place. Many categories of jobs see workers on the road most of the time, including salespeople, maintenance workers, consultants, and those involved in various transportation industries. This trend has been developing for some time; Edwards (2005) said "The number of remote and mobile workers—including frequent business travelers, mobile office workers, telecommuters, remote branch office employees, multi-site workers and non-office workers—will reach approximately 94 million by the start of 2005. That number accounts for nearly 40 percent of all U.S. employment." By now, these numbers will have increased significantly.

- Today many people physically "go to the office" only sporadically, if at all. And a mobile worker does not necessarily do her work from just one physical location. On any given day a mobile worker can be found in a home office, a neighborhood café, an automobile, or at a friend's home and yet still be "at work." (These environments, alternatives to home or a workplace, are sometimes referred to as "third spaces"—see Fig 1.3.)

- Huge numbers of people who physically commute to work on a daily basis often do so via public transportation and thus have available time to communicate and learn using mobile devices on their way to work.

- Young people, sometimes called the "always on" generation, are rapidly becoming the new workforce as baby boomers start to retire. With mobile communications already firmly embedded in their personal lives, members of the new generation expect that mobile communications will also be part of their work lives.

- In many larger organizations there is a demand for greater access to and integration of information, data management, and communications, all delivered in real time whenever possible.

- Mobile communications, including mobile learning, are in great demand in specific industries. There is widespread penetration of mobile learning applications in the health-care field (Wood and Woodill, 2008), in natural resources monitoring, agriculture, emergency services, government, retail, and transportation. The U.S. government is the largest user of BlackBerry smartphones, with over 500,000 units in use (Sweeny, 2009). In terms of its ability to provide reliable communications in emergency situations, the BlackBerry received a huge boost from the 9/11 terrorist

**FIGURE 1.3 Many public spaces are becoming "third spaces" where we go to work and talk to others. Photo by Gail Jade Hamilton.**

attack in New York City. While all other means of communication with people in the twin towers were destroyed during the attack, text-based messaging via BlackBerries kept working.

▶ We live in a mobile society experiencing increasing globalization. Global sourcing and global labor mean that the employees or customers we need to train can be anywhere in the world. Zeleny (2007) argues that, "Mobile knowledge and learning are brought forth by the underlying forces of mobile business and society."

For many people, training has become unhinged from classrooms and entails instead the task of finding the information they need, when they need it. This has been described as a kind of "feral learning" (Hall, 2008) or "foraging for information" (Tselios et al., 2007) (and many people don't think this is a bad thing).

## Business Models for Mobile Learning

The mobile learning industry, as it is currently constituted, consists of a variety of supplier types that use several different revenue models to run their businesses (Hoppe, 2004). *Content providers* develop custom original materials to run on mobile devices. *Content conversion providers* take current print and e-learning content and rework it for display on mobile devices. *Application providers* are software development companies that write applications (apps) specifically for the mobile learning industry. *Hardware providers* are the companies that design, manufacture, and sell the mobile devices that are used in this industry. *Service providers* offer a wide variety of services including project management, translation, consulting, and design. Finally, *solution providers* try to package the entire value chain for mobile learning and manage it from beginning to end.

As the industry grows, companies offering mobile learning earn revenues in a variety of ways (Hoppe, 2004). These include:

- Sales of mobile learning products and devices
  - Consulting fees
  - Custom development fees
- Brokerage fees or commissions
- Membership fees
- Subscription fees
- Advertising revenue from posting messages
- Sale of information to data mining agencies

The corporate mobile learning industry is just starting to develop, so there is a lot of uncertainty and experimentation in business models and growth strategies. We cover the topic of business strategies for mobile learning in Chapter 8.

*Case Study*

## Intuition.com Develops BlackBerry Compliance Training at Merrill Lynch

Merrill Lynch is one of the world's leading wealth management, capital markets, and advisory companies, with offices in 38 countries and territories and total client assets of approximately $1.5 trillion. As a globally dispersed organization, Merrill Lynch has 60,000 employees (learner audience) from three business units employed in 38 countries. Like many organizations, employees at Merrill Lynch struggle to find time for training. Though employees are no strangers to e-learning, as the learning management system is the second most visited site on the company's corporate intranet, completion rates for some courses can be disappointing.

## MOBILE SOLUTION

As Merrill Lynch has more than 22,000 BlackBerry devices in use globally with 500 new devices being added monthly, the potential to leverage these devices beyond their traditional usage was apparent. To test the business case of harnessing the potential of these mobile devices, it was decided to initially pilot the availability of three compliance training courses over a two-month period among a cohort of 2,100 investment bankers and key stakeholders.

The business needs driving the pilot initiative included the desire to:

▶ Enable learning outside the office during naturally occurring down time, such as daily commuting or while people are out of the office on business trips, which equals about 80 percent of a banker's time.

▶ Leverage existing BlackBerry usage habits in this population. BlackBerry users typically access their mobile devices up to 50 times each day and are used to receiving information and taking action through the device while they are out of the office, on trains, in planes, and even in elevators.

▶ Enable employees to complete learning in smaller chunks, at any desired time and place, with no need for connectivity to a telephone network or a PC.

The constraints of the project were as follows:

- *Standards:* The project needed to adhere to the e-Learning industry's Sharable Content Object Reference Model (SCORM) standards.
- *Mobile device limitations:* BlackBerry devices have certain limitations such as limited memory, and small screen size, which needed to be taken into account to ensure success.
- *Full integration with existing LMS:* The authentication, content assignment and tracking needed to synchronize with the existing Merrill Lynch learning management system (LMS). To achieve this the team developed a real-time Web service which linked the LMS with the BlackBerry device and synchronized all learning content downloaded to the device, and the tracking and completion information received from the device.
- *Support of business, learning, and IT teams:* The business, IT/BlackBerry, and learning and development teams needed to work together to deliver the solution.
- *Work locally on device:* Because of the relatively low speed of wireless networks, and also to allow people to work in areas where no signal is available (e.g., trains, planes), all content needed to be downloaded seamlessly and reside locally on the device. This meant that the application on the BlackBerry displayed content on the local device.
- *Ease of deployment:* The application needed to be absolutely simple to install and deploy, with little or no configuration by the end user. This was achieved by wirelessly deploying and configuring the application from the Merrill Lynch BlackBerry enterprise server (BES), requiring no user interaction. The courses were then pushed wirelessly, and all tracking information pushed back up from the device. The users just needed to click on the application icon on their BlackBerry and launch their course of choice.

In addition, one of the principal advantages of using mobile devices for training delivery to a financial services firm such as Merrill Lynch is based on the need for security. Devices are tightly integrated within the corporate network, namely through the BlackBerry Enterprise Server (BES), and many of the technical and security hurdles are already handled by existing application infrastructures, for example, e-mail.

## The Project

The learning objectives of the pilot program were to provide a comparable alternative to online training with no degradation to the learning itself. This was achieved by designing a technology solution that centered around three key guidelines:

1. *Simplistic usability:* Replicate users' behavior in how they use their BlackBerry.
2. *Ubiquitous availability:* Provide users with constant access to the courses with no need for connectivity to a telephone network or PC.
3. *Changing little from existing standards for online learning:* The content or message had to be identical to that offered through online learning; if anything was simplified for mobile, it had to be made identical for the online courses as well.

To foster adoption of this new training delivery medium, the mobile learning system was branded as "GoLearn—a new way to take your training with you."

A Kirkpatrick level-one survey was created that learners could complete directly on their BlackBerry. This survey had the following objectives:

- Identify where the learners took the training.
- Identify if the learners found the balance of text, imagery, and interactions supportive of their learning.
- Determine whether learners liked the training delivery medium.
- Determine whether learners would take more training if it was offered via their mobile device.

## Results

The most important measurable efficiency found from the pilot rollout was that the participants took their courses in 30 percent less time. Given that the senior executives involved were required to take six hours of mandated online content per year, the time required to take these courses was reduced by nearly two hours, while simultaneously it became a more positive learning experience.

Findings indicated that:

- 99 percent felt that the format and presentation supported the learning objectives.
- 100 percent would complete more training in this format.
- Over 75 percent praised the "convenience," "time management," and "training with no distractions" benefits.
- 32 percent completed their learning while traveling for business, 24 percent commuting for work, 26 percent at home, and 18 percent in the office or elsewhere.
- Over 56 percent of active users are at the executive level.
- 12 percent obtained a higher completion rate in 30 percent less time than comparable mandated training programs.

With the pilot's success, Merrill Lynch is now strategically positioned with the mobile enablement of learning and other HR processes and systems. Since the initial pilot, six additional mobile courses have been developed and deployed and GoLearn's ability to wirelessly deliver and track podcasts and branching assessments has been expanded. As of March 2008 all 22,000 current Black-Berry devices and all future devices at Merrill Lynch had GoLearn installed as a standard application—without a doubt a testimonial to the success of the mobile learning initiative.

 ## Benefits of Mobile Learning

For more than 200 years, education and training have been built on a model of the learner as an empty container or sponge that is filled up by the teacher/trainer. The material that is "stuffed" into or "absorbed" by a learner is, for the most part, decided upon and presented by a teacher/trainer. This has been described as the "just-in-case" model; content is delivered to students "just in case" they might have a need for it in the future. The problem with this model is that it doesn't work well in practice. Internationally renowned adult educator Paulo Freire (1970) described it as the "banking approach" to learning where the learner is seen as a bank account in which the teacher makes a deposit each day. But, much of what the learner takes in is soon forgotten unless it is relevant to his or her life, or is useful in an important task.

Mobile learning, when properly designed, can be described as "just in time, just enough, and just for me." It is learning that is "situated" (typically in the field or at the workplace). It is also learning that is "contextualized by mediation with peers and teachers" (Peters, 2007). The key benefits of using mobile devices for learning include:

- Portability
- Any time, any place connectivity
- Flexible and timely access to e-learning resources
- Immediacy of communication
- Empowerment and engagement of learners, particularly those in dispersed communities
- Active learning experiences

Researchers point out other benefits of mobile learning, such as increased computer literacy, communicative skills and community building, improved identity creation, collaborative learning, and mentoring. Looked at more closely, we can discern additional potential benefits to this approach to learning:

- *Improved retention:* Because it is just in time, just enough for the task at hand, and personalized for the learner, the information that the learner takes in is more likely to be retained, especially when the learner knows that she will encounter similar situations in her work.
- *Efficiency:* Mobile learning is very efficient because of the portability of information sources provided by anytime, anywhere connectivity. It allows access to information sources and assistance in a very flexible way that is also empowering and engaging for learners. Mobile learning can also be efficient in that it has the potential to leverage the "idle time" of professionals on the move that would likely otherwise be non-productive.
- *Cost savings:* Mobile learning has cost benefits to large organizations that deploy this approach, because the mobile devices needed are, in most cases, already in the pockets of potential users. (But, to counter this, there is a growing tendency on the part of larger companies to require employees to only use company-issued mobile devices for work).

Of course there are also savings because of reduced requirements for classroom space and for travel by both staff and learners.

▶ *Time savings:* Mobile learning is also immediate—there is usually little or no waiting for the answer to a question. There is no need to schedule classes on a topic or to wait for a presentation. Learning happens following the learner's own time schedule. For example, if an employee can access mobile learning while he is also working with a customer, the customer is better served and doesn't have to wait long for answers. Better still, as we demonstrate in Chapter 4, mobile learning can be delivered directly *to* a customer in the form of customer education or as an immediate answer to a question.

▶ *Increased collaboration and community:* Mobile learning can foster collaboration between colleagues in a company and/or between employees and clients of that company. Together they can form a *community of practice* that supports all participants with timely information as it is needed.

▶ *More granular design:* Mobile learning content is, by necessity, formatted differently from e-learning delivered on laptop or desktop computer screens. What is sent to the learner must be produced in small, discrete pieces of information (sometimes called *mobile learning objects*), which may be easier to digest. For example, in Japan, Masayasu Morita evaluated the use of English language lessons formatted differently for computers and cell phones. He found that 90 percent of cell phone users were still accessing the lessons after 15 days, compared to only 50 percent of computer users (Prensky, 2004).

▶ *Up-to-date information:* Mobile learning is dynamic. It is today's content, not old news. Online experts and up-to-date sources are often available.

▶ *Personalization:* Mobile learning is individual. Learners select activities from a personal menu of learning opportunities most relevant to their background at the moment of their choosing.

▶ *Comprehensiveness:* Mobile learning is comprehensive. It provides learning events from many sources, thus enabling learners to select a favorite format, learning method, or training provider.

With so many changes, it is not hard to conclude that this new way of learning has profound and disruptive implications for present education and training systems. As the use of mobile learning grows, this new way of learning will start to show various *network effects*. As more people use mobile learning and more information is provided to be accessed by learners, the more likely it is for the provision and use of mobile learning to grow quickly. Eventually, mobile learning will become "ubiquitous learning," supplied by pervasive and omnipresent networks that can be accessed from anywhere at any time. Because the same devices and networks can be used for *social media*, network effects are even stronger based on the intersection of both uses.

Of course, there is no point in providing mobile learning if people don't actually learn while using it. Jill Attewell (2005), in her analysis of evidence collected during a three-year study on the impact of mobile learning on students' learning patterns and attitudes toward information and communications technologies (ICTs), found that mobile learning helps to:

- Improve learners' literacy and numeracy skills and to recognize their existing abilities.
- Encourage both independent and collaborative learning experiences.
- Identify areas where learners need assistance and support.
- Combat resistance to the use of ICT and help bridge the gap between mobile phone literacy and ICT literacy.
- Remove some of the formality from the learning experience and engage reluctant learners.
- Keep learners focused for longer periods.
- Raise learners' self-esteem and self-confidence.

These results, as well as other results, indicate that mobile learning has a positive impact on the learning process.

 ## Challenges, Myths, and Misconceptions about Mobile Learning

It would be unfair to simply talk about the benefits of mobile learning without reviewing some of the major challenges, myths, and misconceptions as well. Let's start with the challenges and how they can be overcome.

In many ways, mobile computing is a victim of its own success. The huge growth of mobile data traffic slows down the Internet, and makes it a less than optimal experience. The growth of the Internet in general, and mobile computing in particular, is nothing short of astounding. (You can watch this growth live at a Web site called PhoneCount.com.) One concern of Internet and mobile network operators is that the infrastructure cannot keep up with the massive growth of users and the incredible flow of data that is taking place throughout the network. For example, AT&T's data traffic has grown by 5,000 percent in the past three years. This concern was raised in the February 11, 2010, issue of the *Economist*, which asked in a headline, "Will the rapid growth in data traffic overwhelm wireless networks?"

The greatest growth is happening in mobile phone connections. Mobile phones are replacing fixed-line connections, especially outside of North America. According to a UN report, six in ten people around the world now have mobile phone subscriptions, meaning that mobile phones are the communications technology of choice, especially in poorer countries (Jordans, 2009).

Ten years ago, objections to mobile learning focused on the small size of both the screens and the keyboards of mobile devices. Obviously, small screens *do* limit the amount of information that can be placed on a screen. To meet this challenge, mobile learning requires new "design thinking" to create easily read chunks of information that are delivered as needed and as demanded within the user's specific context. Early mobile phones lacked the processing power that is found in desktop or laptop computers, and early battery technologies required frequent recharging or replacement. Because of their small size, most mobile devices are relatively fragile and can be easily stolen or lost. Connectivity was highly unreliable in the early days of mobile phones, and interoperability among various devices was difficult (McLean, 2003).

"Not all content will be appropriate for mobile learning," notes Jennifer Taylor Arnold (2007), and not all workers are, or need to be, mobile. Those who are already "in the field" are the most obvious potential beneficiaries of mobile learning. Christopher von Koschembahr (2005) of IBM outlines three ways that mobile learning "can help turn field-force automation into field-force enablement":

- ▶ Learn how to use a new device being deployed.
- ▶ Learn how to use new applications being deployed.
- ▶ Receive ongoing training, corporate communications, and critical job-role information on the fly. (p. 41)

But many challenges can arise with a predominately mobile workforce. In many ways, these challenges are similar to those experienced by anyone involved with a "virtual" organization. There is a danger that the workers who mostly use mobile phones will become disconnected from the many informal networks that exist in a face-to-face work setting. These are often used for sharing knowledge and corporate culture and are important for the smooth functioning of an organization. Relationships with colleagues are often harder to develop in a mobile-based work group, and collaboration can take more effort. Identifying interesting opportunities that can arise within a company can become more difficult, and mobile workers can have problems with balancing the demands of home life and work.

In the past decade, many of the original objections to the hardware and network infrastructure of mobile learning have been overcome to a great extent, although the social issues remain and must be well managed. Smartphones have become much more powerful, faster, and more reliable as manufacturers have squeezed more processing power into smaller packages. Mobile phone screens are now somewhat larger, and specialty devices such as tablets and e-book readers are highly portable, yet they come with relatively large screens. At the same time, laptops are much lighter and smaller. A new category of "netbook" computers arrived in 2008 and took the market by storm. With their seven-inch screens, they easily fitted into a briefcase or large purse. While not very powerful, the initial models of netbook computers were able to connect to the Internet and carry out basic office functions. The design of mobile devices reflects the desire of manufacturers to find the best balance of features and size for users on the go. In 2010 we witnessed the introduction of many new tablet computers, including the Apple iPad (Fig. 1.4), that tried to be big enough to read easily while remaining easy to carry. Most likely a few dominant designs will emerge, each aimed at a different segment of the market.

Yet myths about mobile learning persist. Robert Gadd and Katherine Guest (2009) wrote a white paper on some of the "myths and misconceptions" of mobile learning. I have adapted their list of issues here:

▶ *Myth: Mobile Web browsers work fine for accessing existing e-learning content and sites.* While newer mobile phones have improved browsers and displays, most content prepared for desktop access/playback is not properly formatted for mobile-friendly access. As such, most e-learning content "out of the box" isn't ready for mobile delivery. However, proper planning can ensure that online content generated with desktop-focused tools like Adobe Dreamweaver or Microsoft FrontPage can be repurposed for mobile delivery using specialized style sheets and layouts.

**FIGURE 1.4 The Apple iPhone next to an Apple iPad, a touch-screen tablet computer that was introduced to the market in early April 2010. Photo by: Yutaka Tsutano.**

- *Myth: Mobile content can't be as secure as online learning content.* While it's true that mobile devices are more apt to be lost or stolen compared to a laptop or desktop computer, a growing number of enterprise-grade mobile devices and smartphones can actually be considered highly secure and easy to manage.
- *Myth: Mobile learning content should be SCORM compliant.* A key benefit of any mobile device/smartphone is the ability for mobile workers to extend their access to business communications, e-mail, social networks, and training resources while on the go. As such, mobile learners will want to access required content and compliance training while traveling by air or working outside areas where wireless coverage is readily available. Given that most purpose-built online learning materials today conform to a standard protocol called the Sharable Content Object Reference Model (SCORM) and that this requires a connection to a server that is running the SCORM software, strict compliance to this standard is not always possible. Rather, most mature m-learning tools bridge this gap by collecting and managing training session details like, "who, when, for how long, frequency, and test scores/responses" and can send these results back to a SCORM-compliant LMS as soon as direct access to the server again exists.
- *Myth: Mobile learning is not as effective as either instructor led training (ILT) or online learning.* While it is true that mobile devices are not the ideal medium for many types of training delivery, many organizations can provide measurable proof that properly planned and delivered mobile learning can be

just as effective as available instructor led training (ILT) and online learning alternatives. Mobile learners also benefit from the ability to revisit content at the time of need or refresh concepts whenever the mood strikes them.

▶ *Myth: Rich media files are compelling but hard to prepare and distribute.* Rich media files (e.g., video clips, podcasts, slide presentations) are among the most compelling content your users will access using a compatible mobile device, yet many training teams experience trouble converting (transcoding) existing materials into mobile friendly formats. A variety of inexpensive tools is available to capture and deploy content to every major smartphone, thus turning training professionals into media experts.

▶ *Myth: Flash content works easily on any smartphone.* While Adobe Flash files will run on most smartphones, they are not supported on Apple's products such as the iPod, the iPhone and the iPad. As I write this book the BlackBerry does not support Flash files either, but this will be corrected in the second half of 2010. As well, Flash files that are created as e-learning content using rapid authoring tools often will not run on a mobile device because of the small screen sizes and the lack of ability to easily use standard navigation features and "hot spots" included in much of this type of content.

▶ *Myth: You should limit the variety of mobile devices your organization supports for mobile learning.* This approach actually limits the potential use and growth of any new mobile learning initiative. The easier it is to use any available mobile device your users may already have, the easier it will be to get your program accessed, adopted, and reused.

▶ *Myth: Integrating mobile learning results with other learning data can be very difficult.* Once content has successfully been deployed, many organizations face challenges collecting and inputting the gathered results from a mobile learning program back into enterprise management platforms such as a learning management system (LMS), a human resources information system (HRIS), an enterprise resource planning system (ERP), or a talent management system (TMS). There are several different ways this can be done, from simple methods like import templates to more sophisticated platform-to-platform interactions, and even single sign-on connections. (Adapted from Gadd and Guest, 2009, used with permission.)

Hopefully, the list of benefits and the discussion of myths and misconceptions will help you to decide to try mobile learning. This book is designed to bring you up to speed on the state of the mobile learning industry, what is possible today, and what is likely coming in the near future.

# The Mobile Learning Ecosystem

**H**istorians have pieced together an image of early hunters and gatherers as people moving around in small groups, hunting animals that were abundant, and gathering fruit and berries as needed. Back then, learning was not something that happened in schools but was the result of everyday life. Learning on the move was the standard. Eventually, groups of humans developed agriculture, settled down into one geographical area, and lived there for most of their lives. But they still moved around a lot, when compared with modern society. Modern industrial society and the development of compulsory schooling in the nineteenth century confined large numbers of people to either sitting at desks or tending machinery in factories for much of the day. Mobile learning is a development that reverses that trend—freeing us from desks and other specific locations for learning.

> "A learning environment has similar complexities to an ecosystem, especially when situated in a workplace."
> —*Brown and Duguid (1991)*

Mobile learning in the current context is the ability of any given person to use networked mobile technology to access relevant information or store new information, regardless of her physical location. A more precise, technical definition might look like this: *mobile learning is personalized learning that unites the learner's context with cloud computing using a mobile device.* Mobile learning is the opposite of learning that takes place in a traditional classroom where the learner sits, *immobilized,* paying attention to an instructor who stands at the front of the room. Sometimes this classroom type of learning situation is called *tethered learning,* because the learner is tied to a specific resource in a specific location.

The networked mobile technology system that supports mobile learning is a complex mix of multiple forms of mobility, many different mobile technologies, a diversity of carriers, a variety of learners, a multitude of learning contexts, teachers with all levels of experience with mobile learning, and many approaches to the design of mobile content and teaching methods. To understand this complex system, it helps to think of it as a mobile learning "ecosystem" made up of *people* embedded in a particular *cultural context* using *mobile technologies* on a *network* to access or store *information* as part of a *learning experience.* This chapter sets out the context for the rest of the book by describing the infrastructure for mobile learning, the many mobile devices available, and the changing conception of what mobile learning is all about.

Mobile computing is a set of rapidly changing technologies. Nick Jones (2009a), an analyst with Gartner, Inc., commented, "Probably 80 percent of your current mobile technology, architecture, platform and vendor choices will become obsolete inside five years." As I write today, there are over 4 billion mobile phones in the world, more than 5,000 different mobile devices, running at least 30 different Web browsers, on a variety of networks controlled by large companies known as "carriers," which are, in turn, regulated by governments at several different levels. At the same time, unlike the World Wide Web, individual consumers have had little input into the design of mobile learning systems. Like many technologies in rapid development, there are few guidelines or resources to shape the future of mobile learning. Instead, many companies are scrambling to offer technologies, content, and services to a growing market, and are waiting to see how things sort themselves out.

This messy situation is exacerbated by the fact that there are no real standards for the development of mobile computing or mobile learning. One of the surprises for those entering the field is that mobile computing is definitely "not the Web." Rather, it is a parallel universe where things move more slowly and choices are more limited than what is currently available on the Internet. For some people, this is disappointing; but, given another few years, I am confident that mobile computing will catch up to, or surpass, the capabilities of the Internet as we know it today.

Computing methods themselves are in a state of rapid flux. Only a few years ago, the dominant architecture for computing was based on single server technology which was contacted by individual computers known as "clients." Today, this model is being replaced by "mashups," "cloud computing," and "Web services" (Woodill and Oliveira, 2006). This new model of computing is based on distributed content that is accessible from anywhere there is a connection to the Internet. Content from several locations (a cloud) can be pulled together into one application or Web site (a mashup) through "software as a service" (SaaS). The result is that a mobile device can access the Internet, and information can be drawn into, or sent from, the device from any location at any time.

Mobile devices come in many shapes and sizes and have many ways of connecting to and distributing information. These "multimodal inputs" include microphones, cameras, keypads, small keyboards, clickable scroll wheels, mini joysticks, touch pads, touch screens, voice, WiFi, Bluetooth, infrared, accelerometers, magnetic field detectors, and a stylus. Output methods include sound, video, images, digital signals, and various forms of projection onto surfaces or directly into the eyeball.

Let's start to sketch the mobile learning ecosystem by describing the user technologies that can be employed to access a mobile learning system. Many of the possible elements in a mobile learning system are shown in Fig. 2.1.

## Mobile Devices for Learning

A mobile learning ecosystem is be made up of a wide variety of devices connected to different kinds of networks. These can include:

- ▶ Mobile phones
- ▶ Personal digital assistants (PDAs)

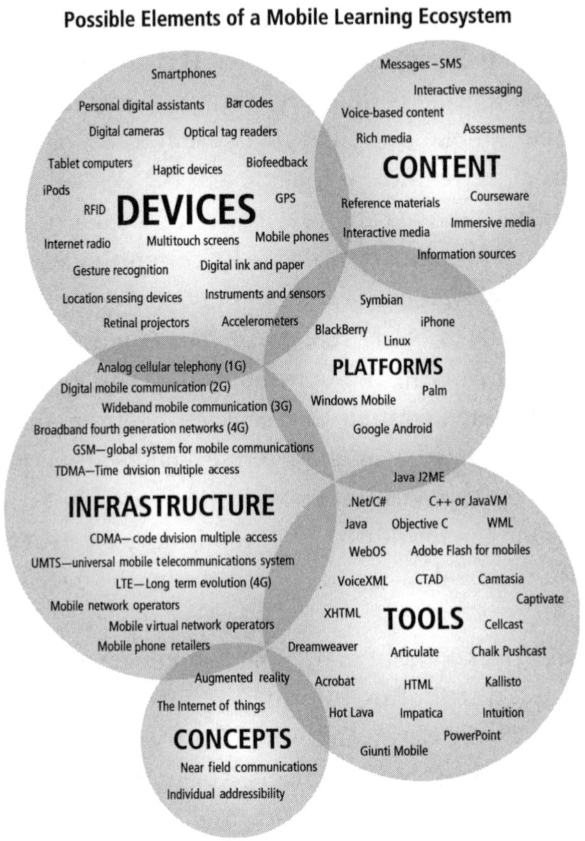

**Possible Elements of a Mobile Learning Ecosystem**

Smartphones

Personal digital assistants    Barcodes

Digital cameras    Optical tag readers

Tablet computers    Haptic devices    Biofeedback

iPods

RFID **DEVICES**    GPS

Internet radio    Multitouch screens    Mobile phones

Gesture recognition    Digital ink and paper

Location sensing devices    Instruments and sensors

Retinal projectors    Accelerometers

Messages – SMS

Interactive messaging

Voice-based content

Rich media    Assessments

**CONTENT**

Reference materials    Courseware

Immersive media

Interactive media

Information sources

Symbian

iPhone

BlackBerry

Linux

**PLATFORMS**    Palm

Windows Mobile

Google Android

Analog cellular telephony (1G)

Digital mobile communication (2G)

Wideband mobile communication (3G)

Broadband fourth generation networks (4G)

GSM—global system for mobile communications

TDMA—Time dvision multiple access

**INFRASTRUCTURE**

CDMA—code dvision multiple access

UMTS—universal mobile telecommunications system

LTE—Long term evolution (4G)

Mobile network operators

Mobile virtual network operators

Mobile phone retailers

Java J2ME

.Net/C#    C++ or JavaVM

Java    Objective C    WML

WebOS    Adobe Flash for mobiles

VoiceXML    CTAD    Camtasia

Captivate

XHTML    **TOOLS**    Cellcast

Dreamweaver    Articulate    Chalk Pushcast

Augmented reality    Acrobat    HTML    Kallisto

The Internet of things    Hot Lava    Impatica    Intuition

**CONCEPTS**    PowerPoint

Giunti Mobile

Near field communications

Individual addressibility

**FIGURE 2.1 A mobile learning ecosystem is made up of many of the elements in each of the categories shown in the above diagram.**

▶ Smartphones
▶ Notebook and netbook computers
▶ Tablet devices and computers
▶ Digital cameras (still and video)
▶ Portable media players, such as iPods and MP3 players
▶ Game consoles and portable gaming devices
▶ Portable navigation devices
▶ Audience response systems (also known as "clickers")
▶ Universal Serial Bus (USB) storage devices
▶ Other mobile learning devices in development include:
  Barcodes

Biofeedback

Digital ink and paper

Digital pens

Footpads

Gesture recognition

Haptic devices

Implanted devices

Instruments and sensors

Internet radio

Location sensing devices

Miniature projectors

Motion recognition devices

Multi-touch screens

Point of View (POV) devices

Radio Frequency Identification (RFID) tags for learning

Ruggidized mobile computers

Speech recognition

Wearable devices

Let's briefly look at each of these types of devices.

## Mobile Phones

By far, the largest category of devices for mobile learning is mobile phones. Mobile phones (also called cell phones) work by connecting through radio signals to special base stations that are linked in a cellular network. As a user moves from one cell area to another, there is a handoff from one base station to the next. Sometimes we even notice the handoff, especially when we lose phone service briefly as we are driving down the highway.

The idea of a cell network for phones was first developed by Bell Labs engineers in the United States in 1947. In 1973, Martin Cooper, a researcher with Motorola, built the first practical handheld phone for use outside an automobile, but it was huge by today's standards (see Fig. 1.2).

In 1979, the NTT Company in Japan built the first fully automated cellular network with 23 base stations covering the 20 million residents of Tokyo. This first cell system is a reference point in naming the "generations" of mobile phone networks. It is now considered a 1G (first generation) network. Currently, we are using 3G networks in most of the world, with 4G networks now deployed in Japan and expanding into select high density markets around the world. 5G networks are in the planning stage.

Mobile phones come in many varieties. Early versions looked like ordinary phone handsets with an antenna; an innovation in the 1990s was the "flip phone," where the lid with a screen on the inside opened up to reveal a keypad. Also, phones became smaller with each new generation.

## Personal Digital Assistants (PDAs)

Personal digital assistants (PDAs), sometimes known as palmtop computers, are mobile devices with multimedia, personal organization software, and office productivity functionality in a very small package. The *term* PDA was first used by Apple Computer CEO John Sculley in 1992 in reference to the Apple Newton, but there were several examples of handheld computers with many of the same capabilities before the Newton. Most early PDAs had a touch screen with a stylus for entering data or for printing letters. Later, many added a miniature keyboard for input. The software on a PDA often includes a calendar, a notepad, an address book, and the ability to display pictures and videos. Most of these capabilities are now built into various versions of smartphones, which are quickly replacing PDAs in the marketplace.

## Smartphones

As mobile phones became smaller, they also took on more features and functions. Paging devices or "beepers," popular in the 1980s, became incorporated into mobile phones such as the BlackBerry from the Canadian company, Research in Motion (RIM). Many phones also developed personal organizing features such as those found in many *personal digital assistants* (PDAs). Gradually, a new type of phone known as a "smartphone" took shape. Current smartphones have taken on some of the functionality of laptop computers, allowing access to e-mail, documents, and office productivity software. Smartphones usually have a miniature QWERTY keyboard, or a virtual keyboard on a touch screen. Smartphones are currently seen as being one of the most suitable platforms for mobile learning purposes.

## Notebook and Netbook Computers

Some people have argued that laptop or notebook computers are not part of mobile computing. Others, including me, see them as part of the mix of technologies that allows people to easily move around and connect to the information cloud wherever they are. Also, notebook and laptop computers have increasingly become thinner, lighter, and smaller, making it even easier for them to be used as mobile learning devices. At the same time, they have become more powerful and much faster than versions available only a few years ago.

New small portal computers, known as *netbooks*, arrived in 2008. They had low-power chips and small screens (usually about seven inches on the diagonal) and were intended mainly for use with the Internet. Their popularity demonstrated that the public wanted lightweight and inexpensive computers that could be put in a bag or purse and used from anywhere with a wireless network connection. Netbook computers clearly fit into the technologies available for mobile learning.

## Tablet Devices and Computers

Tablet computers are special laptop computers shaped like slates which use an electronic stylus or a digital pen to input information onto a touch screen. In 2010, many tablet computers were introduced into the market, including the Apple iPad. Some tablet computers are basically laptop computers with a screen that swivels so that it is on the outside of the computer when it is closed. Other tablet computers have more limited functionality and are used mostly as "e-book readers." These computers, such as the Amazon Kindle, can download documents and books for use by mobile learners at any time.

## Digital Cameras

While both still and video digital cameras are available in a variety of sizes and loaded with many features, they are also being built into the current generation of smartphones and portable media players. Using digital cameras to promote learning through personal production of media is both a learning experience and a way of documenting a learner's activities. Some learners collect what they have done in the form of images and videos to be included in a personal electronic portfolio that can be shown to others whenever they wish.

## Portable Media Players

Portable media players store and play digital media such as audio files, images, and videos. An early, and perhaps the best-known, portable media player is the Apple iPod, launched in October 2001. Because it was early to the market, the term "podcasting" was used to describe the provision of large audio files for playback for educational or informational use. Podcasting is clearly a technology that is part of mobile learning approaches.

While the iPod can play many different audio and video formats, Apple uses a proprietary format (advanced audio coding—AAC) for downloads from its online iTunes store. This means that non-Apple portable media players must play other audio formats, such as MP3. There many brands of MP3 players that compete with the Apple iPod.

As is the case with many other mobile devices, there is a convergence between portable media players and mobile phones, such that many phones can play both audio and video files. Also, there are types of mobile devices that are slightly larger and more conventional than portable media players. Examples include mobile Internet devices (MIDs) and portable DVD players.

## Game Consoles and Portable Gaming Devices

Mobile game-based learning (mGBL) is a rapidly developing subfield that uses general-purpose devices such as mobile phones, portable media players, and PDAs, as well as gaming consoles and handheld gaming devices to deliver educational games. In the United Kingdom, for example, the Royal Navy is using handheld Sony PlayStation Portables (PSPs) to train sailors. This allows sailors to study for tests in confined quarters (*Telegraph*, 2009). Gaming platforms have other mobile learning uses such as doubling as an e-book reader, playing a CD-ROM, or accessing the Internet.

## Portable Navigation Assistants (PNAs)

One of the most common ways we are mobile is when we are driving in a car. Although using mobile devices is dangerous while driving, and in many jurisdictions is now outlawed, several mobile devices are still useful for learning while we drive or as we move around outdoors. For example, portable navigation assistants, using the worldwide global positioning system (GPS), can let us know where we are and guide us to where we are going. GPS devices are also used for exploring the outdoors by guiding a person through an unknown environment or by playing educational location-based games such as "geo-caching." Geo-caching involves players locating hidden trinkets through a set of clues and geographical locations. Using a GPS receiver, the hidden cache is located. The common practice is to remove a trinket from a box, and put another one in its place. You never quite know what you are going to find. Players learn problem-solving techniques, navigation skills, and something about the environment in which the geo-caching game is being played.

As we will see in Chapter 4, location-based applications are a rapidly growing segment of the mobile learning applications market. GPS functionality is built into many smartphones, which has greatly increased the possibilities of using location as a variable in providing information to a learner. This is the basis of a class of applications known as "augmented reality" in which relevant information is overlaid on a picture of the environment in the vicinity of an appropriately equipped mobile learner.

## Audience Response Systems

Audience response systems (also known as personal response systems, electronic voting systems, or "clickers") allow large groups of people in an auditorium or other large venue to vote on a topic or to answer questions. Each member of the audience has a remote control that sends a signal to a receiver, where a computer analyzes the responses and puts out a visualization of the group results. Some people do not believe that these systems should be part of mobile learning because the members of the audience are not mobile. However, audience response systems are now being built into mobile phones, and they allow users to respond to questions appearing on billboards or on television. While the content of such mobile learning is mostly controlled by the producer of the information, learners using audience response systems are becoming increasingly mobile while they interact with this information.

Claims made for an audience response systems include improved attentiveness and engagement, increased knowledge retention, more participation, more fun for learning, quick feedback for instructors on whether an audience is understanding what they are teaching, and, the ability to gather data for input into a database or a learning management system.

## Universal Serial Bus (USB) Storage Devices

USB storage devices (sometimes called "jump drives," "flash drives," or "thumb drives") can be used as a platform for delivery of mobile learning. If learners are not connected to the Internet, software and information can be downloaded into the storage device for playback on a learner's computer. This can be especially useful for field staff when there is not a convenient connection to the Internet. The maximum memory in a USB storage device has been steadily increasing, while costs per gigabyte have steadily dropped. In early 2010 it was possible to buy storage for 256 gigabytes of information on a device that clips onto your keychain.

## Other Mobile Learning Devices in Development

There are many other mobile learning devices that are not well known or widely available, and many more in development. Some of these are special input devices for existing technologies such as mobile phones or PDAs. Others are special output devices that can be used with existing technologies. What they all have in common is that they are only recently on the market, currently in development and being commercialized, or will be on the market in the next two or three years. Many of these devices are discussed later in this book, where we look at uses of mobile learning. Here are brief comments on many of the input and output devices that we look at later:

- ▶ *Bar codes:* A variety of bar codes is available to encode information, and make it available for mobile learners who have the appropriate reader software on their mobile device. Most promising are QR codes (quick response) that can store a message, a URL, or a phone number. Users take a picture of the code that is then processed by special software on their mobile device that interprets the pattern as a web address, phone number or other information. QR codes can be used to link printed materials to mobile phones and Web sites without the user having to type in any information (Fig. 4.7).

▸ *Biofeedback:* Special helmets have been developed that allow the reading of brain waves, which in turn can be used as input into a mobile device. The presenters of a conference paper called"Heart on the Road: HRV Analysis for Monitoring a Driver's Affective State" discuss how to monitor emotions while driving (Riener et al., 2009).

▸ *Digital ink and paper:* Talked about for many years, this technology is still in development. A number of promising prototypes have been developed, including plastic pages that can roll out from a mobile device to form a relatively large screen.

▸ *Digital pens:* Digital pens are input devices that capture handwriting, transform it into digital characters, and store what was written in a computer. They are often used with tablet computers.

▸ *Footpads:* Microsoft has developed a footpad computer interface similar to the one found in the video game *Dance Dance Revolution.*

▸ *Gesture recognition:* New sensing technologies in mobile devices, such as accelerometers and magnetometers, make gesture recognition possible. Chang et al. (2009) report on the Micro-WSNEML project in which classroom gesture detection is possible using a wireless sensor network.

▸ *Haptic devices:* Experimental mobile devices that use the senses of touch and force feedback are already on the market. Ahmad (2008) discusses how multitouch mobile devices can be used to enhance mobile learning capabilities in the workplace. In addition, tangible user interfaces (TUIs) are being developed for use in mobile learning in which the user interacts with information through manipulation of real objects in the environment. For example, in Europe, the WebKit project uses a tangible user interface for navigating the Worldwide Web (WWW) that places priority on direct manipulation—the users control the system and navigate through information by selecting and positioning physical objects, not just icons on a mobile device screen. Holzmann and Hader (2010) discuss how "pressure imaging" can turn everyday objects into input devices for navigation of computer interfaces.

▶ *Implanted devices:* In November 2009, Intel researchers in Pittsburgh announced the development of a "brain chip" that allows the user to surf the Internet, manipulate documents, and play games just by thinking. They claim that these implanted chips will control computers by 2020.

▶ *Instruments and sensors:* An article in the *New York Times* (Nov. 7, 2009) described how the camera in a mobile phone can be adapted as a microscope with some low-cost hardware (Eisenberg, 2009). Mobile phone companies in Japan have developed sensors for smells, allowing a group of mobile phones in a "bad smell network" to detect a pattern of smells, such as the location of a gas leak (Ninh et al., 2007). A wireless sensor network (WSN) can have many sensors that are interconnected. This can be used to extend the possibilities for mobile learning.

▶ *Internet radio:* Internet sites that continually broadcast music and commentary already exist, and many radio networks around the world make their content available on the Internet both live and as an archived file. Blaupunkt, a European audio company, has an Internet car radio ready to go that works via Bluetooth from any mobile phone in the car that has 3G or 4G Internet access through the cell phone network. This technology can be also be used for mobile learning, especially in rural communities without access to conventional radio.

▶ *Location sensing devices:* Many smartphones now have built-in magnetometers used as a compass, an accelerometer for a plumb line, and with GPS capabilities to locate the user. This means that the phone not only knows where the user is located, but which direction the camera on the phone is facing. Additional information, known as "augmented reality," can be overlaid on images of objects at which the camera is pointing. This ability has many applications for mobile learning.

▶ *Miniature or Pico projectors:* 3M has developed a prototype of a miniature LED projector that can shine the output of a smartphone application onto any surface. A company in the United Kingdom, Light Blue Optics, offers a microprojector using holographic laser technology that turns any flat surface into a touch screen. Also, retinal projectors are available as prototypes that project images directly into a person's eye.

▶ *Motion recognition devices:* Accelerometers, which detect motion, have moved from video game platforms like the Wii into mobile phones. This device can monitor exercise performance and bodily movements for playing games. This will increasingly become standard equipment for mobile phones.

▸ *Multitouch screens:* Hand movements, moving several fingers together, pointing, and other gestures are already becoming alternative ways of interacting with computer screens.

▸ *Point of view (POV) devices:* Point of view devices are cameras and microphones that record video from the user's point of view. The cameras and microphones are often built into eyeglasses or other forms of headgear. Point of view recordings are used to document a person's learning, and the resulting video can be stored as part of a personal electronic portfolio.

▸ *RFID tags for learning:* RFID stands for "radio frequency identification," a technology built into electronic tags that can be placed anywhere. The electronic tags broadcast a message over a very short distance, which is then picked up by an RFID receiver in a mobile device. Such devices have been used successfully in outdoor education or as electronic guides at public sites such as museums or zoos.

▸ *Ruggidized Mobile Computers:* Special ruggedized mobile computers can be used for learning materials or delivery of "just-in-time" information in the field (Fig. 2.2).

▸ *Speech recognition:* The use of speech recognition software in mobile devices reduces the amount of typing necessary and improves access for persons with a disability. It can also be used for assessment and diagnostics in the teaching of foreign languages.

▸ *Wearable devices:* Special gloves and headsets, as well as computers built into all types of clothing, are being used on an experimental basis as learning platforms.

# Mobile Network Infrastructure

Mobile devices generally don't work by themselves but are connected to other technologies through mobile networks. Even devices that can be used as standalone units need to be connected to a network or a computer occasionally in order to synchronize their content with a larger pool of information. This

**FIGURE 2.2 Ruggedized mobile computers can be used for mobile learning by workers in outdoor environments. Courtesy of Psion Teklogix.**

section of the book briefly describes the network infrastructure that is used to support mobile learning. (While it is more technical than the rest of the book, it is not overwhelmingly so, and the reader is encouraged to work through it.)

## Mobile Networks

As noted previously in this chapter, the first cellular network for mobile phones was installed in Tokyo in 1979. This first cell system is now considered a 1G (first generation) network. Currently, we are using 3G networks in most of the world, with broadband 4G networks in early release across select markets. Specialized 5G networks for research and education (R&E networks) are now being proposed and discussed (St. Arnaud, 2010a, 2010b). The first four generations have been described as:

- Analog cellular telephony (1G)
- Digital mobile communication (2G)
- Wideband mobile communication (3G)
- Broadband fourth generation networks (4G)

Both fixed-line and mobile phone networks are moving toward convergence with each other, with the aim of phone companies providing each user with access to all services with a single phone. Fig. 2.3 show the architecture of a typical phone network used for mobile learning.

Before a network is set up and seeded with content, there are administrative tasks like planning, budgeting, and implementation that need to be completed. Additionally, content for the mobile learning system needs to be prepared using a variety of software tools (more about creating content in Chapter 9). The information in a mobile learning network is usually stored in multiple core servers in a hosting center, and, if it is an enterprise system for a single company, the information is also usually behind a secure firewall, which is software to prevent unauthorized intruders from having access to the information. The servers can be connected to several other specialized computers, to allow Internet access, to send messages through the company's corporate phone system (Private branch exchange or PBX), to serve voice content through an interactive voice response (IVR) system, or to send out text through a "short message service" (SMS) server. Mobile users connect to either a mobile voice network or an Internet data networks run by one of the major mobile phone carriers or by a voice over Internet protocol (VoIP) provider.

There are several different standards or protocols for transmitting mobile signals throughout networks. However, because this is not a technical book

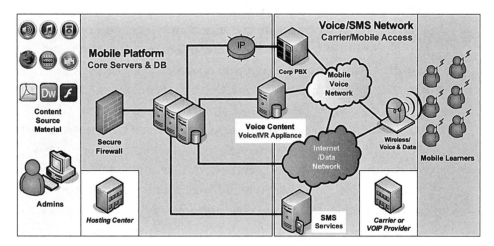

**FIGURE 2.3 A typical mobile learning network infrastructure. Courtesy of OnPoint Digital.**

on mobile phones, we will not delve into the various acronyms and specifications that are available. What is important to note is that many phones work with only one or two different standards and will not necessarily work in all locations around the world. Mobile phone vendors can sell you specific models of phones that switch from one standard to the other as you move around the globe.

The standards and protocols that are used in each network are determined by large companies known as "carriers" in an environment regulated by governments at several different levels. Unlike the Internet, which has little in the way of government regulation, mobile computing is very much under control of these regulatory bodies. The only real way around this is to use "device to device connectivity" and build your own private mobile network. The technologies for doing this are sometimes called ad hoc networks, mesh networks, or peer-to-peer networks.

## Mobile Operating Systems

There is more bad news if you want to have a simple system for mobile learning. Not only are there different standards and protocols on networks around the world, but each mobile phone in a network could also be using a different *mobile operating system* from the next phone. As of 2009, there were at least seven different operating systems in use by mobile phones around the world. The breakdown of use of different operating systems is shown in Fig. 2.4. While Nokia's Symbian operating system (now open source) has about 50 percent of the market for smartphones and is widely used in Europe, in North America the most common operating systems are Research in Motion's BlackBerry OS, Apple's iPhone OS, and Windows Mobile from Microsoft. However, a new open source operating system from Google, known as Android, looks poised to capture a large share of the market in 2010.

The diversity of operating systems will improve in the next few years, as one or two operating systems become dominant and as mobile standards develop. Many new mobile browsers are moving towards a browser layout called WebKit, a new model for displaying Web pages. Much like earlier standards compliant Web browsers helped online content delivery to desktop personal computers running vastly different operating systems (e.g., Microsoft Windows, Apple Mac OS, Linux, Unix) gain universal acceptance, market acceptance of Web-

**Global Smartphone Sales, Q2 2009**

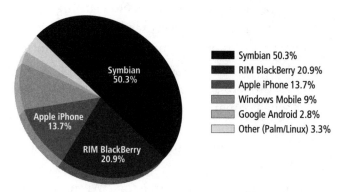

- Symbian 50.3%
- RIM BlackBerry 20.9%
- Apple iPhone 13.7%
- Windows Mobile 9%
- Google Android 2.8%
- Other (Palm/Linux) 3.3%

**FIGURE 2.4 Global smartphone sales by operating system, second quarter, 2009. Source: Wikipedia, used under a Creative Commons license.**

Kit-enabled mobile Web browsers will begin to normalize content delivery to mobile devices and ensure more consistent content presentation to all mobile learners. The Apple Safari browser, and Google's Chrome browser both are built around WebKit, and more mobile phone manufacturers like Research in Motion and Nokia are moving to support this emerging standard.

## Mobile Learning Contexts

Understanding the mobile learning ecosystem is not just a matter of looking at a variety of mobile devices and the structure of mobile networks. Mobile learning takes place in a set of contexts that also adds complexity to understanding what works best.

Mobile learning is often defined by the fact that we're using a mobile device. But there are different ways of being mobile. For example, we may find ourselves in an environment that is mobile, such as a train or airplane. Using embedded or ubiquitous computing applications built into the environment, it is also possible for an individual to access mobile learning while moving by interacting with the environment immediately around him. This will increasingly be the trend as mobile computing technology becomes invisible and simply part of the world we take for granted.

Organizational and business objectives may dictate what kinds of technologies can be used as solutions to learning problems. Within an organization there can be both acceptance of and resistance to change and to the introduction of mobile computing solutions. Introducing a mobile learning ecosystem into a large organization can have a profound effect on how things work within both small groups and the organization as a whole.

Mobile computing is a highly regulated industry. One reason for this is that there is a limited amount of bandwidth available in the wireless radio spectrum. This must be allocated, a job that is usually undertaken by government bodies.

Then, there are human factors. We need to know a lot about the end user of mobile computing in order to properly design a system that works efficiently and positively. Human factors include issues like the locations and settings where mobile learning will take place. What are the lighting, noise levels, and social environments surrounding the users while they're engaged in mobile learning? Is mobile learning likely to take place outdoors or indoors? If it is outdoors, what are potential weather conditions that may make learning difficult? What are the other obstacles in the environment that we need to be aware of?

Knowing the ages and physical characteristics of the end users for mobile learning is also important. When the learners are engaged with information, will they be sitting, standing, or walking? Will they be using one hand or two hands, or another input device that is not based on use of hands at all? What else will they be doing while engaged in mobile learning?

As you can see, there is a lot of information to be gathered and many decisions to be made before we can start developing for mobile learning. I discuss more of these issues when we look at the creation of mobile learning content in Chapter 9.

 ## Mobile Learning Content Sources

We tend to think of mobile learning as being connected to schools or to some form of formal training. But mobile learning is potentially disruptive because it connects us to many sources of information when we need them and from wherever we are located. In the past, teachers and instructors were sources of information, which they tried to pass on through the act of instruction. While the use of classrooms and instruction will continue for some time, there will ultimately be less of a need for the expert to be standing in front of students in a designated room in order for learning to take place.

As any given mobile learning ecosystem develops, learners in that system will be able to draw information and interactive content from a huge variety of sources. These sources include applications and databases that have been purpose-built for mobile learning by organizations at all levels. A new industry is developing for the conversion of traditional classroom content and e-learning content to mobile learning materials. Mobile learning materials tend to be delivered in small chunks, sometimes referred to as "mobile interactive learning objects" (MILOs). Small bits of information are preferred for mobile learning because of the small screens and because learners are not likely to sit for long stretches working through instructional materials.

There are many other sources of information besides custom-developed content. For example, there are different kinds of feeds from the Internet that can be read on mobile devices. Generally these are delivered through a technology called RSS (which may stand for "really simple syndication," although no one is quite sure of its origins). RSS feeds are picked up by special readers that list the headlines for all items in the feed.

Tags of all sorts are being proposed to label the world around us so that it can be read by software inside mobile devices. For example, Inman (2009) suggested that with respect to food choices, "Customers in stores should eventually be able to photograph a product's bar code with their phone, and be directed to the relevant charts and videos."

Location-specific information is rapidly becoming available for many services, but it can also be used for mobile learning. Because your smartphone generally knows where you are and in which direction you are facing if you take a picture, information about the view ahead of you can be provided as an overlay on the image you photograph. Also, smartphones will be able to connect you with friends or experts who are located near where you happen to be at any given moment. And meeting new people could also be mediated by decisions made based on information inside your mobile phone.

By now most of us are quite aware of the Internet and the content of the World Wide Web. As the new mobile computing industry develops, there is a rush to build proprietary applications and information repositories in order to make money in what is seen to be a rapidly rising industry. However, because most smartphones have a Web browser, an alternative to proprietary applications is the placement of information and programs directly on the Internet. These can then be accessed through a browser. The main problem with Web-based content for mobile phones is that HTML is not as powerful as many of the computer languages that are used to create proprietary applications. This difference between browser-based content and native applications may lessen with the release of HTML 5.

For the moment, however, most proprietary applications are available at app stores that sell downloadable programs for as little as 69 cents. There are app stores for each of the major brands of mobile phones, with the iPhone store having the most content available by far. In addition to educational applications, the various app stores sell music, podcasts, e-books, videos, and other forms of content.

Finally, if you want to develop your own content, I have outlined the processes of development and design for mobile learning in Chapter 9.

 ## Mobile Browsers

While developers of *Web-based* mobile learning content can produce applications that are truly cross-platform, they must contend with the fact that (1) Web-based applications are usually not as powerful, fast, or detailed as proprietary apps, and (2) there are over 30 mobile browsers in use that translate HTML content into slightly different formats for display. Developers of Web-based mobile learning content need to test their materials with at least the three or four leading mobile browsers to make sure that everything works the way it was planned.

Browsers, like any other software program, are developed for specific mobile platforms. So it is not surprising to find that the major brands of smartphones each has its own browser. In addition, there are generic mobile browsers that will work on a number of different (but usually not all) mobile operating systems. Opera Mini, available since 2006, is a downloadable mobile browser that works on many brands of smartphones, including, most recently, the Apple iPhone but certain features work differently across the various smartphones. For example, limited support for JavaScript and content frames on BlackBerry devices limits their ability to take full advantage of advanced mobile Web browsers.

# Mobile Learning Applications, Uses, and Experiences

Rounding out the picture of the mobile learning ecosystem are all the applications and uses that been developed for mobile learning to date. Also, it is possible to have mobile learning experiences using existing information services that are not based on specific programs or applications. In the next four chapters, I spend considerable time discussing a variety of uses of mobile learning. In order to make sense of the over 50 uses of mobile learning that I've identified, I've developed three categories of uses of mobile learning that correspond to the next three chapters. In addition, management applications for mobile learning are reviewed in Chapter 7. The uses of mobile learning that are covered in this book are:

## Information Retrieval (Chapter 4)

- ► Customer education
- ► Digital media channels
- ► Feeds
- ► Just-in-time information
- ► Libraries
- ► Location-based information
- ► Maps and satellite photos
- ► Presentations
- ► Search and retrieve
- ► Signs and kiosks
- ► Tags
- ► Translations
- ► Universal Serial Bus (USB) storage devices

## Information Gathering and Analysis (Chapter 5)

- ► Assessment and evaluation
- ► First-person documentation
- ► Monitoring and trend tracking

- Research and data collection
- User-generated information and learning materials

## Communicating, Interacting, and Networking (Chapter 6)

- Network science
- Collaboration and communities
- Mobile games, simulations, and virtual worlds
- Mentoring, support, and cognitive apprenticeships
- Text messaging
- Personal media production
- Social media

## Mobile Management of Learning, Knowledge, and Performance (Chapter 7)

- Classroom uses of mobile technologies
- Emergency and Health-Care Uses of Mobile Learning
- Knowledge management
- Learning management
- Team management
- Shift in power with mobile learning

# Putting It All Together: Building a Mobile Learning System

Ten years ago the first versions of mobile learning were all about putting legacy print materials and e-learning courses on the small screens of mobile phones. The thinking for Mobile 1.0 was based on the traditional model of classroom instruction in which an expert instructor conveys information to a learner who then "absorbs it" and hopefully retains it. It was not surprising, therefore, to see applications such as lectures on mobile phones, stripped-down presentations, simple multiple-choice tests, and text messages as the principal formats of mobile learning materials 10 years ago (Nantel, 2001). Because instructors were in charge, learning management systems, popular on desktop computers at the time, were also developed for mobile use.

The past 8 to 10 years have changed the idea of learning in important ways. There is now an emphasis on the user-centered learning and a push to use the unique "affordances" of mobile learning to do things that previously were not even possible. The characteristics of mobile learning systems that allow this change include:

- *Mobility:* Devices can be taken anywhere and access to the information cloud can be found readily.
- *Ubiquity:* Mobile devices have a very high penetration rate throughout the world, and have evolved into much more than just phones.
- *Accessibility:* The advent of cloud computing coupled with mobile devices has meant that all the information on the Internet, and proprietary sources of information, are available at a moment's notice. This has allowed us to augment our experience in the world with additional information when needed.
- *Connectivity:* Global social networking and communications make it easy to be in touch with anyone around the world who has access to a mobile device. This makes collaboration using mobile devices possible.
- *Context sensitivity:* Mobile devices can sense the user's location and orientation, and thereby know his or her environment. They can also sense the time and store information about the characteristics of the user.
- *Individuality:* Mobile devices are personal, although in some developing countries they may be shared by a community or a group. Because they are personal, mobile learning can be individualized to the needs of each learner.
- *Creativity:* highly capable mobile devices can serve as content generation platforms, allowing the mobile learner to create and contribute to mobile learning materials.

In Chapters 4 to 7 we look at the unique uses for mobile learning that take advantage of these characteristics. In Chapters 8, 9, and 10, with the help of my colleagues David Fell and Sheryl Herle, we discuss how to develop a business strategy for corporate mobile learning, create content and experiences for learners on the move, and implement and manage an enterprisewide mobile learning system.

# Methods for Effective Mobile Learning: Seven Principles for Employee Training

There is little doubt that we are in a period of immense change in terms of teaching and training methodologies. It is hard to grasp the impact of this change simply because we have been so immersed in the heritage of the past 300 years that it has conditioned our responses to teaching and learning.

> "We don't know who discovered water, but it certainly wasn't the fish."
> —*Marshall McLuhan (McLuhan and Fiore, 1968)*

Before the development of modern classrooms in the late 1700s, only a few people actually went to school. Schools were run by schoolmasters, who were usually equipped with a whip to ensure compliance, and the curriculum was mostly about memorizing religious materials. Around 1770, in Prussia (now part of Germany), a devoted group of Protestants known as the Pietists developed modern teaching practices for schools and universities that we now take for granted. The Pietists invented the modern classroom, with such features as having students sitting in long rows facing the teacher, raising of hands, periods of scheduled instruction, detentions, recess, and standardized curricula. To train their teachers, the Pietists also built and ran "normal schools" that modeled this new approach.

Before Gutenberg invented the printing press in the 1430s, books were manuscripts that were copied by hand. With the invention of the printing press, standardization of printed materials was made possible. Now everyone could follow standard textbooks, the printed Bible, and grade-appropriate materials. The new disciplinary structures of the classroom meant that students were *immobilized* in their seats for most of the day. Classrooms, and their associated technologies of desks and blackboards, were the *new* learning technologies of their time. Little has changed in the organization of teaching over the last several hundred years; these same technologies have been part of the learning experiences for most of us today.

Marshall McLuhan once remarked that the initial content of new technologies is the content of the old technologies (McLuhan, 1966). So, it is not surprising to see that the first attempts at using digital technologies for teaching, such as e-learning and mobile learning, were essentially the placement of existing school structures, practices, and processes into electronic formats. Most of the learning software developed for both desktop computers and for use with mobile devices has been software to support online virtual classrooms, learning management systems, computer-based assessments, and online lectures and presentations, complete with instructor controls, "blackboards," "chalk," enrollment lists, and online "raising hands." These are all technologies that either support or mimic the traditional way to teach — by using classrooms and presentations and tests given by instructors.

In many ways, the standard format for schooling has paralleled the bureaucratization of the world whereby humans have been made into just another object in the production system. The sociologist George Ritzer calls this process "McDonaldization" after the well-known chain of hamburger restaurants that profitably applied these principles to the way hamburgers and fries are delivered to the end customer.

These approaches were tried with online teaching in the 1980s, in the early days of e-learning, and were subsequently rejected by many as too mechanistic and controlling for deep learning to take place. The result of treating learners as mechanical objects in a closed system is "the learners' inability to reflect effectively upon their own learning . . . a product of an educational system that fails to hand responsibility for learning and problem-solving over to learners" (Koschmann et al., 1996).

Treating learners as individual objects also fails to take into account the social nature of human beings and the fact that all of us are immersed in a specific cultural context that also greatly influences how we learn.

At this point I want to assure you that I don't intend to develop a complete critique and treatise on the many varieties of learning theories that exist today. There are several excellent summaries of learning theories for mobile learning readily available; outstanding among them is the 2005 document from the MOBIlearn project titled "Pedagogical Methodologies and Paradigms: Guidelines for Learning/Teaching/Tutoring in a Mobile Environment" (O'Malley et al., 2005) and two Web sites—Greg Kearsley's Theory into Practice (TIP) database at http://tip.psychology.org and Martin Ryder's Models of Instructional Design Web site at http://carbon.ucdenver.edu/~mryder/itc/idmodels.html.

It is important to understand that some of the resistance to the use of mobile learning is because it challenges familiar practices of schooling and training along with the learning theories that support these practices. In corporate training, this legacy of traditional schooling can be seen in the overuse of behavioral principles, an overreliance on measurement, and an almost exclusive focus on "performance support." In this view, people are seen as performers who need to increase their output for the sake of improving a business. While improved business efficiency and productivity are always good things, the current practices that are advanced to support that goal do not take into account either the complex nature of human learning or the other interests to which people respond.

Because mobile learning unties the learner from the classroom, it can be seen as a "liberating technology." This can be very disruptive to the traditional ways of doing things. But in a world of constant change, where innovation and creativity are highly valued, disruption may very well be a good thing for a business.

In this chapter I develop seven basic principles about mobile learning for employee training that you will need to know if you are to successfully take on the potentially disruptive (but ultimately rewarding) project of introducing mobile learning to your organization:

*Principle 1*: Employees are adults who learn differently from children.
*Principle 2*: Employees learn from solving problems that matter to them.
*Principle 3*: Employees learn by collaborating as members of cohesive
social groups.

*Principle 4*: Employees learn through conversing with, and listening to, each other.

*Principle 5*: Employees learn by integrating new information with what they already know.

*Principle 6*: Employees learn through active experiences that involve their senses and their bodies.

*Principle 7*: Employees learn best in concrete situations where the context matters to them.

In the rest of this chapter, I explain these principles and show you how best to apply them to the design of mobile learning.

 ## Principle 1: Employees Are Adults Who Learn Differently from Children

While it may seem obvious that employees are adults, it is an important point to make given that most learning theories and empirical studies of learning are based on children of various ages or on animal studies. Early learning theorists studied animals such as rats or pigeons because they thought that learning could be reduced to simple stimulus and response sequences. Children's learning was studied because children were readily accessible and under the control of adults. There have been comparatively fewer studies of learning at various stages of adult life.

But children's learning and adult learning differ in several important ways (Knowles, 1984a, 1984b). Most adults are self-directed and are expected to take responsibility for their actions and decisions. Because adults can make their own decisions, it is important that they be involved in the planning and evaluation of any learning program. Having been through school, most adults are not interested in memorizing more content but like new experiences as the basis of their learning activities.

Adults who are self-directed usually also have a purpose in their lives. This means that learning activities need to be relevant to the learners' interests and goals, and individualized in terms of their learning objectives. Of course, much employee training is, and should be, based on the business objectives of the organization for which the employee works. However, business objectives by themselves generally do not motivate employees to learn except under the threat of dismissal.

Much of what employees learned in school has been long forgotten, or at best is no longer relevant to the employees' current jobs or interests. Any new learning an employee achieves should be based on what she needs to know to do her job or what really interests her. For many employees, school was not an enjoyable experience. Adults want learning to take place at their own pace, when they need it, and at their work site.

## Relevance for Mobile Learning

Designing mobile learning for adults means paying attention to individualization, interactivity, and employee interests, while leveraging meaning, context, and motivation in order to actively engage the adult learner. The content of mobile learning activities should not be frivolous or patronizing. This doesn't mean that adults don't like playing games. On the contrary, many of the young people joining the workforce today have grown up with video games on their computers and on their mobile phones. While young adults are quite comfortable with the social networking aspects of mobile learning, there needs to be a clear separation between hanging out with one's friends and work-related mobile learning.

 # Principle 2: Employees Learn from Solving Problems that Matter to Them

Problem-based learning works well with adult learners, especially when the problems are real and based on issues that matter to the person solving the problem. Problem-based learning is a methodology that seeks to improve learners' critical thinking skills and knowledge base by giving them sample problems similar to the ones that they might encounter in their future jobs or professional practice.

Problem-based learning was first developed in 1969 at McMaster University in Canada as a methodology for medical education. It is still extensively used in the medical field. As trainees explore problems, they document the areas of knowledge they need to further investigate in order to understand and solve the problem. Data are gathered, hypotheses are stated, and plans are drawn up for further inquiry. All of this is done in a very structured manner, and the information that is collected is used to develop a plan that could be applied to a real-life situation: define the problem, find solutions, reflect on the process, and evaluate the outcomes.

When problem-based learning is carried out in a group, it is sometimes referred to as a "community of inquiry" model (Garrison and Anderson, 2003). Inquiry-based learning is similar to problem-based learning in that the learner pursues an issue that is of interest to him. This means that the learner owns the process of searching for answers and exploring options. It also means that he has taken some responsibility for the outcome of his actions.

## Relevance for Mobile Learning

From a learner's perspective, solving real problems that are important to the learner is much more motivating than dealing with curricula that have been selected by others. Authentic learning is sensitive to the learner's orientation, goals, and experiences in the learning process. These factors determine the nature and usability of what is learned. Instruction should be based on problems and activities that are found in the real world (Koschmann et al., 1996). Networked mobile devices link employees to sources of information about the concrete situations in which they find themselves. With networked mobile learning devices, your employees can get out of the classrooms and into the real world and be exactly where meaningful learning happens.

Because the world is complex and always changing, employees learn best with multiple perspectives and sources of information. Also, specific individuals move through the world in a unique path. Because of the ability of mobile devices to track location, the trail of a learner can be recorded and used for both evaluation and feedback. Learning should always have a quality of tentativeness about it because of the rapid change of circumstances and information the learner may encounter.

## Principle 3: Employees Learn by Collaborating as Members of Cohesive Social Groups

All learning is social. That is, without other people in our lives, we would learn very little. We tend to think of ourselves as individuals operating independently of others. But from birth we interact with those around us in terms of learning language, concepts, and behaviors. This social context is with us even when we are by ourselves, because our thoughts and reactions have been deeply influenced by those others with whom we interact on a regular basis.

Being identified with a specific social group is part of our evolutionary history. We hunted, gathered, fought wars, and communicated with each other in the context of a group. In terms of learning, Gerry Stahl (2006) argues that, "The individual is always essentially engaged in a shared world and . . . the network of meanings that define the individual situation are historically, culturally, and socially defined" (p. 235). Stahl goes even further in stating that individual learning may *automatically* take place within collaborative interactions.

> "It may be that group learning often supplies an essential basis for individual learning, providing not only the cultural background, the motivational support, and the interactional location, but also an effective mechanism for ensuring individual learning" (p. 274).

We need to distinguish between *individual learning* through collaboration and developing *collective intelligence* through learning in groups. Collaborative learning can make us more knowledgeable as individuals, but it also adds to the "distributed cognition" of communities and societies as a whole, especially when there is an informational artifact left behind that has been produced as the result of collaboration. In fact, learning is *both* an individual process and a social process; too much emphasis on individual identities in collaborative projects can inhibit group learning.

## Relevance for Mobile Learning

A mobile network can make a significant contribution to the process of learning and collaborating with others. Having rapid access to others at any time and any place facilitates both individual and group learning. When the results of mobile-based collaboration are stored on databases for easy retrieval, the results are the construction of a permanent archive that can be accessed at will by anyone in the group, thus contributing to the growth of collective intelligence within the group.

# Principle 4: Employees Learn through Conversing with, and Listening to, Each Other

Most of our thinking, communicating, and understanding is mediated through the use of language. From our early experiences as children, we build up our language and concepts as a set of metaphors as we interact with others and listen to what they have to say. Metaphors are the building blocks of language; they allow us to group and categorize our thoughts. Metaphors also help us to make connections with our own real experiences which can serve as a basis for understanding new, unfamiliar phenomena. Often we can gain new insights and arrive at innovations simply by changing the metaphors we use (Lakoff and Johnson, 1980).

Learning with others involves conversation. This is true even if the encounter is between a teacher and a student. Professor Diana Laurillard (2002) has developed a "conversational framework for learning." While her original conceptualization involved conversation between the student and teacher, it has been adapted by others to show that the processes Laurillard identified could happen with any conversational partner.

Learning is the process of making sense of the world as the learner knows it to be, as well as expanding the knowledge the learner has of how the world actually is. Learning should not be a question of memorizing facts and repeating them back on a test. This kind of learning is known as "surface learning." "Deep learning," by contrast, happens when the learner takes control of his own learning processes and expands what he knows about the world as a result of searching for answers to questions that matter to him.

All learning can be enhanced by the process of articulation—that is, when a learner explains to another learner what she has learned and in turn listens to others tell what they have learned. But, by itself, articulation, or conversation does not necessarily lead to deep learning. Deep learning is where learning is integrated with the learner's prior knowledge and goes beyond the simple memorization of facts (surface learning).

Deep learning requires reflection—where a learner looks back at what happened—and evaluation—where the learner assesses the outcomes of applying what she has learned. Finally, a deep learning cycle is concluded when the learner is able to make adjustments in her thinking and practices.

## Relevance for Mobile Learning

We already are in the habit of using use mobile phones to talk to each other. This means that mobile phones are especially suited to conversational learning. By way of contrast, many instructors insist that learners in classrooms put their phones away and not use them. Yet mobile phone technology can be used to facilitate deep learning because it affords learners the ability to talk to almost anyone, located anywhere, about what they have just learned. Learning through conversation is supported by such activities as mentoring and "cognitive apprenticeships" in which an experienced person who may very well be physically far removed from the learner, is able, nonetheless, to provide guidance, information, and advice as needed.

# Principle 5: Employees Learn by Integrating Information with What They Already Know

Learning has been shown to be both a process of accommodating new information and integrating it with what a learner already knows. It can also be a process of adaptation in which the conceptual framework of what a learner already knows is changed to take the new information into account. While accumulating new information into a storehouse of knowledge can be useful, it is also often good for learners to shake up their existing conceptual frameworks. Employees often learn when their present understanding of how the world works is disrupted and they must adapt and modify their existing conceptual framework of the world.

Good teachers know that, to have learners grasp a new idea, it is best to start with what they already know and move them along a series of steps toward the new idea. This process has been called *scaffolding* by cognitive psychologist Jerome Bruner (1966). As in the world of construction, scaffolds are used to support the construction of knowledge and are taken away as the learners become more confident about learning a subject by themselves. Scaffolding can take place in any learning encounter, whether it is between an employee and a trainer, a novice and an apprentice, or peer-to-peer teaching. When members of a group learn from each other's experiences and knowledge, this is known as *reciprocal scaffolding*.

Clark Quinn (2007) suggests that scaffolding should follow the "least assistance principle." He says:

> The "Least Assistance" Principle is an extension of minimalism for mobile design. Translated to our mobile devices, the principle is "what small amount could we make available to a person that would make them more, or most, effective?" One of the ways you need to think different is to start thinking about the small things you can do that will make a big difference.

But being a social learner is not just a matter of having other people, more experienced than us, teaching us what we need to know. It is also the fact that we are embedded in a culture that we observe and in which we act and share a common life with others. Language tools such as speech and writing are developed within a culture and carry meaning and concepts in their words. These words mediate the social environment through which each of us moves. As we absorb and reproduce language, we move to higher thinking skills through the manipulation of verbal concepts.

## Relevance for Mobile Learning

Because mobile learning connects learners to each other, as well as to trainers and experts, the idea of scaffolding argues for a personalized/individualized approach to designing mobile learning experiences and content. As much as possible, learners need to take control of their own learning processes and use mobile learning as a way of gaining information about a problem that they are working on *in their present environment*. In order to integrate what is being learned through a mobile experience with a learner's own knowledge base, it is best that learners be in charge of their own learning. Trainers involved with mobile learning can play a facilitation role that leads to scaffolding, rather than just providing instruction based on a set curriculum.

## Principle 6: Employees Learn through Active Experiences that Involve Their Senses and Their Bodies

While we tend to think of learning as mostly involving the brain, it in fact involves the whole body. Learning is experiential and not separate from the direct experience of living as an embodied being in a physical world. Even when we read something, for example, we are having a physical experience. The words on the page evoke images and concepts in our minds that relate to the physical world that we move through on a daily basis. As George Lakoff and Mark Johnson have argued in their 1980 book *Metaphors We Live By*, words stimulate our imagination because they are often metaphors that help us recall our past physical experiences whether those experiences are from our childhood or from our current lives.

One immediate way to learn is through direct, active experiences. All our senses constantly take in information that is then processed by our brain at an unconscious level. These sensations are integrated with already existing memories of other similar experiences. We are conscious of only a small fraction of the information that is available to us through our senses at any given time. And, even if we are conscious of learning something, it gradually becomes part of our unconscious thinking.

A learner usually has a particular task or activity to accomplish. This task or activity is mediated by a set of tools, as well as by the sociocultural context that the learner inhabits. The actions of the learner must be understood through the lens of the rules of the community in which she is embedded. Teachers and trainers must consider the whole activity in which the learner is engaged in order to properly evaluate both the learning environments and the tools we might want to use.

### Relevance for Mobile Learning

Learning is not an activity that is isolated in the brain. Mobile devices are mediating tools that can help create rich and meaningful learning experiences. Learning takes place when there is a relevant activity from which the learner is able to gain new insights and knowledge.

## Principle 7: Employees Learn Best in Concrete Situations Where the Context Matters to Them

Employees are always part of particular social situation, and they are always found at a specific, physical location. In other words, learning is both socially and physically situated and contextual. The role of the trainer is to help employees to get into situations—both social and locational—that will be productive for learning, and to facilitate employee learning where employees are socially and physically located. This process is sometimes referred to as a *cognitive apprenticeship.*

> The situated learning paradigm holds that learning is not merely the acquisition of knowledge by individuals, but instead is a process of social participation . . . the idea of cognitive apprenticeship [is] where teachers (the experts) work alongside students (the apprentices) to create situations where the students can begin to work on problems even before they fully understand them. (Naismith et al., 2004)

Context awareness refers to trainers being aware of what is going on around the learner in order to provide learners with the most relevant information and activities for learning. Traditional education and training tries to reduce contexts and standardize the environments for learning. Contextual learning does the opposite—it uses the changing contexts to increase the opportunities for learning.

## Relevance for Mobile Learning

Mobile learning is ideally built around a series of learning activities where mobile devices are mediating accessories to the experience and not the focus of attention. Mobile devices can now detect many aspects of the learner's context and provide personalized learning experiences. Mobile devices move with the learner. This means that they are especially suited to context-aware applications because they are available wherever the learner is located. The best use of mobile devices for contextual learning is to have learners focus on the world around them and use the mobile device to augment the information that is already available in the physical environment.

Activities such as outdoor games, tours of museums and galleries, and the use of augmented reality to supplement information in each location are some of the activities that are best suited to this kind of mobile learning.

# Learning Theories and Mobile Learning

There are many theories that try to explain how people learn; over 50 are listed and described on the Theories into Practice (TIP) Web site. Most are variations on three major theoretical orientations—behaviorism, cognitivism, and constructivism. These three approaches have been criticized as being inadequate for describing the new world of digital learning technologies, and mobile learning in particular. New theories that more accurately describe what is happening in mobile learning are emerging.

## Behaviorism

Behaviorism is based on the idea that only observable behavior can be studied scientifically. It reduces human behavior to simple operators such as stimulus and response and punishment and reward, and it proposes a set of principles and processes for how these operators work together. It ignores the internal experiences of people and minimizes the role of social groups in learning. Behaviorists advocate the teaching of simple tasks, which added together, can produce a more complex set of behaviors.

Standardizing how people are treated simplifies the task of teaching, and in the minds of many, makes the enterprise more efficient. It is not surprising, then, to find that early learning theories such as behaviorism treated people as reducible to discrete objects. Behaviorism spawned teaching machines and mechanical approaches to "programmed learning," a method of continuous presentation of facts followed by tests, along with appropriate rewards for getting answers correct. Perhaps its biggest impact on the field of adult learning was the formulation of the methods of instructional systems design (ISD) and "mastery learning." As Alessi and Trollip (2001) explain:

> ISD procedures are largely based on behavioral psychology. Their emphasis is on specifying behavioral objectives (statements of things the learner will be able to do at the end of instruction), analyzing learning tasks and activities and teaching to specific levels of learner performance. The ISD model begins at the curriculum level with analysis of content, definition of overall objectives, and delineation of sequences and subsequences of the curriculum. It proceeds with the selection of instructional methods and media, designing individual lessons to enhance learner mastery of the objectives, developing delivery systems for the individual lessons, and ends with the evaluation of the lessons and the entire instructional system. Evaluation in ISD emphasizes measurement of observable target behaviors.

Mobile learning activities based on this simplistic view of human learning include various types of flashcard games, and drill and practice types of exercises and games. As O'Malley et al. (2005) note, behavioral models of teaching are "Very much a transmission model of teaching, with the tutor seen as driving the learning lessons." One attempt to overcome the objections to behaviorism was to formulate new theories based on the operation of the brain, based on new findings and theories in neurological research. This approach is known as cognitivism.

## Cognitivism

Cognitivism is a theoretical approach to learning that looks at how we process information. It focuses on unobservable constructs, "such as the mind, memory, attitudes, motivation, thinking, reflection, and other presumed internal processes" (Alessi and Trollip, 2001). It models itself on how computers work, referring to inputs and outputs, as well as how information is transformed in the brain. It is concerned with both long-term and short-term memory and the construction of concepts in the developing mind. Cognitive psychologists don't necessarily reject behavioral principles and insights; they often see both approaches as working together to give a more complete view of learning and thinking.

Because cognitive psychology is focused on the operations of an individual brain, it is quite inadequate as a theory for mobile learning. It doesn't address the fact that mobile learners are networked or that each learner can have a unique experience of learning while on the move. The fact that we all learn differently and that the content of what we learn is unique to each individual is addressed by a third learning theory known as constructivism.

## Constructivism

The seventeenth- century philosopher John Locke thought that children were born as "blank slates" and needed to be written on by the processes of education and training. We now know that this view is wrong. Children are born with certain capacities for action and with a motivation to learn about the world. But, according to constructivism, each person actively constructs an understanding of the world throughout life, taking in certain experiences and rejecting others as sources of knowledge. This doesn't mean that sociocultural influences don't matter; rather, it means that each of us pulls together a view of the world that is uniquely ours but that also has much in common with the view of others. We share a culture with those closest to us, and in this way we learn about what is acceptable to do or say in any given situation.

In present day culture we are bombarded with an overwhelming amount of information and experiences vying for our attention. We select those things that fit with our identities and with the goals and purposes in we have in life.

The constructivist perspective argues that our knowledge about the social world and our ideas about what is good and desirable and what is worthy of pursuing are all "socially constructed." The constructivist perspective is the leading learning theory of the present time, and it incorporates many of the seven principles articulated above. But, for understanding mobile learning, it is not enough.

Employees learn deeply when they take charge of their own learning, embark on a voyage of discovery, and "learn how to learn" (a process known as "metacognition"). Adult learners need to approach the task of learning as strategists and agents (Wintrup et al., 2009). They need to take charge of their own learning and decide on which aspects of a learning environment they should focus their attention. This sense of agency is important to being an adult in a democratic society:

> Personal agency requires not only purpose, but knowledge of processes, cultures and norms, in order to influence relationships and access learning opportunities. Easily accessible information about entitlements, risks, rules—and when these change—is essential to students, as needed. Working students, with little time to waste, require strategic approaches to study: organising time and study methods, understanding assessment, self-regulating effort and developing meta-cognition. It is unusual though, for such approaches to be explicitly encouraged and facilitated; students described taking many months or even years to work this out. (Wintrup et al., 2009).

Mobile learning supports a constructivist learning philosophy because it advocates that learners be afforded information when they need and want it, and not that the learner receives his information because it is pushed at him during a lecture in which a trainer delivers a standard curriculum. But constructivism doesn't go far enough as a theory to explain all aspects of why and how mobile learning works. Two new theories, connectivism and enactivism, are very useful for understanding the dynamics of mobile learning.

## Connectivism

The three learning theories briefly described above were all formulated before the current explosion of the use of digital media in education and training. They don't take into account the impact of being connected to others via computer or mobile phone networks, or the changes in the amount and variety of information that is available online today. In the early 2000s, two Canadians, George Siemens and Stephen Downes, separately, and then together, began to formulate a new learning theory for the digital age called "connectivism."

Connectivism borrows concepts from a variety of sources, including chaos/complexity theory, network science, and personal learning and organizational learning. Some of the principles of connectivism, as described in George Siemens's original 2004 article, are:

- Learning and knowledge rest in diversity of opinions.
- Learning is a process of connecting specialized "nodes" or information sources.
- Learning may reside in nonhuman appliances.
- Capacity to know more is more critical than what is currently known.
- Nurturing and maintaining connections are needed to facilitate continual learning.
- Ability to see connections between fields, ideas, and concepts is a core skill.
- Currency (accurate, up-to-date knowledge) is the intent of all connectivist learning activities.
- Decision making is itself a learning process. Choosing what to learn and the meaning of incoming information is seen through the lens of a shifting reality. While there is a right answer now, it may be wrong tomorrow because of alterations in the information climate affecting the decision.

Connectivism makes a lot of sense in terms of a theory of mobile learning, which can be seen as personal and organizational, and self-directed and connected, all at the same time. But, connectivism doesn't look at how our bodies and senses directly affect the ways we learn and what we can know. This seems important to me because we are coming to realize that technologies are often a form of "prosthesis" that extends our human bodies, while, at the same time, they are also limited by the functioning of our bodies. This point of view is articulated in a new theory of cognition and learning called enactivism.

## Enactivism

Enactivism is an emerging learning theory that focuses on how we learn through our bodies and senses. Our bodies are always situated in the world, which is the context for what we learn. The theory emphasizes the way that all organisms organize themselves by interacting with their environment and experiencing the world through their senses and nervous systems or brains. From an enactive learning point of view, we learn through perception and our actions, through experiencing and doing. Enactive learning is social learning, based on our relationships at many different levels. Therefore, our knowledge and learning depend on the situation in which we find ourselves (Davis, Sumara, & Luce-Kapler, 2000).

According to cognitive psychologist Jerome Bruner (1966), we learn mostly through symbols and icons. In contrast, with enactive learning we learn through the active use of our bodies. New enactive interface designs for both computers and mobile devices involve a mix of several senses in a more natural way than the use of a keyboard and a mouse.

Mobile learning is complex, connecting individual learners to information sources on an as-needed basis and to other people for collaboration, socializing, and learning. People learn while moving, or with the potential to change locations, leading to a loss of control for those in positions of power, such as instructors and managers. Each of the above learning theories subsumes the insights and concerns of the previous theories and adds a unique focus of its own (Fig. 3.1). By using them all, we can begin to understand the complexities of mobile learning.

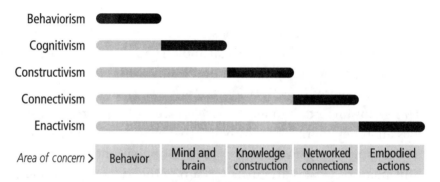

**FIGURE 3.1 Major areas of concern for different learning theories.**

# From "Just-in-Case Training" to "Just-in-Time Training"

Mobile learning requires us to rethink how learning takes place and to reformulate our approaches to training. The early uses of mobile learning, such as managing classrooms, retrieving information, doing assessments, and watching media presentations can be supported by traditional teaching methods where an instructor controls the activities of a classroom, or an online class. But as soon as we realize that mobile technologies have unique "affordances" that are not part of classroom instruction, then our methods change. Arnedillo-Sánchez et al. (2007) identify seven categories of mobile learning systems: (1) administration, (2) referential, (3) interactive, (4) microworlds, (5) data collection, (6) location-aware, and (7) collaborative. They say, "Systems in the first four categories tend to replicate learning experiences that were until recently enabled by more traditional, 'static' technology. Whereas systems in the last three categories leverage off the unique attributes of handheld devices allowing for the creation of learning opportunities which would not be possible without mobile technology."

The sheer amount of information available to each of us as an adult means that we need to pick and choose the information that is most relevant to our needs, interests, and desires, and which best supports the jobs that we carry out. The shift is to *doing and experiencing* learning activities on mobile devices as apps, supported by mobile technologies as we move around the real world. This new approach to pedagogy means that learners need to be strategists and agents of change rather than waiting for directions from training staff about what they should study. Training personnel, to the extent that they are actually needed, become guides and facilitators, helping learners scaffold to new levels of knowledge. Learning has become a do-it-yourself (DIY), just-in-time (JIT) exploration of many sources, constructing knowledge for a particular goal or interest.

Because it challenges the way things have been done in traditional education and training, mobile learning is likely to be highly disruptive of previous systems. At the same time, mobile learning creates new and innovative ways of learning that were previously untried. For example, the idea of mobile "augmented reality" is something that has not been used in employee training. This involves having a mobile device detect the location and orientation of the learner and supply information that is relevant to the context in which the learner is located. Sometimes this can be accomplished when the learner points a camera at the scene. Software recognizes the location and then supplies relevant information to the learner about the scene he is viewing.

Another example is the use of mobile devices as data collectors for research. Mobile phones are two-way communications devices. Not only can information be sent to the learner, but a learner can send information back to a central database to be used later by peer collaborators.

These are only two of the many exciting new uses of mobile learning. In the next four chapters I provide you with further details about how mobile learning is transforming the way that adults learn.

# Retrieving Information: Anywhere, Anytime

**M**obile learning involves the flow of information
to and from a learner or group of learners.
In this chapter I review the flow of information from a server to a learner's mobile
device by looking at the many ways that users can retrieve information using
mobile technologies. Retrieving information can include learning materials
prepared by instructors or it can be information that is available to the learner
on an "on-demand" basis as public information. But, because of the rise of
mobile learning technologies, there is a definite shift from just-in-case training to just-in-time training (Tucker, 2009).

Examples of retrieving information using mobile learning technologies
include:

> "The future of learning
> is DIY (Do It Yourself)."
> —*Harold Jarche (2007)*

- ▶ Customer education
- ▶ Digital media channels
- ▶ Feeds
- ▶ Just-in-time information
- ▶ Libraries

- Location-based information
- Maps and satellite photos
- Presentations
- Search and retrieve
- Signs and kiosks
- Tags
- Translations
- Universal Serial Bus (USB) storage devices

Let's look at each of these uses of information retrieval for mobile learning.

## Customer Education

Customer education via mobile devices is the provision of mobile learning programs and information for people who buy a company's products and/or services. Mobile customer education can take the form of short video clips, answers to frequently asked questions, interactive tutorials, and searchable help files.

Customer education is a very new application of mobile learning in corporate environments. Not surprisingly, the mobile phone companies—both carriers and handset suppliers—are among the first to offer customer education as part of their services. For example, MetroPCS, the fifth largest mobile carrier in the United States, now sends educational "idle screen" messages to customers based on their interests and needs. Customers sign up through the MyExtras service in order to receive these screens. "New customers are welcomed with a comprehensive introduction to their wireless service. MyExtras also educates users about their current rate plan, offers tutorials on advanced wireless services, and provides answers to frequently-asked-questions. MetroPCS subscribers may elect to receive optional content messages, like weather forecasts, local gas prices, and sports scores, along with occasional offers from local and national retailers" (Ankeny, 2009). Behind the scenes, a mobile customer relationship management (CRM) program supports the customer education program.

The mobile banking industry is also using customer education delivered via mobile phones to train customers in the proper use of banking protocols and procedures, especially in relation to online security. When customers are educated, their confidence levels are raised. It also will increase customer loyalty and make it unappealing for customers to switch to another system where they would have to learn how to do things all over again.

A third group that is pioneering customer education on mobile phones is the health-care industry. If questions can be answered and information provided using mobile learning technologies, then there is less need for direct patient visits to a clinic or hospital, or for health-care staff to see people in their homes. Even within a hospital, giving patients "mobile patient communicators" can free up nurses' time normally spent in answering questions, finding rooms, or educating patients about their medical conditions (International Medical Solutions, 2009). Given the high costs of health care, the cost benefit to using mobile learning in these settings can be considerable.

Normally, a sale is made at the beginning of a relationship with a customer, who then disappears from the radar of the seller until it is time to market to the customer again whenever the seller thinks that the customer is ready. For example, when people buy a new house, they don't usually continue an active relationship with their real estate agent. However, smart real estate agents will work at keeping in contact by sending cards and useful information to their clients in order to get referrals from them and to be there when the clients decide that they want to move. The new model of business relationships is one of continuing involvement with customers after the sale until they are ready to buy the next iteration of a product or service. By keeping the relationship, it is much easier to initiate a sales process at a later date.

Given the high rate of penetration of mobile phones, it is not surprising that marketers get excited by the prospect of sending their messages to the mobile devices in people's pockets. But, as the Norwegian digital marketing guru Helge Tenno points out (Tenno, 2009b), marketing in the postdigital era is not about pushing messages toward people but about adding value to people's lives so that they will come to you when they need you. For example, using mobile learning for customer education, even when it is not about your product or service, is a form of marketing that customers appreciate. When they are ready to buy, having experienced an engaging multimedia program that they find relevant and enjoyable, or having a continuing relationship with you, will help drive customers to contact you again for another sale.

# Digital Media Channels

In the first half of the twentieth century, families regularly gathered around a central radio and listened to scheduled broadcasts. In the second half of the twentieth century, families gathered around a television set to watch scheduled programs broadcast by a few major networks. The first decade of the twenty-first century has seen a fragmentation of media as dozens of new broadcast channels were added, incredible video sources grew on the Internet, and the devices for watching and listening to media content became personal and pocket-sized.

At the same time, an ethic of "information wants to be free" permeated the online world as a new generation found ways of copying and sharing music, books, video clips, and movies without paying for them. This led to the development of innovations such as Amazon's Kindle line of e-book readers and the iTunes music store, where digital content can be obtained legally for a fraction of its price in analog format.

At the beginning of 2010, Amazon had over 330,000 copyrighted books available for sale for its Kindle electronic readers. Other e-book readers boasted having over 1.5 million free public domain titles available for their models, mostly scanned by Google in its efforts to digitize the world's literature. In early 2009, Google launched a mobile version of its Book Search service, with the announcement of a Books Browser for iPhone. Rob De Lorenzo (2009), a Canadian teacher, lists 10 e-book resources for downloading educational materials to a smartphone:

1. Project Gutenberg: Over 28,000 free public domain ebooks.
2. iTunes: Purchase a wide variety of high quality audiobooks.
3. Librivox: A large database of audiobooks read by volunteers. All books are in the public domain.
4. Manybooks.net: Contains a vast database of ebooks that can be downloaded in a variety of different formats for a variety of different media players/cell phones.
5. WOWIO.com: Free ebooks comics and graphic novels that you can take with you!

6. Lit2Go: Contains a large library children's literature in audiobook format.
7. Wattpad: An ebook sharing community.
8. Open Culture: A blog post of free ebooks from a variety of sources.
9. Free Classic Audio Books: The title of the site says it all!
10. MobiPocket Reader: Free ebook reader for your PC, PDA and smart phone.

Other numbers for digital media are also astounding. By early 2010, the iTunes store listed over 11 million high-quality songs priced at $.69, $.99, or $1.29 (U.S. dollars). The online photography storage site Flickr claimed to host more than 4 billion images as of October 2009. The well-known blog TechCrunch estimates that YouTube (owned by Google) puts out more than 1.2 billion video streams each day. The fact that you can shoot a video on an iPhone and immediately post it to YouTube means that the number of videos on YouTube will continue to grow at an astonishing rate. Both Flickr and YouTube have special versions of their Web sites that are designed specifically for viewing on mobile devices. For Flickr, use your mobile browser to go to m.flickr.com and for YouTube go to m.youtube.com.

The videos on YouTube have been posted for downloading or for direct viewing. Live streaming video is another variation of video use where a video feed of an event is sent out in real time. To experience this, try the QIK site at qik.com. Live streaming video is great for immediately sharing knowledge or teaching on the go.

Television itself has migrated to the Internet with the advent of IPTV (Internet protocol television). Major networks have placed portions of their television shows on their own Web sites or through services like Hulu.com (only available in the United States). MobiTV is a service that allows users to access 35 channels of network television on their mobile phones.

Groups other than the TV networks have also set up streaming video sites featuring regular broadcasts. For example, for several years, Rocketboom.com has offered daily satirical commentary on the news and Internet culture. Blip. tv is a Web site that delivers videos from universities and conferences on an ongoing basis.

Perhaps the most successful use of digital media for mobile learning to date has been the development and deployment of audio and video podcasts. Podcasting is the name for sharing media files designed for devices like the iPod and other digital audio-video players. It is another way of distributing content online that is now being used in education and training settings. Eva Kaplan-Leiserson (2005) explains: "The term podcasting is an amalgamation of two other words: iPod, the popular digital music player from Apple, and broadcasting. But podcasting is a bit of a misnomer. Podcasts are digital audio programs that can be subscribed to and downloaded by listeners . . . [and] can be accessed on a variety of digital audio devices, including a desktop computer."

Audio is an important component of many learning experiences. According to Crofts et al. (2005), the growth of podcasting is being shaped by a number of social factors, including the following:

- Podcasting allows listeners to engage in time-shifting while providing place independence, (i.e., the ability to listen to media at a time and place that are convenient).
- Consumers view traditional radio as having too much advertising.
- Listeners are frustrated with the homogeneous nature of traditional radio programming.
- Traditional media are being fragmented—from mass broadcasting to media that are tailored to individual needs, (i.e., to personalized media). This fragmentation is fueled, in part, by podcasting—a technology that allows individuals to share their expertise and interests with others.

Using sound to convey understanding and knowledge has a long history, being the main form of communication in preliterate societies. Podcasts are short audio programs placed on a Web site and downloaded into an iPod or MP3 player. Podcasts don't *need* to be downloaded into a portable media player but can also be played on any computer. The potential for mobile learning is evident: employees can access these programs whenever (and whereever) it is convenient. "The benefits of podcasting are substantial because employees don't have to stop working to learn. The format's time-shift capability enables more productive load-balancing during the workday, and the ability to listen on the go while driving to client meetings or work, walking the dog, or running on the treadmill, transforms downtime into constructive time" (Gronstedt, 2007).

To produce good quality audio podcasts requires some basic equipment such as microphones and a simple mixer, along with some sound editing software. It is even possible to use a mobile phone to produce a podcast, a technique known as "cellcasting," pioneered by OnPoint Digital in Savannah, Georgia.

A number of software-based audio editors are available on the Internet, including:

- *Adobe Audition (formerly Cool Edit Pro):* This product from Adobe is for recording, mixing, editing, and mastering sound on Windows-based computers. It costs approximately $350.
- *Adobe Soundbooth:* This software from Adobe is designed for less technical people such as Web designers and video editors. It costs $199 and runs on Windows computers
- *Ardour:* A free, Linux-based open source program for recording and editing sounds. Developer requests a voluntary fee of $35 for downloading the software.
- *Audacity:* A free, open-source program for recording and editing sounds from soundforge.net. Available for Mac OS X, Microsoft Windows, GNU/Linux, and other operating systems.
- *Bias Peak:* This sound editing software for Macintosh computers comes in a number of different editions: Peak Express, $29.95; Peak LE, $129; Peak Pro,$599; and Peak Pro XT, $1,199.
- *Bremmers Audio Design MultitrackStudio:* This Windows software is especially designed for "one-man band" home recordings, where users can add one track at a time, or for live multitrack recording, where all tracks are recorded simultaneously. There is a free Lite edition of the software, as well as Professional ($69) and Pro Plus ($199) editions with additional features.
- *Cakewalk SONAR:* This sound editing software has been developed by musicians and runs on both Windows and Macintosh computers. It costs $139.
- *GarageBand:* This popular software is from Apple and runs only on Macintosh computers. It comes in a package called iLife, which also includes iPhoto, iMovie, iWeb, and iDVD, all for $79.
- *Levelator:* This is free sound editing software that runs on Windows, Mac OS X, and Linux, and is specifically designed for mixing sound for podcasts.
- *Mixcraft:* This software has been called "GarageBand for the PC." In fact, it can work with output from GarageBand. Price: $64.95.
- *Music creator:* This software is designed for people without previous recording experience. It guides users through initial setup, making it

easy to plug in an instrument or microphone and immediately start recording.

▶ *Sonic Foundry Mediasite:* This sound software is for producing Webcasts—audio programs sent live via the Internet. Mediasite records lectures and Webcasts and sends them live over the Internet automatically. Learners can then watch in real-time, later on-demand or listen on the go with podcasting. Price: $22,490.

▶ *WavePad:* This is audio editing software that runs on Windows, Mac OS X, and mobile devices with Pocket PC. It is designed to be very intuitive and easy to use. Price: $59.95.

It should be noted that there are limitations to the exclusive use of audio as an educational medium. It is almost impossible to skim or speed-hear an audio file. You can't add your own notes, and you can't put hyperlinks in the middle of an audio stream the way you can with text. But for learners on the move, audio in the form of podcasts can be a very useful tool.

All the above forms of digital media can be mixed together (sometimes called a mashup) to provide mobile learning opportunities. In a real sense, these developments in digital media have provided the infrastructure for creating mobile learning content and having it readily available on a Web site or mobile device. For example, while iTunes was originally an online music store, it is now used to access videos, and many universities are using it (in the form of iTunes University) to store and deliver digital versions of professors' lectures.

## Case Study

## Cognizant's iPod-based Conversational Language Training

Content and Design Services (C&DS) is an organizational entity of Cognizant that provides both internal and external consulting and training. With over 60,000 employees, Cognizant has a huge resource base that requires regular training and skill-set enrichment. Over 80 percent of its associates are based in India.

With a majority of customers based in the United States and Europe, English is the primary language of communication. However, English is not a native language in India. This results in language problems like the following:

▶ Clients and associates are unable to understand each other properly.
▶ Project requirements are not captured correctly.
▶ Cost and effort overruns occur because of gaps in understanding and the need to rework projects.

The existing training methodology at Cognizant consisted of classroom sessions followed up by Web-based courses and evaluation. By analyzing the data, the company found that over 80 percent of the registered associates attended the classroom sessions, but only 50 percent completed the Web-based courses and evaluation. The feedback from the learners presented the following constraints:

▶ Instructor-led courses:
  –Three-day classroom training was too short in duration.
  –Learners forgot easily because of lack of follow-up reviews or interactive sessions.
  –Regular travel affected attendance and course completion percentage.
▶ Web-based courses:
  –Little or no time to access course during working hours.
  –Existing project-specific Web-based training courses (WBT) were given priority.
  –Courses could not be downloaded and used on the move (only assistant managers and above have laptops).

The existing training methodology was not up to par. An innovative solution was required that would be available anywhere and anytime. It would need to be short and appealing. It would also have to cater to previous cohorts as they were not happy with their training.

A detailed target audience survey was conducted, with the following results:

▶ Associates felt they are wasting two hours every day commuting. Most associates in India travel to the office on company buses for approximately two hours each day (both ways). This is idle time that could be used constructively.

- ▸ Frequent business travel also means that employees were wasting time during flight travel and transit time.
- ▸ Courses of 10 to 15 minutes duration and not involving computers would also help employees take a break from work. Members of the audience felt that small learning nugget-based programs would help them take breaks during work hours.

## MOBILE SOLUTION

As part of its celebrations in exceeding $2 billion in revenue, Cognizant gave all its associates an Apple iPod that supported video playback. The iPod was a platform that could potentially support informal, mobile learning.

The mobile-blended solution that was created included multiple stages. The learner would:

1. Sign up for the training and go through the reading material.
2. Attend a five-day classroom session that would be a focused training session. This session also provided an overview of the mobile learning platform.
3. Download and complete iPod-based learning nuggets.
4. Attend a virtual classroom for reinforcement (LiveMeeting).
5. Take an online audio-based assessment, consisting of listening and comprehension tests.

The iPod-based learning nuggets would be available as part of the new mobile-blended solution as well as a stand-alone solution for learners who wanted to review and refresh their knowledge (i.e., previous cohorts of students):

- ▸ *The learning objective:* To improve the conversational skills of associates through the use of a nontraditional, informal training medium.
- ▸ *The solution:* The iPod Notes feature allows the iPod to support interactive personal multimedia presentations. Notes can be linked together as well as to audio clips, images, and videos to enhance the experience and provide navigation features such as branching, previous and next, and home.

A single iPod-based course is usually around 10 minutes long and is structured as follows:

- Introduction
- Scenario (video)
- Discussion on the scenario (video)
- Quiz with feedback
- Summary

## Results

A total of 7,320 associates have benefitted from 33 course nuggets that amounted to approximately 200 minutes of learning. Cognizant did a learning analytics exercise based on Donald Kirkpatrick's learning evaluation model (Kirkpatrick, 1994).

- *Learner satisfaction survey:* Every learner who completes a course also submits a rating on a scale of 1 to 5. In 2007, when the original training methodology was being used, the aggregate score was 2.9. In 2008, after the introduction of the iPod-based blended training, the aggregate scores rose to 4.4.
- *Course completion survey:* Though over 5,000 associates signed up for training in 2007, only around 2,500 completed the training. In 2008, over 7,000 associates completed the training out of the approximately 8,700 who signed up. The new mobile-based blended learning model had resulted in 80 percent completion compared to a dismal 50 percent in the previous year.
- *Average learning duration per month:* In 2007, associates would spend an average of 11 hours a month in training. In 2008, this duration rose to around 27 hours a month.
- *Assessment pass percentage:* In 2007, around 70 percent of the associates who completed the training program passed the final assessment. In 2008, with the introduction of the mobile-blended program, this percentage increased to 83 percent.

▶ *Calls supervised by project leaders/managers:* In 2007, almost 90 percent of all client calls needed to be supervised by managers. This was essentially as a result of the manager's lack of confidence in associates who were weak in English communication. The survey in 2008 indicated that only 54 percent of the calls were monitored by managers.

▶ *Client communication reviewed per month:* In 2007, about 80 percent of all client communication, such as meeting notes and e-mails, would be reviewed by managers before being sent to the clients. In 2008, less than 50 percent of the communication needed to be reviewed.

▶ *Return on investment:* A survey shows that managers saved approximately 1,000 hours a month by *not* having to attend client calls and review client communication. This resulted in an approximate cost saving (time away from business) of $26,000 per month.

One of the main roadblocks to the use of mobile technology was the company's ability to easily supply it for a vast audience. With the blended approach and also by the leveraging of the iPod gift, Cognizant was able to break the roadblock by making it not a future concept but a present learning concept which is providing a very healthy ROI from a business and a training effectiveness perspective.

 ## Feeds

An alternative method for gathering information from the Internet is to subscribe to an Internet feed. The most common type of feed technology is RSS (no one is quite sure of the origins of this acronym, but it is thought to originally stand for "really simple syndication" or "rich site summary"). There are also several alternative technologies, the most common one being Atom.

In order to receive content from an RSS feed, you need to have a feed reader. Fortunately, there are several RSS readers for mobile devices. These include:

▶ Avant Reader
▶ Bloglines Mobile
▶ Egress
▶ FeederReader

- Google Reader Mobile
- Litefeeds
- NewsBreak
- NewsGator Go!
- Pocket Express
- PocketRSS
- pRSSreader
- Smartfeed
- Spb Insight
- Sublimobi
- TopStory
- Viigo
- WiWi
- ZDNet.com Mobile Reader

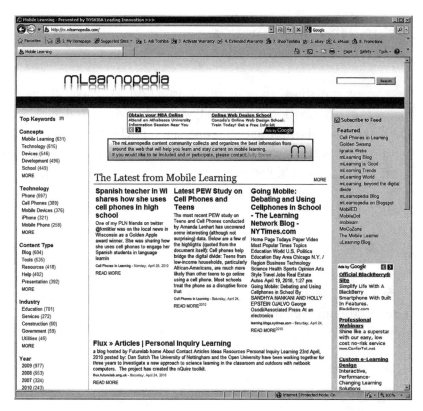

**FIGURE 4.1 The mLearnopedia Web site aggregates a number of RSS feeds about mobile learning into one (see http://cc.mlearnopedia.com).**

There are several advantages to using an RSS feed to receive content. First, users choose what information to receive, and because it is not e-mail, no spam is received along with the requested content. Second, any mobile learning application or Web site can have an RSS feed to show when there is something new for the learner to download or look at.

If there is no change when you go to look at your reader's listing of subscriptions, then there's no need to visit that Web site. This is an efficient way to monitor a lot of content in a short amount of time.

In addition to following RSS feeds in a reader, there are also Web sites known as aggregators that combine a set of RSS feeds on a particular topic into one view. For mobile learning, the best example of an aggregator is the cc.mLearnopedia.com site, maintained by mobile learning analyst Judy Brown (Fig. 4.1).

# Just-in-Time Information

Because of the sheer amount of information available, memorizing large amounts of information on any subject is now not advisable, especially when you know that this information is only a few clicks away on a mobile phone or small computer. Instead, just-in-time applications deliver the knowledge you need when you need it. Following are some examples of the use of just-in-time information in mobile learning.

## Guides

Virtual tours, field trips, and guided visits to museums and galleries can now be set up and supported by mobile devices. For example, the Socialight application for the iPhone is a great way to mix/edit your own mobile walking tour.

## Job Aids

Given that most people own a mobile phone, it is not surprising that analysts predict that mobile learning will include giving just-in-time assistance to people on the job. This type of assistance is often referred to as performance support, meaning that the business objective is to help employees work more efficiently and effectively by having easy and immediate access to the information. Training and development experts Bob Mosher and Conrad Gottfredson (2009) even see the need to distinguish between m-learning and m-support.

Job aids are especially appropriate for a mobile workforce. On the road there is often a need to find out a specific answer to a question, look up a set of directions, or to refresh one's memory about a certain process. Sometimes, in emergency situations, we are called upon to carry out procedures for which we have no training. A mobile device can be very useful if it contains a set of instructions that we need or if we can contact an expert at another location who can then guide us through the emergency situation. Already there are examples of this in the medical field where a doctor, who was not trained in a specialized procedure, was able to perform that procedure while receiving text messages from a colleague who was familiar with it.

 ## Libraries

A few libraries of information are available for mobile phones, but for the most part, library materials need to be modified for mobile learning. There is a lot of interest in making library materials available on mobile devices, so much interest, in fact, that international conferences on m-libraries were held in 2007 and 2009, with more being planned. And, the Library Success Wiki at www.libsuccess.org has a special section on "m-libraries" that lists 9 libraries that offer "mobile collections" and over 50 libraries worldwide that provide "mobile services," including SMS notification of when a book is available or overdue. Libraries offering mobile collections of audiobooks, e-books, audio language courses, streaming music, films, and images which can be used on mobile devices include:

- *Crouch Fine Arts Library at Baylor University:* Audio streaming databases.
- *C/W MARS library network in Massachusetts:* E-books and audiobooks.
- *Duke University Libraries:* Digitized image collections (over 32,000 images).
- *New York Public Library:* E-books and audiobooks.
- *St. Joseph County Public Library:* Audiobooks on iPod.
- *Thomas Ford Memorial Library:* Lends iPod audiobooks to the public.

▶ *University of Alaska Fairbanks:* Audiobooks.

▶ *University of Virginia Library Electronic Text Center*

▶ *IEEE Xplore Mobile:* Free search of all IEEE Xplore documents directly on your mobile device.

While there is an overwhelming amount of education and training information on the Internet, most of it is *not* formatted for mobile devices. Most mobile phones have a Web browser, but the content of the majority of Web sites is too wide and long to be read easily on the small screens of most mobile phones. However, things are improving. Larger screen e-book readers and tablet computers are being developed, for example, and in the near future a wide variety of mobile devices will accommodate most Web-based materials.

Athabasca University (AU), a pioneer in providing distance education using mobile devices, developed a digital reading room (DRR) a few years ago. McGreal et al. (2005) describe what was involved:

> By accommodating and encouraging the inclusion of resources in a variety of formats, the DRR could support a wider range of learning objectives and styles. This project has fully exploited these capabilities by:
>
> ▶ Developing AU mobile device ready learning objects, including an MP3 version of journal articles, and M-learning compatible video clips and e-books;
> ▶ Identifying and organizing existing AU library electronic resources for M-learning;
> ▶ Generating a Mlibrary website (The website will include links to materials pertinent to a mobile library, mobile learning and teaching);
> ▶ Creating a comprehensive list of mobile learning application tools and software helpers to post on the website; and
> ▶ Compiling a best-practice document for M-learning instructional design.

Other efforts have been made to make university libraries mobile-ready. The University of Adelaide in Australia, for example, has developed mobile versions of its library pages, including catalog search, contact information, hours of opening, maps, podcasts, databases, computer availability, and information for configuring an iPhone. While Hahn (2008) found that "mobile learning has seen increased service development, but has not yet evolved to be a robust field in librarianship," other libraries are certain to follow the trend in providing service to students with mobile devices.

It is not necessary to go through a physical library to have a mobile library. For example, the Google Books app for the iPhone allows it to be used as an e-book reader, opening up access to thousands of books on your mobile phone. Digital libraries are available from most of the vendors of e-book readers, including Amazon's Kindle and many new e-book readers coming onto the market.

Finally, we need to mention the very active blog called *Spectrum: Mobile Learning, Libraries, and Technologies*, which tracks developments in this field (Fig. 4.2).

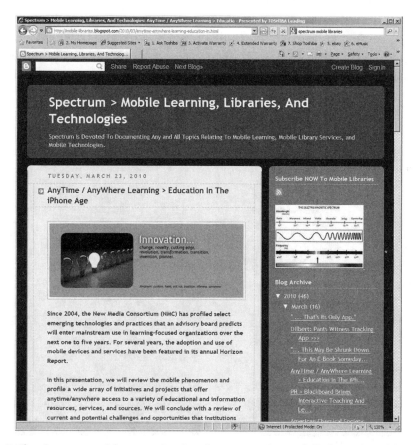

**FIGURE 4.2 The Spectrum blog tracks developments in mobile learning, libraries, and technologies.**

# Location-Based Information

Knowing the location of users is one of the most important pieces of information needed for designing mobile learning experiences. Wang (2004) adds:

> Besides identifying the geographical position of the user, it makes sense to introduce some sort of meta-information that enables the system to distinguish between locations used for different purposes. In learning settings, for example, these "meta-locations" could be classroom, home or outdoors, thus enabling the system to adapt to the current learning situation.

Retrieving information to lie on top of a picture of what you are looking at is now possible with several "augmented reality" applications. For example, Fig. 4.3 shows two iPhone screens from the Junaio app that tells the user the distance to the nearest subway station in San Francisco and how long before

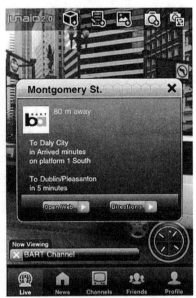

**FIGURE 4.3 Junaio, an augmented reality application for the iPhone directs users to the nearest subway station in San Francisco, and tells them when the next train will arrive. Courtesy of Metaio, Inc. Used with permission.**

the next train arrives. Augmented reality can go well beyond information overlays and can include virtual objects as well.

Most new smartphones have mobile positioning system (GPS) functionality, and an accelerometer and a magnetometer to measure the user's location, for both verticality and directionality. In other words, the software in the phone can generally figure out what is showing in the camera's viewfinder. Then information about what the camera is showing is downloaded from a server and displayed as an information overlay.

In addition to knowing where you are located, a smartphone can be programmed to know a lot about you, the user. This means that information can be brought to the user that is not only relevant to the location that he or she is in, but is also relevant to his or her own personal needs.

Software applications that enable information overlays on pictures or that give more information about immediate surroundings include:

- *Acrossair:* In New York, will show users the nearest subway station with information on the distance from the user's current location.
- *Layar:* A browser that adds layers of information on top of images of a user's immediate surroundings.
- *Wikitude:* Shows information that has been collaboratively produced about locations that a user points at with a smartphone camera.
- *Yelp:* Collects shopping and restaurant reviews of businesses in the United States, Ireland, and the United Kingdom. Shows information about the nearest shops and restaurants based on a user's current location.

Mobile learning uses for information overlays are just being developed but have immense potential. For example, tours of a company's facilities using a smartphone could allow employees to learn whatever they need to know about the location that they are visiting at any given time.

 ## Maps and Satellite Photos

Given that users can take mobile devices almost everywhere they go, the provision of maps and satellite views of a particular geographic area is a natural fit. The two main map providers on the Internet, Mapquest and Google, both support mobile versions of their products. The inclusion of global positioning system (GPS) functionality in most smartphones today means that any mobile device can track its user's location on a map in real time.

Mapquest 4 Mobile is an application for both iPhones and BlackBerry smartphones, and provides maps, directions, and local search on request. Maps that you create and save on your computer can be retrieved and used by the Mapquest 4 Mobile program. Mapquest Navigator takes this one step further, providing voice-guided navigation using your phone's GPS information. Mapquest provides a software development kit (SDK) for iPhone for those who want to build mobile mapping applications using the Mapquest platform.

Google Maps allows all the same functionality as Mapquest 4 Mobile and much more. Because Google has so many more information sources than any other mapping company, it is able to do more by integrating these sources into new mashup sites. Having Google Maps Mobile on your phone allows you to:

- Find your current location with or without GPS (using cell tower triangulation).
- Receive both driving and transit directions, including real-time traffic information, where available.
- Look up phone numbers and addresses for local businesses.
- If available, get Street View for your current location.
- Obtain reviews and walking directions for nearby businesses.
- Start the Latitude application to find your friends' locations and status messages.
- Locate places of interest with information, reviews, photos, and Wikipedia articles.
- View "favorite places" of local experts in cities around the globe.
- Choose to display different layers of information with your maps.

Google Earth has similar capabilities to Google Maps, but with the added feature of being able to see a satellite view of any location of interest (Fig. 4.4). Google Earth Enterprise Portable Edition allows you to download Google Earth's geographical data for a particular area, and then play it back on a laptop. The purpose is to make Google Earth functionality available to staff in field operations without high speed access to the Internet.

FIGURE 4.4 Google Earth can show a satellite view of anywhere on the earth on a mobile phone. I spent a year as a teacher in this remote location. Can you find it on Google Earth? (See end of chapter for answer).

Perhaps the most powerful aspect of Google Maps and Google Earth is the provision of an application programming interface (API) for each that allows third-party developers to add functionality through "geotagging" and create a mashup application that combines one or more other applications with the Google offerings. You can build personalized maps without programming through Google's MyMaps program, or by using a Web site like Wayfaring or Map Builder. Or you can create your own mashups with a bit of programming skills using Javascript or XML (basic instructions are found at programmableweb.com).

# Presentations

Whether we like it or not, "frontal teaching"—a single instructor in front of a class presenting information—will continue to be a predominant method of training for at least the next few years. A major change from the teaching practices of 20 years ago is the replacement of overhead projection materials with digital presentation software. Because of this, instructor-led or expert-led presentations will continue to be a relatively popular way of delivering mobile learning materials. Perhaps the most ubiquitous tool for presenting materials in the classroom and on the Internet is Microsoft's PowerPoint, and now there are versions for various mobile devices. Software exists that will convert PowerPoint from its native format on a computer to formats for various mobile operating systems.

Prezi is a Web-based alternative to PowerPoint worth investigating. It uses a large canvas rather than a set of slides and allows you to move around the elements that you have placed on the canvas and relate them as you wish. This means that you don't need to order your presentation in a fixed linear sequence but that you can move around at will. For mobile devices, you simply need to size the window panes containing information to be mobile friendly.

Other presentation software is not based on slides or images, but on capturing live lectures for later viewing on the Internet or on a mobile device. Windows Mobile Lecture Recorder is an example of this genre of software. Over a dozen vendors offer similar programs. Captured lectures can be loaded into iTunes University, an educational content Web site sponsored by Apple. Students in a focus group at the London School of Economics reflected on captured lectures by noting that they "were more likely to dip into certain parts of the lecture rather than watch the whole lecture again. This approach was particularly useful for revision (studying) but also really helpful for grasping a point they might initially not have understood. Students talked about how lectures could be extremely content rich or 'dense' and that the ability to go back and review the material really helped their learning" (Secker, 2008).

Even though the use of digital presentation materials is usually instructor-centered, learners can transform these materials for their own use. There is a lot to be learned by students making their own presentations and showing them to others either directly or virtually. For example, Peter Byrne and Brendan Tangney (2006) explain how students at Trinity College, Dublin, produce their own animations on mobile phones. This facilitates "powerful learning experiences by enabling collaborative learning and encouraging creativity and self-expression."

For those who want to improve their presentation skills, there is the Presenter Pro app for the iPhone ($.99 in the iTunes store). The content includes presentation skills techniques with supporting graphics, audio, and video; hundreds of quick tips accessible by shaking the device; a checklist feature to capture and e-mail any content for later review; notes capability; practice exercises; and knowledge check quizzes. Another useful app for presentations is called Clicker. It turns your iPhone into a Bluetooth presentation controller so that you can stroll around the room and not have to be tethered to your laptop.

Presentations will continue to be a major format for mobile learning. But they will be just one of dozens of possibilities as the world of adult learning moves to more learner-centered methods.

 ## Search and Retrieve

Digital search and retrieval of information is by far the most common learning technology in use. Because of the vast store of available information on the Internet, searching for what we are looking for is a form of informal learning that we have come to take for granted. Searching the Internet has become so commonplace that "to Google" has become a well-used verb for many people. In 2002 it was chosen as the most useful word of the year, and in 2006 it was officially added to the *Oxford English Dictionary.*

In the United States, Google, with about 65 percent of the market share, processes over 300 million queries a day. There are many reasons why people undertake an online search, but finding information that leads to learning has got to be near or at the top of the list.

Of course, Google is not the only search engine available even though it dominates the market. Other prominent search engines in English-speaking countries include Yahoo!, Microsoft Bing, Time Warner, and Ask. There are also lots of specialized search engines. comScore, a search engine tracking service, follows over 150 different search sites.

Most of the major search engines have mobile versions that simplify the search process and return the results formatted for a small screen. Google Mobile is a specially formatted suite of mobile applications developed for most major smartphone platforms that includes Search, Maps, Gmail, YouTube, Earth, Voice, Talk, Latitude, and SMS. The actual makeup of the Google Mobile suite will depend on your particular smartphone make and model (Fig. 4.5).

**FIGURE 4.5 Google Mobile is a simplified version of the Google interface design for desktop and laptop computers.**

The use of a search engine with a mobile phone is not just about retrieving information. In many ways, the fact that we can find and retrieve what we want at a moment's notice means that the mobile phone connecting to the cloud of information resources extends us so that we don't have to memorize as much information as we used to. It has become a "prosthesis" for the mind; a way of extending brain functioning beyond our physical body, (Clark, 2008).

 ## Signs and Kiosks

The shift to thinking of mobile learning as being about learners on the move, rather than the use of mobile technologies, means that ubiquitous, ambient computing (ubicomp) can be seen as a means of mobile learning. Not only do most of us have digital information appliances available in our pockets, but digital information surrounds us in many public spaces. For people who don't have a mobile phone or who don't want to use one, digital signage and public kiosks can deliver useful information, especially in emergency situations or in public education campaigns.

Paul Gragtmans (2010), a partner with ET Group in Toronto, says this about the digital signage system that his company supports:

> Digital signage and mobile messaging platforms have the ability to allow field workers to interact with a digital signage network in real time by updating the ticker/marquee messages on the digital sign from their mobile device. This means workers at a railway or subway could be using their mobile phone and send updates to a network of digital signs. The system also provides the ability for the mobile workers to take pictures from their mobile phone and send them in real time for instant display on the digital signage network or on a central control and command centre display wall. It can also stream live video to the central command centre or to the digital signage network. Conversely, a central command centre can forward messages, pictures or any type of video stream to the mobile device of their field personnel.

A kiosk is just a different form of digital sign that can be integrated with a mobile device. A digital sign or kiosk can be programmed to ask mobile phone users to send a text message to a certain number which in turn can trigger many different kind of events, including being able to change the content being displayed on a kiosk or digital sign. In Fig. 4.6 we see a sign for wireless Internet service accessed by touching this large digital screen in the Gare du Nord train station in Paris.

Billboards and signs that react to users have been in development for several years. Their displays change into personalized messages as the mobile phone system senses that a user is nearby, information that can be gleaned from the GPS data that are provided by the newest mobile phones (Wally et al., 2009). In the other direction, billboards can be used to gather opinions of people by posing a set of choices. Mobile users can text their vote to a number, which can then update the billboard with the results of the survey and/or the number of respondents.

 ## Tags

There are various ways to attach information to a place or an object, which is then readable by a properly equipped mobile reader. The reader may be a spe-

**FIGURE 4.6 This large sign in the Gare du Nord train station in Paris, France, says, "Touch this screen or the keyboard to use the Internet." Photo by Peter Kaminski. Used under a Creative Commons license.**

cial purpose device, such as a meter reader, that is designed to read data from a specific type of object. Or the reader can be software in a general purpose computing device, such as a smartphone.

There are several types of tags, divided into two main categories. One category is electronic tags that transmit information to a receiver, and the other category is optical tags that reveal their information when a picture is taken of them by an optical tag reader and decoded by appropriate software. The best known example of an electronic tag is called a radio frequency identification (RFID) tag. Barcodes are a well known example of an optical tag. A type of bar code called a Quick Response (QR) code is becoming popular with smartphone users who can use it to exchange information between two suitably equipped phones, or to read information from a QR code in a book or on a computer screen. QR codes can be placed on the pages of a book linking a printed page with Web site information. For example, clicking on the QR code below will take you to my Web site (http://garywoodill.com). If you have a QR code reader in your smartphone, you can try it (Fig. 4.7).

RFID tags have many different uses. They are familiar to shoppers who set off alarms when they leave stores with items that have not been desensitized; there is usually an RFID tag in the item that transmits a signal to the scanners at the door, thereby setting off an alarm. In Florida, RFID tags are the source of information for traffic reports on more than 200 miles of toll roads—the RFID tags are built into the more than 1 million transponders that are used by commuters. RFID tags can be sewn into children's clothing so that, for safety reasons, schools can monitor their comings and goings. GPS-enabled RFID tags can be attached to the ears of cattle for herd management. More relevant for mobile learning is the experimental use of RFID tags in libraries, both for speeding up checkout procedures and for leading users to the most appropriate books for their particular research interests.

In the near future, RFID tags will be used to send product information directly to shoppers with receivers in their "smart" shopping cart as they pass

**FIGURE 4.7 A sample quick response code. Try clicking on it if your mobile phone has a QR reader.**

a product on a shelf. Because newer RFID tags can transmit up to 64 kilo-bytes of information to a mobile device, they can be used to label items in a museum or other form of educational display. They have been used in outdoor education as a way of labeling plants and rocks, for example. The information sent by an RFID tag can be displayed using the smartphone's Web browser. An example of the use of RFID tags in mobile learning is the study by Horng et al. (2007) that combined paper maps with electronic guide resources. By waving a handheld computer equipped with an RFID reader over a region of interest on the map, additional information was provided from a database about the specified region.

The use of tagging is part of the movement toward "ambient findability" (Morville, 2005), the labeling of the environment so that it speaks directly to us through our mobile devices.

 ## Translations

Sometimes we want information that is available only in another language. While CD-ROM based translation software has been on the market for many years, it is not very good. Similarly, Web-based translation software, both standalone and embedded in browsers, has been very rough. However, the new Google Translate software is much improved, and is therefore much more useful. It is also available in a mobile version. Just go to Google.com, and click on the word "more" at the top of the screen to find the Translate application.

There are many companies working on translation software for mobile phones. Mobile Translator is an online translation and dictionary application that is optimized for mobile phones. You can translate words and phrases from any Web-enabled mobile phone (including iPhone) as well as any mobile browser such as Opera Mini. It lets you translate to and from English, Russian, French, Portuguese, Korean, Japanese, Dutch, German, Spanish, Italian, and Chinese. Trippo is a program that allows you to type in common phrases in English; have them translated into Spanish, Italian, and French; and then spoken by your mobile phone. You can also translate from the three supported languages back into English.

iLingo is another talking language phrase book, specifically developed for the iPhone.

Other companies, such as Toshiba (Gangar, 2009), are working on real-time translation software for smartphones, but not based on set phrases. Here you can type or speak into a phone, and a translation will arrive immediately. This is no small feat, given the limited computing power and memory in most phones, and the significant processing requirements of translation software. This is expected to be a growth area for development in the next five years.

 ## USB Storage Devices

USB storage devices (sometimes called "jump drives," "flash drives," or "thumb drives") are essentially a memory chip attached to a USB plug. We carry them around in our pockets or on our key chains without thinking very much about them. But they can be used to carry lots of information from place to place and therefore can be seen as another device to support mobile learning. USB storage devices have the advantage of being widely distributed and inexpensive. They can easily be passed around or given to another person, and the content recorded on these devices is easily copied.

For example, salespeople in the field could have complete product information on a high-capacity USB storage device that could be loaded into their laptops to provide them with instant information on their products. In 2007 Rich Hoeg reported on his blog *eContent* that "Northwest [Airlines] is exploring the concept of running a pilot flight simulator off a thumb drive" (Hoeg, 2007). Rosselle et al. (2009) explored the use of a USB key for "nomadic learning" by medical students and noted that "the value of a program that runs on a USB key is to allow its owner to work on any computer and retrieve his complete environment, his parameters, like his software. Moreover, this work leaves no trace on the host of the USB key." They also found that the use of USB storage devices was easier for the technicians who supported the medical students in the study. The software being used was configured for each student on the USB key, and not on the various host computers that the mobile students might use in a given day.

Using USB storage devices is a simple form of mobile learning technology; nevertheless, it should be considered and used when appropriate.

 ## Information Retrieval Uses of Mobile Learning

At the simplest level, mobile devices can act as clients that retrieve information from servers—whether the server is a massive server farm "in the cloud," or a simple coded tag on an object. This means that the information is not necessarily stored in the learner's memory, but is updated and used "just-in-time." But, we need to remember that this is a one-way transaction. Information is requested and sent to the user. Or information is "pushed" to users if they have subscribed to a feed of that information.

In the next chapter, I look at the other direction of information flow, where information is gathered by the user and then sent to a server for storage and/or analysis. This reverses the direction of information flow that usually takes place in a classroom, although an assessment—a kind of "confession" by the learner—does allow information to flow back to the instructor and then be stored in the learner's record. Beyond assessments, however, the use of mobile devices to gather information makes each user a node in a network that can be used to drive a kind of collective intelligence. In addition to each learner gaining new knowledge, a *group* of networked learners can also become smarter.

Note: The place shown using Google Earth in Figure 4.4 is Cartwright, Labrador, Canada. The author spent 1971-72 there as a school teacher.

# Gathering Information with Mobile Devices

Traditionally, education and training have been mostly unidirectional activities. Since the advent of the modern classrooms in the 1770s, learning has been dominated by a model in which an expert instructor conveys information to a student, usually in

a classroom. Mobile learning radically changes that model to one in which communications are more balanced and where learners can send information to instructors or to database applications, as well as interact with each other and with immersive programs in real time. In this chapter, we look at how users who are moving about in the world can use a mobile device to gather information from their environment and send it back to a server, an application, another person, or a network.

This doesn't mean that mobile device-using learners have become all-powerful; it means simply that, with mobile communications, learning can now be a true two-way street. For mobile learners, this has several powerful advantages. First, many young people are attracted to mobile learning because it involves using a technology that is very familiar to most of them. Second, it enables problem-based learning approaches where learners gather information based on their own inquiries and issues. And the same mobile learners can generate information and data that can be used by others (Fig. 5.1).

There are four types of applications that use mobile devices for gathering information that in turn can be used for learning purposes. These are:

- Assessment and evaluation.
- First-person documentation.
- Monitoring and trend tracking.
- Research and data collection.

Learners who use mobile devices to gather information can contribute to their own learning as well as to the learning of others. Using learner-generated materials shifts the emphasis from instructor-led training (ILT) to true learner-centric education. This has profound implications for the future of education and training. But first let's look at a more traditional approach to gathering information—the use of mobile devices for assessment and evaluation of learners.

**FIGURE 5.1 User-generated content: ordinary people are documenting their experiences in the world and making them available to others. Source: istock.com.**

# Assessment and Evaluation

We can't look inside a person's head to see what he knows or how much he has learned. Instead, we use indirect measures of knowledge and learning based on observations of what a person says and does, including the results of formal testing. Based on these observations, we make judgments about the level of a person's knowledge or progress in learning. This process is known as "assessment and evaluation."

In the business world, assessment and evaluation have traditionally been the task of trainers who have direct contact with employees in training. Typically, these trainers administer a quiz or test to assess a learner's knowledge. With mobile learning, trainers do not have to be present in order to gather information about the level of learning that has taken place. Assessment tools such as exams and tests, observation checklists, rating scales, and surveys can all be made available through mobile phones. Exams and tests usually have a variety of question types ranging from fill in the blank, true and false, short-answer, and multiple choice. For high-stakes assessments, the camera on a smartphone can be used to verify the person taking the test. Smartphones can be used by a learner to build an electronic portfolio that can be evaluated at a later date.

Assessment as part of e-learning has been available since the 1980s, but online assessments may be more accepted using mobile devices because of the novelty of the method. Other benefits of mobile assessment include the increased speed of results available to both learners and instructors, the efficiency of data collection, improved scalability (many learners can be assessed on the same system), integration of assessment results with a learning management system (LMS), question and test analysis, and reporting on test performance parameters.

Traditional assessment is seen by many educators as inadequate in that a small amount of data is used to describe and summarize a person's total learning and knowledge. There is a movement in education and training toward "authentic assessment," an effort to have a more holistic approach to assessment and evaluation. Authentic assessment is a move away from traditional multiple-choice, standardized achievement tests to the inclusion of direct observations of learner performance on meaningful tasks that are relevant to the learner's job (Burke, 1999). Mobile assessments that use "first-person documentation" (see next section on page 114), electronic portfolios, and remote observation can go a long way toward making assessments more authentic.

In performing assessment and evaluation, it is important to identify the specific use of various procedures. Seven different kinds of assessments can be identified, and each can be facilitated by the use of mobile technologies.

- *Formative assessment and evaluation* are used for feedback while learning (e.g., "continuous improvement" methods). For example, by using a headset built into a pair of glasses, a mentor could "listen in" to a medical student speaking with a patient and provide real-time coaching.
- *Adaptive assessment and evaluation* are used to change or individualize the curriculum or further assessments. A preliminary quiz on a mobile phone could determine the current level of knowledge of a trainee and then provide the "next step" that he or she needs to know in order to move to the next level of a procedure.
- *Demonstrative assessment and evaluation* are used to show what a person has done and can do, often compared to a specific set of criteria. Sensors on a mobile device could be used to judge an athletic performance, to be followed by a demonstration video that shows the correct techniques. Speech recognition software on a mobile phone can listen to a person speaking a foreign language and intervene to provide the learner with the correct word when needed.
- *Summative assessment and evaluation* summarize achievement levels, assess program effectiveness, and are used as criteria for granting credentials. Mobile versions of learning management systems are now used to track and report on learner progress in many different kinds of tasks.
- *Diagnostic assessment and evaluation* are used to diagnose the presence of a defined diagnostic construct. Software now exists to diagnose depression from the sound of a person's voice on a mobile phone, and preliminary diagnosis is possible for some diseases by having a person cough into a phone.
- *Normative assessment and evaluation* summarize the results of assessments from many learners to provide a set of statistics (or "norms") for an identified group. For example, surveys and polls on mobile devices can be used to judge political trends or preferences.

▶ *Research* is used to answer specific questions, make predictions, or supply data for other software applications. Using mobile devices may be the best option for gathering data in many cases.

In Europe, the Assessment and Learning in Practice Settings (ALPS) project assessed learners in 16 different subject areas from a wide range of health- and social-care courses to see that they had the skills needed to be effective in the workplace (Little, 2007). In Australia, organizations affiliated with the National Audit and Registration Agency provided online learners with Webcams and used Skype to verify the learner's identity for assessment. "Trainers can download . . . assessment tools to a [mobile] device, assess learners in a practical, hands-on environment, upload the results, and collect and store electronic evidence such as photos, video and audio. This evidence can be emailed back into the organization's IT systems and can be easily accessed by an auditor" (Clark, 2009).

Workplace assessments often require the gathering of data to show competency in a number of predetermined areas. Mobile applications can be helpful in a variety of ways. For example, digital cameras can be used to capture work in progress or a finished product. Digital video from a mobile camera can show an employee performing a skill. The audio recorder in many PDAs or smartphones can be used to store comments by an assessor who might be observing a worker in an on-the-job assessment. Or the assessor can be using a touch screen to fill out a checklist while observing. Tests or exams on a mobile phone are another option. All these ideas are just in the experimental stages as training departments begin to see the potential of mobile learning and assessment.

The assessment approaches suggested above are similar to classroom-based assessment techniques. But there are also approaches that can go well beyond assessment and evaluation methods that have been traditionally used in classrooms. For example, mobile interactive training games that have an assessment component have entered the market and are now used in training departments (Klopfer, 2008). Virtual worlds, such as Second Life, will soon be available on mobile phones and will be used to assess such skills as strategy, leadership, and decision making under pressure (Heiphetz and Woodill, 2010).

Sande Chen and David Michael (2005) discuss the challenges and issues of assessing game-based learning, whether mobile or not, and suggest that there are three main types of assessments used in serious games:

▶ *Completion assessment*: Did the player complete the lesson or pass the test?

▶ *In-process assessment*: How did the players choose their actions? Did they change their mind? If so, at what point?

▶ *Assessor evaluation*: Based on observations of the student, does the assessor think the learner now knows and understands the material?

In addition to the above types of assessments, training managers may be interested in the actual scores that players achieve, although there are many factors that can lead to a particular score. The most relevant question concerning assessment is, "Just what is being learned?" Belanich et al. (2003) categorized the information presented in a computer-based game along two dimensions: (1) type of information (i.e., factual, procedural, and episodic) and (2) relevance to game play (for example, does the information help a player progress through the game scenario?). They say, "Results indicated that participants were most likely to recall procedural information followed by episodic and then factual information. Regarding relevance to game-play, participants were more likely to recall information that either was required or helpful for player progress in the game compared to information that was tangential to the game's objectives."

Mobile learning technologies are also useful for peer assessment and self-assessment. Liu (2004) described a model of peer and self-assessment with the following steps:

1. Instructor presents the educational objectives of peer and self-assessment in the beginning and uses some real samples to prepare students for later assessment activities.
2. Instructor repeats the following steps for each assignment.
3. Instructor reviews the relevant course materials covered in the semester.
4. Students and instructor jointly discuss assignments and the criteria for marking.
5. The assignment completed by the students is uploaded to the peer assessment system.
6. The peer assessment system randomly assigns reviewers (each reviewer marks three assignments).
7. Reviewers assign a score (1 to 5, from worst to best) to the assignment.

8. At the same time, reviewers also assign a score to their own work.
9. The instructor marks each student's work without seeing the students' ratings.
10. The peer assessment software notifies the students of their grades and any comments given by their peers. They can also compare peer and self-assessments.
11. Based on this feedback, each student makes corrections or modifications accordingly. (This step is optional, and can be repeated one or two times.)

Perhaps the best strategy is a blend of three approaches—instructor assessment, peer assessment and self-assessment. Wali (2007) advocates ". . . tracking and triangulating students' learning activities and self reports." Let's look at how self-reporting can be done with mobile phones.

## Case Study

## Brainvisa Develops a Mobile Apps Portal for Ngee Ann Polytechnic in Singapore

Ngee Ann Polytechnic is one of Singapore's leading institutions of higher learning. Its eight academic schools offer a total of 47 full-time diploma courses. They also offer a range of part-time diploma courses. The polytechnic offers students a holistic learning experience through the Ngee Ann learning model (NLM), which emphasizes balanced and broad-based education. To ensure that its courses and students are in tune with current market developments, the polytechnic maintains close industry ties and devotes expertise and resources to assist the development of local enterprises.

The learners at Ngee Ann are between the ages of 16 and 19. This age group comes with a high degree of dynamism and a desire to do *everything* with their mobile devices, including manage their social, school, and work lives. The new generation of millennial students expects a learning experience that accommodates a mobile lifestyle, integrates today's digital tools, adapts to personalized learning styles, and features collaboration and teamwork. This means that Ngee Ann Polytechnic required the following:

► A vision for lifestyle-driven m-learning to accommodate the way millennial students work, study, and socialize.
► The transformation of the entire learning experience to using mobile technology.
► A new paradigm in formal and informal learning, using a mobile platform.

Some of the constraints and challenges that the project team faced included the need to engage a highly dynamic and mobile generation of 16- to 19-year-olds. The platform and content had to be exciting enough to attract the users to use the platform for learning. And the solution had to move away from the boundaries of a traditional learning platform. This posed a set of design and implementation challenges that included:

► The mobile interface design, given the limited screen size.
► Navigation and information design needed to be clear, avoid clutter, minimize scrolling, and use high color contrasts for an engaging experience.
► Limited storage and memory capacity.
► Need for rich interactivity.
► Flexibility of content for updates, reusability, and expandability
► Personalization to adapt to each learner's context and preferences.
► Search capabilities.
► Utilities for collaboration and communication.
► Utilities for assessment and feedback.
► Interoperability among various mobile phones

 ## MOBILE SOLUTION

Brainvisa, an instructional design company with offices in a number of countries, was instrumental in the design and development of the Ngee Ann Appstore Portal, which was called MobiLearn. This portal was created to operate within the Ngee Ann WiFi campus. The Ngee Ann Appstore is used for hosting iPhone/iTouch based applications and other mobile content such as e-books, podcasts, and vodcasts. The applications are categorized under various headings such as educational, social, gaming, e-books, and videos. Students are able to both upload and download applications from this portal. The portal hosts both native and Web-based applications for the iPhone/iTouch. Brainvisa was also involved in the design and development of specific applications for this portal.

The MobiLearn platform was resident to numerous downloadable iPhone applications. These applications were created with the objective of providing fun learning content to students on the move. Here are some of the applications created by Brainvisa for Ngee Ann Polytechnic:

1. *Shuttle bus service*: This is a native application residing on the iPhone/iTouch. It is used by students and staff to find bus schedules and pickup points.
2. *Academic calendar service*: This is a native application residing on the iPhone/iTouch. It is used mainly by students looking for their semester time table. It is preloaded with the known events and deadlines for the semester (e.g., teaching weeks, study week, exams, vacation period). Students can also log custom event reminders into the calendar.
3. *Nursing mobile report taking (iMART):* This application for the iPod Touch platform is a patient shift report application that aims to facilitate efficient and effective shift-to-shift communication among nurses. There is access to information relating to patient care, including health history, health status, recent laboratory or diagnostic tests, medications, and so on. This information is stored locally in the iPhone/iTouch and can be beamed from one student to another as part of the handover to an incoming nurse on the next shift. A critical feature is for the data file to be saved locally on the device in a non-WiFi equipped hospital and transferred later to the Polytechnic server through WiFi. This data file can then be downloaded to a personal computer or laptop.
4. *Mobile translator:* This application for the iPhone/iTouch includes a database of approximately 500 phrases, categorized into under various headers related to health sciences, including clinical specialties, hospital items, health-care professionals, and so forth. For each phrase there is a corresponding translation and pronunciation sound clip in four languages—Mandarin with Han Yu Pin Yin, Cantonese, Hokkien, and Malay.

5. *Co-Curricular Activities (CCA) Planner:* An application that allows students to calculate their CCA points. All students are awarded CCA points for their involvement in co-curricular activities throughout their two- or three-year course at Ngee Ann. This iPhone/iTouch application allows students to manually enter their activities into the application which stores these details across sessions.

## Results

The MobiLearn portal is an exchange Web site, a marketplace, and an ecosystem for the aggregation and distribution of mobile learning content. It is a highly engaging and exciting platform for students to learn and collaborate with each other that was more suited and acceptable to prevailing student lifestyles. It was designed to support on-demand, anytime, anywhere learning, using a multifaceted approach that included traditional curriculum-based content, video and audio content, e-books, game-based assessments, and collaborative learning applications. The portal is now live on the Internet. Apart from being an effective learning platform, it is also a great branding vehicle for the university.

 # First-Person Documentation

Assessments of learning and performance have traditionally been based on tests, quizzes, and observations from instructors or examining bodies. First-person documentation using mobile technologies changes all that. Instead of being surveyed by the power of the "teacher's gaze," first-person documentation allows the learner to control what is being seen and revealed. Many of the technologies are built around head-mounted cameras and microphones that produce video or still images. Consequently, these are also called "point of view" (POV) technologies.

Mobile devices in the form of smartphones and small laptops are usually powerful enough to record sounds, images, and video. They often also allow for editing and playback of multimedia productions created in this way. A collection of these productions can be placed on a hard drive for storage as an *electronic portfolio* (or e-portfolio). An e-portfolio is a way of storing evidence of a learner's skill and knowledge. It is useful for showing competencies and showcasing a learner's achievements.

Selena Chan (2006) in New Zealand describes how apprentice bakers are assessed and evaluated at different stages of their training using mobile technologies. She reports that both formative and summative assessments for the theory of baking, and the written part of a workplace-based competencies evaluation, were delivered and answers collected via mobile phones using "texting" through SMS (short message service). Additional evidence of competence was gathered by mobile phones taking photos or videos, and storing them in an online e-portfolio. The e-portfolio was linked to the institution's learning management system (Moodle) for reporting and tracking of its contents. In addition to all this, the bakers-in-training were able to check on reference materials using mobile Web browsing. These materials were then collated and used for further reflection in interviews with instructors at the college they were attending (Chan and Ford, 2007).

From their work with apprentice bakers, Chan and Ford (2007) identified five levels of e-portfolios:

▶ Level 1 basically revolves around a scrapbook concept.
▶ Level 2 provides more structure to bring [the student's electronic portfolio] up to curriculum vitae status.
▶ Level 3 is a working portfolio that showcases a student's work.
▶ Level 4 opens the Web folio up to feedback from other parties who may include a student's families, employers (current and potential), various mentors, and faculty.
▶ Level 5 is achieved when the Web folio becomes authentic and authoritative evidence that links the contents of the folio to standards, programs "other descriptors including higher order taxonomies."

There are many other examples of the use of e-portfolios for student learning. With mobile phones, the amount and types of evidence of achievements can be greatly expanded.

The ultimate in first-person documentation is the vision of collecting everything possible about a person through his or her entire life. This is the goal of the MyLifeBits project at Microsoft Research, led by computer pioneer Gordon Bell. His vision is to capture and store every moment on digital audio and video from the moment a child is born until he or she dies. The purpose of this is to be able to recall at will any particular time in one's life. In their 2009 book, *Total Recall: How the E-Memory Revolution Will Change Everything*, Gordon Bell and Jim Gemmell explain the purpose of this project:

> E-memories will provide every person who embraces them with a different sense of their whole lives. It won't erase human nature's capacity for self-deception, but it will surely make the truth of what we did and what happened around us more available, clearer, and less obscured by nostalgic make-believe. The benefits will also be distinctly practical . . . higher productivity, more vitality and longer life spans, deeper and wider knowledge of our world and ways to accomplish things in it—these are all wonderful practical consequences of this coming technological revolution. But there will also be psychological implications. Enhanced self-insight, the ability to relive one's own life story in Proustian detail, the freedom to memorize less and think and creatively more, and even a measure of earthly immortality by being cyberized—these are all potentially transformational psychological phenomena. (page 8)

Even more radical is the idea of continuously broadcasting ones life to the world (at least to anyone on the Internet who is interested in watching what you are doing). Called *lifecasting*, this practice involves having a head-mounted camera and microphone that is connected wirelessly to a Web application that broadcasts the media stream throughout the Internet. As the person with the equipment moves around, everything that she says or does can be broadcast to an audience on the Internet or recorded on a pocket digital video recorder (DVR) (Fig. 5.2).

 ## Monitoring and Trend Tracking

Mobile phones are ideal as devices to collect information and send it back to a central database or a cloud computing application such as Google Docs. If

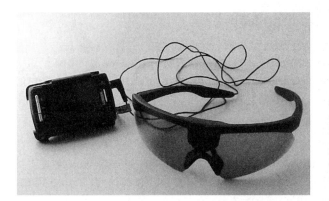

**FIGURE 5.2 The equipment for first-person documentation has become simple to use and relatively inexpensive. Here we see glasses with a camera and microphone attached to a pocket digital video recorder. Courtesy of EDUPOV Pty. Ltd, Australia.**

thousands or even millions of people do this, then it will be possible to monitor all sorts of situations and to track trends as they happen. This also enables a form of *collective learning* that is based on mobile technologies that can be recording from anywhere around the world. There are already many examples of collective learning through mobile technologies. For example, election monitoring is now much more efficient and faster because of the use of mobile technologies to send back comments and data (*Economist*, 2008). What used to take days to report can now be accomplished in close to real time.

Monitoring subtle social signals is now possible thanks to mobile devices. Professor Alex (Sandy) Pentland (2008) of MIT has invented a "sociometer," a specially designed digital sensor worn like an ID badge that monitors and analyzes social interactions among groups of people. Pentland suggests that by "reading" our social networks with these devices, "we can become more successful at pitching an idea, getting a job, or closing a deal."

Environmental monitoring using mobile technologies has also taken off. Because most mobile phones now have geographic positioning system (GPS) functionality, special software that monitors hundreds of thousands of mobile phones by location can look at such events as traffic jams, or advise drivers on improving fuel consumption based on their speed, location, and driving habits. The *Economist* (2008) reports that specially equipped taxis with pollution sensors were able to map the areas of Istanbul, Turkey, with the highest level of pollution, causing some taxi drivers to change their routes.

## Health Education and Monitoring

The potential of using mobile networks to track diseases is now well recognized. The SARS outbreak of 2003 resulted in hundreds of deaths and billions of dollars in economic losses. There was evidence of this disease on the Internet as early as November 2002. Since that time, the tracking of diseases and disasters through mobile technologies has improved greatly. An Internet application called HealthMap (healthmap.org) now tracks diseases by location as they are reported (Fig. 5.3). A mobile phone-based health project called DISAMAR allows Peruvian military doctors to report disease outbreaks and ask for help with treatment (Marwaha, 2009). Laboratories that test for diseases, traditionally isolated from each other, are now being connected by computer networks in order to share results and to integrate the inflow of data about diseases (Bellina and Missoni, 2009).

Health monitoring can also go beyond the use of mobile phones. For example, subscriber identity module (SIM) cards, normally found in phones, can be attached to medicine bottles in order to monitor whether patients are taking their medicine. When this was done in South Africa, the percentage of

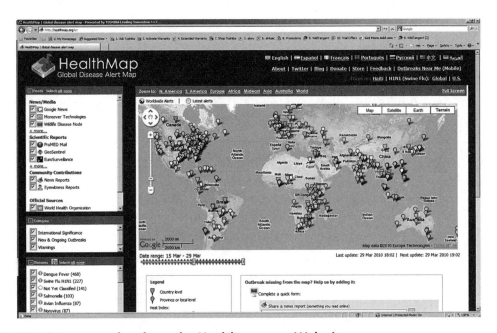

**FIGURE 5.3 A screen shot from the Healthmap.org Web site.**

people keeping up with their medicine rose from 22 to 90 percent (Marwaha, 2009). Wireless implanted heart monitors can send readings to doctors on a daily or even continuous basis, with alerts if it appears that there may be an impending problem (Woodill, 2009).

Mobile phones can be used for remote diagnosis. Current applications include the early detection of depression by monitoring a person's speech, and phones that listen to coughing so that doctors can distinguish between a healthy, voluntary cough and the involuntary cough of a sick person (Huss, 2009). Dr. Aydogan Ozcan, a University of California Electrical Engineering professor, has developed the Cellophone while Dr. Daniel Fletcher, a University of California Bioengineering professor has created the CellScope, both diagnostic imaging tools made from everyday camera phones. Medical personnel in remote locations can now place samples of blood, urine or other bodily fluids into a modified mobile phone and have images sent from the field to medical laboratories for diagnosis (Nightingale, 2009).

Moving beyond diagnosis, we enter the field of "computer assisted rehabilitation." There are implanted devices that monitor hearts, record activity levels, and check on other bodily functions. Some of these are built into clothing such as underwear or vests. A number of mobile medical monitoring devices can be integrated to form a wireless body area network (WBAN) that combines miniature computers with wireless communications and sensors to derive a detailed picture of a person's current state of health. Sensors can include:

- An ECG (electrocardiogram) sensor for monitoring heart activity
- An EMG (electromyography) sensor for monitoring muscle activity
- An EEG (electroencephalography) sensor for monitoring brain electrical activity
- A blood pressure sensor
- A tilt sensor for monitoring trunk position
- A breathing sensor for monitoring respiration
- Movement sensors used to estimate user's activity
- A "smart sock" sensor or a sensor-equipped shoe insole used to delineate phases of individual steps (Jovanov et al., 2005)

It may seem like a stretch to include health monitoring devices as examples of mobile learning, but all these sensors control messages sent to the person being monitored in order to teach people how to take good care of their bodies. As Greenemeier (2009) says, "If all goes well, look for MBANs [mobile body area networks] to fall into three categories in the near future those used to monitor a patient's general health or 'wellness,' those measuring the health of the elderly, and those used to monitor patients with long-term medical conditions such as Parkinson's disease or epilepsy."

# Research and Data Collection

Mobile phones are not just for phone calls, but they can also be used to collect data in several different formats and send them to a central server. There the data can be aggregated and analyzed, with tables and visualizations automatically generated. What is new is the sheer number of observation points that are potentially available by using mobile phones. With over 4 billion phones in use worldwide, the mobile phone network is emerging as a form of "global brain" with sensors everywhere. In addition, there are companies such as Fourier Systems that provide purpose-built mobile devices that are specifically designed for science experiments in schools and for data logging in any science project.

## Surveys, Questionnaires, Polls, and Voting

Because they are carried around by people, mobile phones seem particularly useful for research in the social sciences. Surveys, questionnaires, and polls are similar to assessment techniques (discussed above) and can be administered using mobile phones and lightweight tablet and notebook computers. Voting for a choice among several alternatives is like answering a multiple-choice question. This mobile technology has been available for at least a decade and is increasingly being used in developing countries as a way of contacting and connecting citizens and helping them to organize for a better life. One Web site dedicated to mobile technologies for social activism is MobileActive. org. This site lists a large number of data collection applications available for mobile phones, some of which are also designed for use in business. Here is a selection of data collection applications from MobileActive.org and other sources that might be of interest:

- *CS Pro Mobile:* CS Pro Mobile is a census and survey processing system for capturing household and other survey data directly on PDAs.
- *DigitalICS:* DigitalICS is a mobile phone application for filling out surveys, recording audio, and taking pictures. Developed at the University of California, Berkeley.
- *EpiCollect:* Allows two-way communication between field workers and their project databases, as well as polling and voting. Many different researchers can submit their field data and GPS data to a common Web database. There the data can be displayed and analyzed, along with previously collected data, and then plotted on Google Maps. Developed at Imperial College, London, U.K.
- *EpiSurveyor Mobile:* A mobile phone-based application for collecting data with a GPS stamp in field-based surveys. Displays results on Google Maps.
- *GATHERdata:* An application for mobile data collection, including forms development, deployment, analysis, alerting, reporting, and data transfer.
- *gReporter:* Allows reporters to upload photos, audio, and text with GPS information attached.
- *JavaRosa:* An open-source platform for data collection on mobile devices.
- *LimeSurvey:* The world's leading open-source survey tool, used by government, business, and various software houses.
- *Mobile Researcher:* The Mobile Researcher is an application that can be installed on a fieldworker's mobile phone, and used to download surveys, collect data, and upload the results.
- *Mobile-SPS:* A Web tool for easy creation and distribution of any kind of surveys to mobile devices. Users buy credit and use it up. Free trial.
- *Open Data Kit (ODK):* A suite of open-source tools developed at the University of Washington to help organizations collect, aggregate, and visualize their data. ODK runs on Android-based mobile phones.
- *Poll Everywhere:* This application facilitates live audience polling. Answers to questions can be sent via SMS text messages, Twitter, or the Web. Real-time results can be displayed in a Web browser or PowerPoint.

▶ *Polls by Pollimath:* Another Android mobile phone application used to conduct opinion polls.

▶ *RapidSMS:* A free and open-source framework for dynamic data collection, logistics coordination, and communication. Developed by UNICEF.

▶ *TextMarks:* A commercial data collection tool, but there is a free version with ads.

▶ *Wildform:* Enables users to create their own mobile recording forms for receiving and capturing data on location.

But what if you want to go beyond surveys and questionnaires and get more in-depth descriptive information from people via their mobile phones? There's even an application developed for *that*. Textonic is an open-source Web interface for processing text-based data with Amazon Mechanical Turk, a "crowdsourcing" application that uses people to sort data into categories, something that computers with artificial intelligence still find difficult to do. Textonic allows for tagging and categorizing text messages sent from mobile phones to a centralized database. These messages are then automatically submitted as human intelligence tasks (HITs) to MTurk. This procedure can quickly and cheaply generate custom metadata for each message.

## Sensor Networks

While we should be rightly concerned about invasion of individual privacy through surveillance by mobile devices, there is also tremendous potential in using individual mobile devices as sensing nodes in a larger network. The practice of *participatory sensing* and the building of *sensor networks* to gather information from many different sources in order to construct a picture of what might be happening within any group in society or at any location has been with us for the past decade. For example, the *Economist* (2008) reports that researchers at Purdue University revealed that they are constructing a network of mobile phones to detect and track radiation. A nuclear leak or a "dirty bomb" would set off the sensors in a large number of phones that would then identify their location through GPS. This would allow authorities to pinpoint the source of radiation. The *Economist* article continues:

The idea that phones should have sensors is far from outlandish. Phones already incorporate primitive versions, including the sensor that picks up the cellular signal, light sensors that dim the keyboard, and acceleration sensors that notice when the user lifts the phone to his ear. "Today, everybody can look at his phone and say how many signal bars he has," says Eric Paulos, a researcher at Intel, the world's largest chipmaker. "In a few years, everybody will look at his phone and see what the pollen count is."

. . . Carbon monoxide, ozone, pollen, sun intensity and temperature are among the things that Mr Paulos considers particularly easy to measure by tweaking mobile phones in ways that consumers would not even notice. Any such data would need to be collected in a discreet way to assure the privacy of consumers. But eventually, thinks Mr Paulos, this new twist to the everyday mobility of ordinary people could lead to "grassroots citizen science."

"Citizen science" is already happening in a big way, aided by the widespread distribution of smartphones. The What's Invasive project uses community data collection with mobile phones to locate and track invasive weeds that are threatening native plants and animals in several different locations in the world (Fig. 5.4). Other citizens are gathering information on pollution sources, identifying birds, or plotting bicycle use, and feeding their data into applications that analyze patterns from this information. Researchers in the SixthSense project at MIT are building prototypes for wearable devices that will automatically collect data as the wearers move around their environment. The potential for citizen science using mobile devices is enormous.

 # User-Generated Information and Learning Materials

The design of the modern classroom, with confining desks all facing the same way, essentially *immobilized* learners by forcing them to sit in one place for long periods of time (Fig. 5.5). The teacher/instructor/trainer was then able to lecture to the group and could easily see who was not paying attention. Mobile learning reverses that by allowing learners to move and to respond

**FIGURE 5.4 A screen shot of the What's Invasive project Web site (www.whatsinvasive.com).**

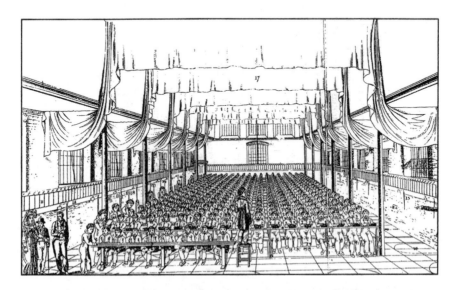

**FIGURE 5.5 Modern classrooms, first designed in the late eighteenth century in Europe, were designed to immobilize students by controlling all aspects of bodily movement.**

to the trainer, or to even ignore him or her in their pursuit of knowledge by going directly to sources of information that are relevant and of interest. For adults in training, we are moving from the practice of instruction to the practice of "do-it-yourself" (DIY) learning (Jarche, 2007).

While there are good legitimate concerns that the technologies for monitoring individuals can lead to extensive *surveillance* by authorities, the same technologies give rise to *sousveillance*, the ability to look back and report on the activities of those in power. The power to document the world around can be held by anyone with a minimal investment in equipment and time. This means that there is also a risk to businesses—either that someone will maliciously show something to embarrass a company or that genuine abuses and bad practices will be exposed.

On a positive note, more and more people are creating their own learning materials and are making them available to others at no charge. Still other users are documenting their little corner of the world and assigning their photos, audio recordings, and videos to open Web sites where they are available to others under a "Creative Commons" license. This alternative to copyright allows others the right to use uploaded materials in a way that is defined by the copyright holder. Often this means "noncommercial" uses, but many people designate their work as freely available to others provided proper credit is given. Learning materials that are created by others are sometimes referred to as user-generated and may include many forms of media or simply be the tags attached to Web sites that users find educational and useful. For example, there is an emerging genre of "mobilography" in which images are collected using mobile camera phones and later used to stimulate reflective learning.

After materials had been captured by a mobile device, they then can be uploaded into the information cloud that is available through any connection to the Internet. One popular place to store information is Google Docs. There is a version of Google Docs for mobile phones (m.google.com/docs) where you can edit the materials that you store there. Leo Gaggl (2009) in Australia describes how this all works:

> Along with the use of 2D barcodes, this will open a few interesting m-learning possibilities for educators that would previously have required custom coding to achieve. I can see this being very useful in situations where you have students being in the field and allowing them to enter data gathered using a standard mobile phone. The barcodes could point students to the location of

the spreadsheet (avoiding the need to type the information) . . . The data gathered can easily be embedded into LMS course pages for review. . . . The (quite capable) graphing tools in Google Spreadsheets can be used to visualize the results gathered (Gaggl, 2009).

As I have demonstrated in this chapter, mobile learning is definitely a two-way street. Instead of information coming at students from experts, learners can document their own world and send the results into the information cloud where it can be used by others. However, we can even go beyond that and see how learning can take place by using social and interactive applications on mobile devices. This is a topic for the next chapter.

6

# Learning by Communicating, Interacting, and Networking

It is in the use of networking, interactive applications, and multiparty communications through networking that mobile technologies shine as tools to support learning. It is also these new uses of mobile technologies that are the most disruptive of traditional ways of teaching and training. Mobile learning technologies allow for collaborative learning, social networking, building of communities of practice, learning games, simulations, virtual worlds, immersive language learning, mentoring, and messaging. They allow learners to work on projects from anywhere in the world while they are mobile.

Because the use of mobile learning tools involves other people, we refer to the kinds of learning these tools support as social learning. The older methods of education and training are often referred to as formal learning because they involve structured institutionalized procedures and fixed specified curricula. Yet, as many of us know from experience, much of what we learned in formal settings is promptly forgotten right after the test, unless it turns out to be relevant and useful to what we are doing at the time. Instead, possibly up to

80 percent of what we learn and retain is based on informal learning, the learning that happens every day as we encounter new situations. Jay Cross, author of the book *Informal Learning: Rediscovering the Pathways that Inspire Innovation and Performance* (2006), says on his blog:

> People acquire the skills they use at work informally—talking, observing others, trial-and-error, and simply working with people in the know. Formal training and workshops account for only 10 to 20 percent of what people learn at work. Most corporations over-invest in formal training while leaving the more natural, simple ways we learn to chance.

Although training departments are looking at how to incorporate mobile learning into their training programs, many are hesitant because of the loss of control that potentially accompanies mobile learning in the workplace. In Chapter 10, management consultant Sheryl Herle grapples with this and other issues involved in actually implementing a program of mobile learning in a large enterprise setting.

Educational researchers are only now trying to conceptualize informal learning in a rigorous way. Tselios et al. (2007a, 2007b) have developed an "information foraging theory" to describe how we deal with the mountain of information that is available to us. Several writers use the image of "feral learning" (Hall, 2008) invoking the metaphor of a wild child or an animal dashing about, picking up whatever information it needs when it needs it.

But foraging for information and feral learning don't capture the fact that for thousands of years, much of what humans have learned has been achieved within stable social groups—family, friends and community—and not in schools or training departments. In Western societies, the institution of compulsory schooling is only about 150 years old.

We learn within a culture that has a history, located in a specific geographical region, usually embedded in a family group that belongs to a specific social class and income level. As individuals, we can move out from these groups and come back to them as needed. As noted previously in Chapter 3, Gerry Stahl (2006) argues that group learning comes before individual learning because we learn within a specific cultural background and geographical location, stimulated and encouraged by other people around us.

# Network Science

Mobile learning may have a greater potential for profound change than we realize. It disturbs the normal social relations that most people experience in growing up, by allowing us to form bonds with others who are not in close physical proximity to us and who may not be in our traditional social groups. These ideas are being studied under the label of "network science," which provides us with insights about the impact that mobile communications in general are having on our society.

Human interactions can happen in many ways, including (1) one-to-one relationships, (2) few-to-few relationships, (3) one-to-many relationships, (4) many-to-one relationships, and (5) many-to-many relationships. One-to-one relationships are generally two directional and therefore social. In networking theory terms, these connections are or have the potential to become "strong ties." Examples include face-to-face interactions, telephone calls, e-mail, and text messages, all between two people.

Few-to-few relationships are a pattern characteristic of small tightly knit groups in which there are strong ties among all the members of the group. The group size is usually between three and thirty. This size of group is often the most powerful in terms of learning from peers. Examples include a family, a gang, and small groups that work and collaborate together.

One-to-many relationships are usually unidirectional in terms of flows of power and communications and therefore are not very social. These are not networks but hierarchies, and are familiar to us as the "command and control" structures of the military, some religious groups, and schools. Examples include classroom instruction and lectures, meetings dominated by one person, and any form of broadcasting.

Many-to-one relationships are also unidirectional. They occur where many people supply data to a single central source which then aggregates the information into a view of the "will of the people." Online social polling/survey tools, feedback forums, group decision support tools, and "crowd sourcing" (many people working on a piece of a larger problem to find a solution) are all examples.

Finally, many-to-many relationships are multidirectional but are often superficial because of the short amount of time spent on each connection in the network of relationships. These relationships usually remain as "weak ties" in a network, although individuals may form one-to-one or small group connections as "strong ties" (Fig. 6.1). Note that in networking theory weak ties are very useful for the diffusion of new ideas. Examples include large group collaboration, group chat, group games, participation in discussion in blogs and online media sites, online meetings, and the use of large-scale social media platforms such as Twitter, Facebook, and MySpace.

What is interesting about mobile technologies is that they can support all these levels of relationships at the same time. The potential for mobile learning is present in each of these network configurations. What is exciting is that it is a new mix; a new way of relating that has literally never been seen before. In his essay, "Going Nomadic," Bryan Alexander (2004) writes:

> The physical vs. the digital, the sedentary vs. the nomadic—the wireless, mobile, student-owned learning impulse cuts across our institutional sectors, silos, and expertise-propagation structures. How do we respond to such across-the-grain learning? Is this a budding venue for curricular transformation, wedding student interest to institutional practice?

## Knowledge Flow – Organizational Perspective

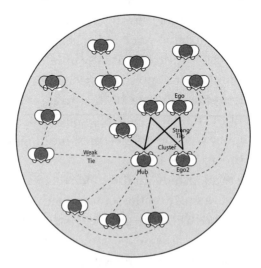

**FIGURE 6.1 Social relationships can be characterized by a series of "strong ties" and "weak ties."**

In the rest of this chapter we examine how the five forms of social relationships outlined on page 129 work for mobile learning in a way that has the potential to be both disruptive and transformational of the way we all learn.

 ## Collaboration and Community

As social beings, humans are naturally attracted to being part of a community. Computer networking allows the development of many more connections among people then were possible in the past. With mobile technology, remaining connected to one's network is now possible regardless of where one is physically located. As Mary Chayko (2008) notes in *Portable Communities: The Social Dynamics of Online and Mobile Connectedness,* we can now take our social relationships with us wherever we go. Chayko says that members of online communities "think in tandem"; they share a "cognitive connectedness" through stories and collective memories. The feeling of connectedness involved when people are connected electronically can be just as strong as the bonds between people who meet each other face to face. When these bonds of connectedness and support grow to the point that we feel we are part of a virtual group of coworkers and fellow professionals, we then can speak of being part of a "community of practice."

One of the most powerful ways to learn is through collaboration with others. In the past, this has generally meant being in the same room with coworkers in order to work together on projects. The more of us there are who work virtually and connect to our colleagues through mobile devices, the more mobile collaboration is a reality for many.

Collaboration using mobile devices can take place at several different levels. At the lowest level, collaboration simply means being able to access e-mail or instant messages from colleagues and send replies. Often, this requires software to coordinate a company's servers with the various mobile devices that employees take with them when they are mobile.

The second level of collaboration using mobile technologies is to enable people to meet while some or all of the participants are on the road. The easiest way to achieve this is through a conference call involving all participants.

It can also be achieved through laptop or mobile phone connections with high-speed WiFi networks, often available at hotels.

A third level is to use online meeting software that is specifically designed to include mobile devices. Vendors now offer products that will support mobile collaboration at all these levels. Unified communication and collaboration (UCC) is a concept promoted by many different vendors although it is relatively expensive to set up. In 2008, Johna Johnson of *Network World* estimated that the average cost for a mobile employee is around $2,200 per year, including hardware, software, services, and support.

Even though collaboration technologies are now available, research shows that collaboration will not spontaneously take place without a structured and regulated socially shared learning process (Järvelä, Volet, and Järvenoja, 2005). Organizing mobile collaboration tasks as "mobimissions" that include challenges and a sense of adventure motivate collaborators to work together.

Another motivator for mobile collaboration can be a shared sense of social purpose. For example, the MobileActive.org Web site brings together activists who are using mobile technology to achieve social change. Another type of mobile collaboration involves asking individuals to make small contributions to a larger collective project. Known as "crowd sourcing," this movement harnesses volunteers and paid workers to solve problems that are difficult for an individual or small group to solve on their own.

For organizations, mobile collaboration will most likely happen as part of the work of virtual project teams. One of the new business skills to emerge is the ability to both motivate and manage mobile virtual project teams. Leading and managing such teams can be more difficult than contending with a face-to-face group. In a Canadian study (Hambley et al., 2007), qualitative data were collected through comprehensive interviews with nine virtual team leaders and members from six different organizations. The most common challenge appears to have involved solving problems across multiple time zones. Study participants also believed that ineffective leaders lacked vision, strategy, and direction, and that they were unable to run effective virtual team meetings or to "read" and "hear" cues from team members while using virtual conferencing software.

Other issues involved with leading virtual project teams include lack of facial and body language cues to validate team members, participants' fears of isolation from each other, communicating changes in operating procedures, and a higher demand for individual accountability because of delays resulting from lack of preparedness. All these issues are exacerbated for those leading virtual project teams, and recovering from making errors takes longer than it does when teams work together face to face.

One solution to this problem is that leadership of mobile virtual project teams can be shared so that no one person actually manages the functioning of the group alone. When no designated leader is assigned to a group, we say that the group has "shared leadership" or is "self-managed." Once the members of a mobile virtual team are integrated into a social group, their mobile phones can become the means of "hypercoordination" where members continuously send messages to each other updating their status, location, and thoughts.

Much advice about leading mobile virtual teams revolves around fostering positive and respectful relationships among team members who hold each other accountable and support each other through difficult situations. The same also holds true of professional relationships in the onsite workplace; however, mobile virtual relationships face unique challenges that take more work to maintain and nurture. But if a collaborative mobile virtual team is right for your organization, the rewards can be well worth the effort.

Mobile collaboration is a relatively new phenomenon that will develop new methods and new technologies in the near future. Nick Jones (2009c) expects that we will see voice-controlled wikis (a wiki is an online document that anyone can edit), shared mobile screens, and multiple points of view merged together on mobile phones in the near future.

## Mobile Games, Simulations, and Virtual Worlds

Mobile games, simulations, and virtual worlds are all based on similar technologies. *Virtual worlds* are environments in which characters, called "avatars" move around and take actions. When the virtual world is similar to a real place and the actions of the user approximate what might be done in real life, we speak of this as a *simulation*. If the controllers of the characters in a virtual world have specific objectives and can achieve a higher score than others involved in the same virtual world, then we have set up a *game*. What virtual worlds, simulations, and games have in common is that they are generally engaging for those involved. This is important because the world of employee training is rapidly changing. No longer are people willing to simply sit in seats and listen to an instructor who, at the end of the "course," hands out another three-ring binder to be put on a shelf. Instead, employees want to be engaged. They want to be immersed in a task that grips them and motivates them and moves them along in terms of confidence and knowledge.

It is not just training that is changing but work itself. To quote Diego Rodriguez of the design consultancy IDEO, "The future of work is here; it's just disguised as a game" (cited by Quinn-Votaw, 2009). This doesn't mean that work is not serious or not hard. Rather, people want work to be engaging and fulfilling. We are now largely motivated by interests, not by duty. We are no longer just cogs in a system but self-fashioning actors in charge of our own learning. At least that is the direction in which we are moving.

One direction that is very promising is playing serious games in nonworkplace environments using mobile handheld devices (Fig. 6.2). This allows the players to be freed from their desk, and allows the game designer to incorporate elements of the user's location into the game play. Being mobile allows the learner to connect to the "information cloud" for just-in-time instructions or data. Also, mobile devices with geographical positioning system (GPS) capabilities allow computer programs to assess the user's location and provide information that is specific to his or her context. Klopfer (2008) argues that, "Designing good applications for handhelds and mobiles requires taking advantage of the platform and the context in which these games are used."

**FIGURE 6.2 Screen shots of a driving challenge game from Audi.**

While there are viable learning games based entirely in virtual worlds, there is an advantage to "being there" when learning about a specific location in the world. In this way augmented reality has a number of advantages over virtual reality. These advantages are referred to by Klopfer as "mobile game affordances." They include:

- ▶ What constitutes a game is in the eye of the beholder; mobile games don't have to look like traditional games.
- ▶ Previous experience can be important; in designing mobile games, experiences with role-play, drama, and simulations are all useful.
- ▶ There is better access for mobile games. Mobile devices can be easily and inexpensively deployed and maintained.
- ▶ There needs to be a balance of on-screen and off-screen time. Mobile augmented reality games don't require full attention to a screen, and therefore activities can be added to a game that don't need to be read from a screen.
- ▶ Mobile games have "temporal flexibility" in that short bursts of game activity can be integrated into the ongoing lives of learners.
- ▶ Mobile games can incorporate natural communications. Face-to-face and phone conversations can be part of the game.
- ▶ Learning is situated; mobile games can be set in a social and physical context that readily becomes part of the game.
- ▶ Learning is embodied; players can both communicate and think with their bodies using the physical context of games. It is easy to make physical connections with a game set in the physical world.
- ▶ Knowledge is constructed; players construct knowledge as they play the game.
- ▶ Transfer of learning is easier. With real-world role-play, players experience the situation from perspectives that closely resemble real-life roles.
- ▶ Mobile games excel at connecting to existing classroom ecologies and extend them in powerful new directions.

I personally experienced the motivational effects of playing a mobile simulation game while attending the 2009 mLearn Conference in Orlando, Florida. One evening, the conference participants were divided into several small groups and given an assignment—to be a personal bodyguard for singer Jimmy Buffett. We moved around a theme park looking for Jimmy Buffett, all the while receiving instructions on our mobile phones. Once we had completed one task, we sent a message to security control and received our next set of instructions. This mobile *alternate reality* game was challenging, educational, and entertaining, and it alerted me to some of the possibilities of this emerging genre of training methods.

## Case Study

## A Mobile Learning Game to Orient Employees at Turkcell

GSM-based mobile communications started in Turkey when Turkcell began its operations in February 1994. As of December 31, 2007, Turkcell had invested $8 billion in Turkey, excluding the price of its operating license. With 35.4 million subscribers, Turkcell is the second largest GSM operator in Europe in terms of subscriber base. Turkcell is still the first and only Turkish company ever to be listed on the New York Stock Exchange (NYSE).

Turkcell Academy is the corporate university of Turkcell Communications Plc., responsible for the general training activities of the employees in the Turkcell Group and the developer ecosystem. The corporate university uses a virtual campus, e-learning, m-learning, and traditional training activities to strengthen employees' technical and nontechnical competencies, which in turn improves their business processes and results.

Turkcell perceives that the need for standards for mobile learning is essential for mass applications and usage as well as establishing a content developer ecosystem. Turkcell is working together with Bogaziçi University in Istanbul to set standard requirements and to contribute to international e-learning and m-learning standards bodies.

Turkcell Technology and Turkcell Academy have collaborated on a mobile learning project to develop an infrastructure that will bring together *mobile communications technology* and *learning*. Turkcell has built a platform where users may access mobile learning content just as they would access any other Internet service via a mobile device. The platform includes application programming interfaces (APIs) for user-generated content to be developed through a Web 2.0 approach, a learning management system (LMS), a digital rights management (DRM) infrastructure, integration with a mobile operator network, and multimedia support.

The main goal of the m-learning project is to provide Turkcell Group employees with the opportunity to access training materials while they are on the move. At Turkcell, mobile learning is used for various learner groups:

- ▶ New employees in the orientation program.
- ▶ Sales representatives at flagship shops.
- ▶ Employees who need to be informed regarding the latest developments in new telecommunications technologies.
- ▶ Hobby training (stress handling, managing people).

## MOBILE SOLUTION

"Kim Tutar Cell'i" is a mobile learning game for the new employees attending the company's orientation program. In the orientation program, the newcomers first attend classroom training where they learn the history, corporate culture, and values of Turkcell and Turkcell Group. Information on basic GSM infrastructure and enterprise IT software training is provided as e-learning.

Apart from the above topics, there has been a need for the newcomers to understand the physical environment and get a feel for the organization's corporate business processes. Consequently, we designed a "treasure hunt" game in which participants go around the offices (scattered in different commercial buildings around Istanbul) and meet people they will have to work with in their corporate future, in order to understand the company's methods of doing business. The Kim Tutar Cell'i game is administered on the last day of the orientation program.

The English translation of "Kim Tutar Cell'i" is "Who Can Stop The 'Cellbuddy'?" (Cellbuddies are Turkcell's mascots.) The game lasts a whole day, and it has been in the orientation program since November 2005. At the start, it was played with paper envelopes and clues handed out to the participating teams. Later on, the m-learning platform became operational and the game was adapted to the mobile environment.

One of the main constraints was the need to have mobile phones that support Flash. New employees usually do not yet have a company phone that is m-learning–compatible. However, since only a single phone is necessary for each group, a total of five phones are needed. Lack of user experience in mobile learning is also a problem during the initial phases. The new employees need to become familiar with the user interface of the phone they are using, and the Web-based management software that is used for the game.

Playing Kim Tutar Cell'i itself requires participants to be mobile. It is very important for Turkcell to show new employees the endless possibilities of the mobile world, and the game provides a very effective way of achieving this goal. Logistically, the game is now much easier, because there is no need to distribute envelopes all around the different commercial buildings a day in advance.

## Results

The Kim Tutar Cell'i game helps new hires to become comfortable with the physical environment of the company and to learn specific processes that they will use in the course of their corporate life. Starting to work with mobile learning familiarizes the new employees with the mobile learning environment that they will be using to access other learning content, such as training in first aid or how to deal with stress.

The new employees' participation rate for e-learning is now higher than it was previously, showing that new employees can creatively adapt to an electronic environment. The number of questions asked by newcomers about the "critical processes" learned in this game is now lower than it was before. Also, transferring Kim Tutar Cell'i from an "envelope" environment to "mobile" environment saved Turkcell Academy about 15–20 hours of logistical support that had to be spent for preparation and play each time the game was offered. This adds up to a savings of 40 hours a month, not to mention the amount of paper saved.

We get the participants to write at least a paragraph about how they feel after the game. The comments indicate that the game assists new employees in seeing the organization as a whole, knowing the importance of each person working in the company, and feeling oriented enough to tackle the tasks and missions ahead. Furthermore, one of the most frequent comments is that participants appreciate that they received information about company business processes directly from the people doing the jobs, information that could not be as effectively taught in a classroom environment. Almost all participants enjoy the game and remember everything they learned, which goes to prove the efficacy of game-based learning.

There is usually a very serious purpose to playing mobile learning games. Andersen (2004) describes a mobile first-aid training system for training doctors in stabilizing casualties on site. Emergency personnel can use virtual worlds on mobile devices to act out a wide variety of scenarios, especially situations that would happen only rarely in real life. Other examples are language learning games, which, when coupled with augmented reality text overlays, can greatly enhance the learning of a foreign language when people are traveling in a country where that language is spoken.

The field of mobile educational games, simulations, and virtual worlds is rapidly developing. Other examples include training hotel staff using gaming consoles, the organization of large groups for weekend "hide and seek" games played throughout a city, and text-based adventure games that use SMS messages to receive instructions and gather clues. As smartphones become location-aware, they can use geographical information to locate players, provide information, and keep score of large-scale games that are played over a wide area. Immersive mobile learning games are being used to teach languages by having learners move through a virtual world conversing (in the language they are trying to learn) with other people they meet. Tracking software can assess whether their language is appropriate and grammatically correct.

 ## Mentoring, Support, and Cognitive Apprenticeships

Even if we move away from the classroom model of training, learners often need mentoring, psychological support, and direction in terms of what they need to know. Instead of being removed from the real job situation where knowledge is needed, mobile communications make expertise available to learners as they are performing a task. Attewell and Webster (2004) describe a study of hard-to-reach young people where mobile availability of mentoring made a positive difference in outcomes for them:

> One mentor has been working with a homeless young adult who regularly truanted while at school and subsequently left school without any qualifications. The mentor reports that as a result of participation in the m-learning project, her client has not only developed a greater confidence in his current

reading and writing abilities, but he has also been inspired to seek help to improve his mathematical skills from the local Adult Basic Education Centre. Another mentor, working with a group of displaced young adults studying ESOL (English for Speakers of Other Languages), reports that a number of learners who had previously avoided using PCs seem much more confident about using technology. . . . One mentor noticed that learners were more focused for longer periods when involved in m-learning, compared with traditional classroom lessons.

There many are other examples of the use of mobile communications for just-in-time performance support and coaching, especially in the field of health care and medicine. The United Nations Foundation reports that the National Leadership and Innovation Agency for Healthcare introduced a radical approach to mentoring using social networking with guided learning principles. The University of Southampton's MPLAT Project supported health-care students in clinical placements with a mobile learning toolkit that included practice-based learning, mentoring, and assessment using mobile devices.

Workers in the oil sands industry in Canada can take courses from Keyano College through a mobile electrical apprenticeship program. This allows the students to continue working through their apprenticeship with no increase in their living expenses. The employers have the benefit of a steady workforce of highly skilled workers.

 ## Text Messaging

All mobile phones have basic text messaging capabilities. Known as short messaging service (SMS), text messages can be used for learning purposes in many different ways. Because of the difficulty of typing on a small keyboard where several letters can be assigned to one key, users have developed a form of shorthand to send their messages. For example, try reading this text message:

My smmr hols wr CWOT. B4, we usd 2go2 NY 2C my bro, his GF & thr 3 :- kds FTF. ILNY, it's a gr8 plc.

Translated into normal English, the above message reads as follows:

My summer holidays were a complete waste of time. Before, we used to go to New York to see my brother, his girlfriend, and their three screaming kids face to face. I love New York, it's a great place.

(From Sugden and Soon, 2007)

Fig 6.3 shows a message received on a BlackBerry. Can you decipher it? (The answer is at the end of this chapter.)

Text messaging has proven to be a reliable and inexpensive way of sending information to those who need it. For example, a South African instant messaging network is being used to provide counseling for drug addicts and people with HIV (Ananthaswamy, 2009). After the earthquake in Haiti in early 2010, text messaging was used to locate survivors and missing people; report fires; and make requests for food, water, and medical supplies. Much of

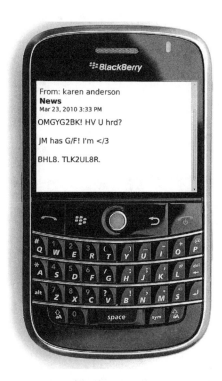

**FIGURE 6.3 A message received on a Blackberry. Can you make out the message?**

the messaging was coordinated by a 4636 texting service set up in Kenya and run by volunteers from all over the world.

Because text messaging is such a basic service on all mobile phones, it is used by social activists around the world. For example, the MobileActive.org Web site lists 68 different education projects in developing countries that use SMS for their communications (Fig. 6.4).

There are three types of SMS campaigns—text blasting, keyword response, and smart texting. With text blasting recipients need to opt in and be placed on a list of recipients for SMS messages. Then a text message can be sent to the entire list in one operation. It is important that recipients be able to opt out of the list at any time. Key-word response generates an automatic reply when someone sends a specific word to a designated phone number. Once the word is received, the program sends back a standard message. Smart texting allows incoming SMS messages to contain a query containing a variable. The

**FIGURE 6.4 The MobileActive.org Web site has a directory of inexpensive software resources for those wanting to help others.**

program looks up information in a database and sends a response based on the information in the incoming query.

Several universities have begun to use SMS text services for teaching and learning. In New Zealand, Auckland University has successfully implemented an SMS-based "learning on demand" service for its students. Operating since October 2005, the service provides small amounts of information to students to be stored on their mobile phones for later recall. Similarly, the Universiti Sains Malaysia pushes snippets of information via SMS to second-year students in its distance learning physics course. The University of South Africa uses SMS messaging to connect isolated students with groups so that they can study together. Tretiakov and Kinshuk (2005) are university researchers who are looking at how SMS messaging can be used as a "pervasive testing environment." This movement for universities to use mobile phone messaging is the beginning of a trend that will likely grow.

 ## Personal Media Production

Not only do mobile technologies allow you to be both mobile and connected, but they often have built-in capabilities that allow you to produce your own creative or learning materials. These capabilities further erode the power and influence of trainers and teachers as experts and the dominant source of knowledge. Do-it-yourself learning means that you find things yourself and produce your own works. Creating your own media productions is a great way to learn about creative processes as well as the subject matter of your production.

To that end, the newest smartphones have built-in digital still cameras, video cameras, audio recorders, note-taking programs, and graphics software. The newest smartphones, such as the iPhone 4, have two built-in cameras—one for taking pictures and videos, and one facing the user for high definition videoconferencing. Digital pens and paper attached to mobile phones can record handwriting and later turn it into word processing text. Sensors in phones respond to your touch and your breathing. Some mobile devices can even be turned into musical instruments. For example, the iPhone app *Ocarina* makes your mobile phone sound like an ancient flutelike instrument.

Automatic speech recognition software allows you to dictate basic commands on mobile phones; it is not quite ready for transcribing narrative text. But it's coming.

Bryan Alexander had it right in 2004 when he wrote that we were becoming ". . . creative, communicative participants rather than passive, reception-only consumers." He added, "We lack a term for describing the world as a writeable and readable service, encompassing mobile phones forming communities, P2P handheld gaming, moblogging, and uploading to RFID chips."

Personal media production has resulted in the phenomenon of "m-novels," entire works of fiction written on a mobile phone. Depending on which phone one owns, this can be a relatively slow and painful process. Nevertheless, it shows that, given the tools, people want to express themselves. Other mobile devices, such as miniaturized video cameras, digital cameras, audio recorders, and appropriately equipped smartphones are all being used to produce creative works of art and literature or to document the world around us. And all the above can be supported with a variety of mobile phone "personal organizers" that allow a person to enter text notes, video or audio memos, new tasks, and appointments at any time.

 ## Social Media

Social media refers to Internet and mobile technologies that allow networked social interaction (because they are networked, social media was originally referred to as "social networking"). Well-known examples of social media include blogs; wikis; microblogging sites like Facebook, MySpace, and Twitter; tagging and voting sites like Delicious and Digg; and media collection sites such as Flickr and YouTube. There are hundreds more social media applications, but these are some of the best-known ones.

In particular, social media refer to new technologies that allow many-to-many relationships rather than connections that are dominated by one person. Social media are part of what is referred to as Web 2.0, but Web 2.0 is a broader term that also refers to other aspects of information technologies such as access to databases and distributed content. Almost all social media are available both on the Web and in versions for mobile phones.

Social media have exploded onto the learning and development scene in the past year or two. For example, Facebook now has over 400 million users. Social media present whole new opportunities for connecting people and letting them self-organize. For businesses, social media clearly present a dilemma; does a company try to ban social media in the workplace as a distraction and a potential security hazard, or does it embrace this new technology, allowing the company to be talked about openly (hopefully in a positive light) and become transparent in terms of its methods, culture, and proprietary information? Many businesses are struggling to find the right balance between these two extremes.

One problem is that the use of mobile phones and social media has become ubiquitous and second nature to the younger generation that is entering the workforce. A new study by the Kaiser Family Foundation found that 8- to 18-year -olds are, on average, spending more than 50 hours a week with digital media (Rideout et al., 2010).

Social media have changed social behaviors. We have learned that material that is posted on the Internet or sent over a mobile phone is no longer private. What we do and share can remain forever. Because you cannot control what others post about you, social media have led to more transparency and loss of privacy, thus requiring people to be careful about what they do in public. Mobile computing means that cameras are everywhere, ready to record any behavior for posterity.

Because information is coming at us from our television sets, our computer monitors, and our mobile phone screens, many people find themselves always multitasking, continuously dividing their attention among competing attractors. But, according to MIT sociologist Sherry Turkle, this can be problematic. "Because technology makes it easy, we've all wanted to think it is good for us, a new kind of thinking, an expansion of our ability to reason and cycle through complicated things —do more and be more efficient. Unfortunately, the new research is coming in that says when you multitask, everything gets done a little worse" (Turkle, 2009).

Actually, the first hints of problems with multitasking came from Canadian researcher Pierre Jolicoeur in 1999. He showed test subjects a computer display that flashed either an X or a Y. The participants simply had to identify the letter, but the task became harder when a tone was introduced at the same time and they were asked to differentiate between high and low pitches while still naming the letters. Jolicoeur demonstrated that the brain has "restricted attentional capacity," that is, it can really only think about one thing at a time.

New research from a team at Stanford University verifies the earlier research (Ophir et al., 2009). The team surveyed 262 students on their media habits. The 19 students who multitasked the most and the 22 students who multitasked the least then took two computer-based tests. In the first test they had to remember how sets of red rectangles surrounded by blue rectangles were oriented. In the second test, they had to categorize a random string of words and then repeat that categorization leaving out words that had been preceded by a beep. A third test involved a new group of 30 students that was classified as high or low in multitasking. The participants were asked to identify target letters on the screen. The test was repeated, and students had to remember whether the letters had been included in previous runs of the test. In *every test*, students who were low multitaskers performed much better than those who were high multitaskers. In an article summarizing this research, Adam Gorlick (2009) commented:

> People who are regularly bombarded with several streams of electronic information do not pay attention, control their memory or switch from one job to another as well as those who prefer to complete one task at a time. . . . High-tech jugglers are everywhere—keeping up several e-mail and instant message conversations at once, text messaging while watching television and jumping from one website to another while plowing through homework assignments. But after putting about 100 students through a series of three tests, the researchers realized those heavy media multitaskers are paying a big mental price.

This research indicates that we can overuse social media to the detriment of performance. Each form of social media can be seen as a particular tool in a toolset. Each tool has a use for which it was designed, and a set of best practices on how it can be used. But it is bad practice to try to use many tools all at the same time.

The use of social media in corporate training is very new, so resistance to change is to be expected. Vendors are also scrambling to develop imitations of the big social media sites but with more controls over who can join and what can take place within a corporate site that uses the new versions of social media. If you want to introduce one or more of the many forms of social media into your organization, you need to:

▶ Manage expectations. Discussion with sponsors, project team members, and users need to take place. Social media will often disrupt the usual way of doing things, and your colleagues need to be aware of that.
▶ Create a common base of knowledge about social media. After all, social media are about sharing. Develop an internal knowledge base where best practices are stored and where useful information gained from using social media can be shared.
▶ Make a social collaboration code of conduct that is extremely clear for all members of the organization.
▶ Don't just demonstrate the technology. Reinforce hands-on use from the outset of introduction and provide facilitated use as an option for everyone, not just the executives.
▶ Create multiple and ongoing reasons to use social media.
▶ Expect and reward organizational use of social media.
▶ Make it difficult not to adopt social media tools. Make it the new way of working.

In the end, it is very difficult, if not impossible, to stop a social movement. For businesses, this means embracing change and developing new business models to work with the new realities.

Note: The translation of the text message in Figure 6.3 is as follows:
"Oh my God! You've got to be kidding! Have you heard? J.M. has a girl-friend! I'm broken-hearted. Be home late. Talk to you later."

# Management of Mobile Learning, Knowledge, and Performance

In addition to being useful for learners, mobile technologies can be helpful to managers of learning, knowledge, and performance. In this chapter I present mobile learning from the point of view of those in charge of training, tracking and reporting of training results, and planning for how employees learn and develop knowledge. The use of desktop technologies to track learners who are using mobile devices allows mobile learning to be tracked and managed from a distance.

> "It's easy to educate for the routine, and hard to educate for the novel."
> —*Jonathan Rosenberg (2008)*

Although I stress that mobile learning revolutionizes the methods of teaching because learners do not have to be in a classroom, it is equally possible for teachers and trainers to bring mobile technology into the classroom in order to try these new modes of teaching. This use of mobile technology allows teachers and trainers to extend instructor-led training into the mobile world by using the devices in the settings that are most familiar to them. However, just using mobile phones in the classroom, without freeing the learners from that location, seems to me to be a poor use of what mobile learning technologies can provide.

In addition to classroom management, mobile technologies are used to inform employees about and help them manage emergencies, and to help employees learn about and manage their own health. They are also used to track learning results and changes in on-the-job performance via mobile learning management systems, and to track organizational knowledge by integrating mobile technologies with a company's knowledge management system. Finally, given that the members of mobile teams are widely distributed geographically, mobile technologies are used more and more for virtual team management.

# Classroom Uses of Mobile Technologies

Today, most students or trainees who come into a classroom bring their laptops and mobile phones with them, and for some teachers this is a disturbing trend. It is also now common for conference attendees to bring both laptops and mobile phones into sessions and to interact with them while the presenter is speaking (Fig. 7.1). Members of university teaching staffs report that many students talk on their cell phones during lectures, or that the phones often ring during a class. Rules about the use of mobile phones during class time need to be established at the beginning of each term. Students respond to requests to shut off their phones with a sense of panic, a feeling that they will be cut off from their world of personal relationships. This feeling, taken to its extreme, has been dubbed "nomophobia," the fear of being forced to shut off a phone, or the obsessive worry of losing a phone. There is even a support Web site for nomophobics.

Some trainers have tried to embrace the new mobile technologies and use them in a strategic way while teaching. For example, course materials can be made available for downloading into mobile phones for later review. Mobile phones can be used to elicit responses and feedback from students during class time. By using mobile phones, students can physically work alone and still remain connected to resources and other learners. They can interact with other students or access "smart boards" or the Internet. Mobile phones can be used in a classroom for educational learning games or digital scavenger hunts.

**FIGURE 7.1 Simultaneous use of laptops while someone is presenting has become quite common at conferences. Photo by Justin. Used under a Creative Commons license.**

Homework assignments can be scheduled and downloaded into students' mobile phones. At Ball State University in the United States, nursing students use their mobile phones to access lab books, medical dictionaries, diagnostic literature, and other medical resources whenever they need them.

One Asian university is using iPhones to take attendance. As students enter the lecture hall, they simply type their ID numbers and a class number into an iPhone application. To prevent students from cheating by logging in from home or elsewhere, the application checks their location using GPS data (Alexander, 2009). Strictly speaking, this is not mobile learning, but the use of mobile devices and software to manage learners.

One obvious use of mobile technologies in classrooms is to allow students to access lectures on their mobile phones at a later date in order to review them or to see what they missed if they didn't attend the class. While some professors worry that putting their lectures online will encourage students to skip lectures, new research has indicated that the student's likelihood of skipping class is not correlated with whether or not a professor puts her lectures online.

Instead, attendance is much more related to whether or not the lecturer is engaging. In a 2008 study at the University of Wisconsin at Madison, 78 percent of undergraduate respondents said that having lectures available online would help them retain lecture material, while 76 percent said that they thought it would improve their test scores. More than a dozen vendors now offer "lecture capture" solutions to professors who want to use this technology.

However, many professors have been highly resistant to lecture capture technology, even refusing to press the start button at the beginning of their lectures. Some universities have turned to automated software that doesn't require the professors' cooperation in order to capture their presentations. Of course this has caused concerns about faculty members' traditional rights to "academic freedom" and disputes about the ownership of intellectual property delivered at a university. Businesses need to be aware of these issues and review copyright provisions in contracts with training staff to make sure that all parties are satisfied with and clear about the ownership of intellectual property used in training.

For some students, the use of mobile phones represents a break between higher education courses and their workplace. Smith (2009) describes the impact that access to learning materials on a mobile phone had for one college student:

> She explained there was usually a tension between the college method of hairdressing and the salon's. The college and the salon rarely met, so the focus for this tension would often be on the student who was corrected in the use of the college method by the salon and vice-versa by the college. Having her learning materials in-depth on her iPhone meant that she could show the salon manager in detail what she had been learning. The manager could then see why or how different methods were being applied and put her workplace learning into context. The relationship between college, student and workplace was transformed and she felt her learning improved. It's a beautiful thing.

Another classroom use of mobile technologies is to alert staff and students of a threat to their health or safety. For example, AlertU is a Web-based emergency text (SMS) messaging platform that has been developed for enterprises, institutions, and school campus communities. Administrators can easily send text messages to mobile devices in real time as needed. Sometimes it is a crisis that persuades traditional teaching and training staff that mobile learning can work. Omar et al. (2008) agree:

> M-learning will change the organisation and technological infrastructure of institutions. Since most organisations and people are resistant to paradigm changes, the migration from a traditional institution to an m-learning campus can take decades to be successful. Nature can sometimes quicken this change. . . . Southern University at New Orleans (SUNO) succeeded in becoming an electronic-learning campus after Hurricane Rita and Hurricane Katrina in particular. In addition to providing basic continuous education to its displaced students, the institution was able to migrate and utilise m-learning to move forward with its mission of providing higher education to students from diverse backgrounds.

 ## Emergency and Health-Care Uses of Mobile Learning

Around the world, people experience emergencies from such events as a terrorist attack, a hurricane, or an earthquake. As I write this section of the book on February 27, 2010, the news channels alert me to a major earthquake that took place last night in Chile, with the threat of tsunamis all along the Pacific Rim in the next 24 hours. Mobile technologies and social media like Twitter bring news to us as it happens and can alert us when we are in immediate danger. When the pilot of a U.S. Airways flight had to ditch his plane in the Hudson River in New York, it was images from the Twitter application Twitpic, sent by a passenger on a nearby ferry from his iPhone that gave the world its first view of this accident.

More importantly, mobile emergency channels can tell us what to do to protect ourselves and get out of danger, even as events unfold. Fig. 7.2 shows a message sent by police to residents of the state of Victoria, Australia, warning of impending danger because of brush fires.

Several emergencies in the past decade have highlighted the important role that mobile learning can play in managing crises. The terrible terrorist

**FIGURE 7.2 Message from police to residents of the state of Victoria, Australia, regarding the danger of brush fires. Photo by Avlxyz. Used under a Creative Commons license.**

attack on the World Trade Center in New York on September 11, 2001, showed the importance of having the BlackBerry text messaging network available when all other means of communications into the burning twin towers were severed. When Hurricane Katrina rolled over New Orleans in 2005, dozens of Web sites were set up to help find people and to respond to victims' requests for help. But, without coordination, the result was chaos because it was impossible to keep track of the many different databases and sites available. In contrast, when the earthquake hit Haiti hard in early 2010, the Ushahidi Web site in Kenya, which had already been set up to track emergencies, sprang into action to coordinate the different forms of social media specifically set up in response to the Haitian earthquake. Anyone with a mobile phone was able to send text messages to 4636 and have them relayed to the proper authorities. Mullins (2010) describes how this worked:

> The translators on 4636, most of whom have never met, are continually asking each other advice in a chatroom. Twitter has played a big role in relaying

news, and many aid agencies log their activities on Facebook. But most of all, it is the knowledge that large-scale activities can be coordinated through online networks that has given individuals and organisations the confidence to collaborate in this way.

The professional groups most advanced in the use of mobile learning for management of crises are those in medicine and health care. Patients increasingly are being given mobile technologies to manage their health care on a day-to-day basis. Mobile phones are used for weight management, to provide personal coaching for physical fitness, to monitor medications, and to collect data from sensors that measure body fat, pulse, and even bad breath. They can be used as pedometers to determine activity levels and energy consumption. Increasingly they are used in diagnosis, as portable microscopes that send pictures of tissue and blood samples back to physicians and laboratories. In Japan, mobile phone cameras are used by home health-care workers to assist in the care of the elderly. Cameras in the phones are used to take photo assessments of patients in rural communities which are then sent to their physicians (Wood and Woodill, 2008).

## Knowledge Management

Many large organizations have formal knowledge management systems that are centralized databases where proprietary information about the organization is stored. Others rely on storing information in third-party applications such as Google Docs that can be accessed by everyone with proper authorization. Either way, programs exist for gaining remote access to knowledge management systems via mobile phones. Such a system of mobile knowledge management (mKM) allows an organization's information to be available anytime, anywhere as needed. In turn, mobile users can add to the storehouse of knowledge in a company's knowledge base.

At this stage of technological development, mKM is a matter of integrating handheld devices into the knowledge management loop that already exists. One project that has worked on this problem is the European Union-funded MUMMY system, which adds contextually correct information to your appointments when you enter them into your mobile phone calendar. When you reach your location, this additional information is then available for you to review. The 2004 report of the MUMMY project (Finke et al., 2004) states that the most important goals of mobile knowledge management are:

- Facilitating the registration and sharing of insights without pushing the technique into the foreground and distracting mobile workers from the actual work.
- Exploiting available and accessible resources for optimized task handling, whether workers are remote (at home, in the office, or on the Web) or local (at their company or at a customer's site).
- Privacy-aware situational support for mobile workers, especially when confronted with ad hoc situations.

Mobile knowledge management systems must not only provide mobile access to existing KM systems but also contribute to these management goals.

 ## Learning Management

The purpose of a learning management system (LMS) is to automate the administration of training. Most LMSs register users, display a catalog of courses, map learning paths, launch courses, track and report on learners' educational activities and progress on assessments, and link to Web-based educational resources. Many LMSs also have a "virtual classroom," which is usually an online whiteboard with voice, text chat, and audio capabilities. In addition to these core features, some LMSs are able to provide "analytics" (such as the calculation of ROI), classroom management, certification management, competency management and skill-gap analysis, performance support with job aids, and some degree of content authoring. At the present time, mobile learning management systems tend to be miniature versions of desktop LMSs.

## Case Study

## Mobile HIV/AIDS Training for Health-Care Workers in Peru

The Institute of Tropical Medicine Alexander von Humboldt in Lima, Peru, and the Institute of Tropical Medicine, in Antwerp, Belgium, cooperated on a project to deliver continuing medical education (CME) modules to health-care workers (HCWs) in Peru, working in HIV/AIDS care. It is very difficult for HCWs working in low-resource settings to access continuing professional education. Although the Internet is growing steadily, its infrastructure and content demand a lot of investment from both companies and governments. Because of rapidly changing technological developments and decreasing costs, many developing countries have leapfrogged into mobile technology as their primary access to the Internet.

HCWs in Peru often travel to see patients in remote areas that don't have the Internet. A mobile learning solution was needed to give them cheap and easy access to continuing education course modules that would let them switch among ADSL, WiFi (because it is less expensive) and the 3G Internet. To enable this, the HCWs were given a mobile plug-and-play router that could be plugged in wherever an Internet connection was available. The router enabled the HCWs to download big files via WiFi into their phones, without having to pass through the very expensive 3G network. Once they had downloaded the latest mobile course content, they could then look at it while traveling in remote areas. The 3G network could still be used for brief communications.

HCWs in the field are highly experienced people who have obtained a high level of individual knowledge in their area(s) of expertise. The HCWs in Peru indicated their need for an autonomous mobile solution that would provide them with access to the latest medical information and low-cost lifelong learning materials, as well as a solution that would allow them to exchange field cases with peers through social media. Mobile devices can create an inexpensive, reliable, lifelong learning environment among health-care workers, both for one-to-one personal learning and for collaborative learning among colleagues in a network. An m-Learning project can strengthen the community of practitioners (CoP) in Peru, allowing high-end knowledge exchange.

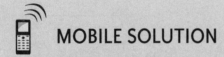

## MOBILE SOLUTION

A set of learning scenarios was developed for mobile devices to simulate interactive clinical cases for physicians working on HIV/AIDS care. Learning outcomes of the acquired knowledge were assessed by multiple-choice questions at end of each module. The technology maintained links to trustworthy sources of information (e.g., Pub Med, WHO library) and backup resources for additional assistance. Many tools were used to support the development of mobile courses for the HCWs including: Moodle, Skype, iClone, Moviestorm, iTunes, Facebook, Screenflow, and iMovie.

Complications with Moodle pushed the team to develop a completely new application that would enable iPhone users to access Moodle with all its features. Application development focused on the iPhone, because it became clear that the iPhone was perceived as more user friendly than the Nokia phones. The development team decided to release the code under a Creative Commons general public (CC GNU GPL) license, which allows people to access the code, run the program for any purpose, to study and adapt the code, and to release it to the public. This choice was made in order to open up mobile learning to other less financially strong regions.

The group developed 3D animations using iClone and Moviestorm that featured recognizable characters who spoke in Peruvian Spanish. The characters played out a real-life scenario that could easily have taken place between a patient and a physician. Screenflow and iMovie were used to build multimedia files. Facebook and Skype were used to facilitate peer-to-peer knowledge exchange, enabling learners to build on their own experience and knowledge. RSS, podcasts and iTunes were used to facilitate quick retrieval of additional materials.

Mobile devices were selected on the basis of their available options—for their ability to facilitate peer-to-peer discussion, their capacity to connect to a television set, and their ease of mobile access. The technical challenges of this project pushed the development team to write ground-breaking code that enabled a much bigger array of smartphones to connect to the mobile learning platform. Selecting mobile devices that could be connected to television sets gave learners two extra benefits: (1) a television set would give them access to a bigger screen, and (2) a television screen enabled the learners to share their content with other colleagues, so they would benefit from it as well (multiplication effect).

When the team started out, it opted to go for high-end smartphones. But, by continually exploring and developing new options, it found that an iPod with WiFi capability could offer the same functionalities as the selected smartphones. This means that the cost for a personal training device is reduced considerably.

## Results

Peer-to-peer knowledge exchange enables problem-based learning (PBL) to occur. Problem-based learning is becoming increasingly important in technology-enhanced learning, including mobile learning, as it fits the constructivist learning theory model and enables a more thorough understanding of the content that is discussed. In this project, problem-based learning was learner-centered as the HCWs were asked to put their own cases up to be discussed with their peer learners.

The mobile project enabled HCWs who previously did not have access to HIV/AIDS training to benefit from continuing medical education while they were traveling in remote areas. This had a big effect, as the selected HCWs covered clinics that treated 70 percent of the HIV/AIDS patients in Peru. Updated medical knowledge has an immediate effect, as the treatment can be made more effective, thus relieving the cost of medical health care in those regions and within the affected families.

With this mobile learning project, new HCWs got access to training because they no longer had to leave their region. Experienced HCWs can keep on doing their professional work while updating their knowledge. And, because the training is offered online, they no longer have to pay travel expenses to a conference or training program. Overall this was a very rewarding project for both the development team and the learners.

# Mobile Learning Management Systems

Applications are under development that will integrate desktop learning management systems with various types of smartphones. For example, several developers have produced ways for mobile phones to interact with Moodle, the well-known open source learning management system. Also, a number of vendors have announced fully functioning learning management systems that will run on a smartphone, without needing to be connected to a desktop LMS.

Commercial and open-source mobile learning management systems currently available include:

- *Blackboard Learn*: This application for the iPhone/iTouch lets users receive notification of updates to their Blackboard courses, including new assignments, course content, study group updates, community discussions, and grades.
- *CellCast*: This learning program from OnPoint Digital allows users to create, notify, deliver, and track audio learning content on a wide variety of smartphones and netbook computers. It also allows for the delivery and tracking of mobile Web content, Web and PDF files, videos, animated narrated slide presentations, and spoken word and text-based assessments.
- *Chalk Pushcast* (formerly Mobile Chalkboard): Pushcast runs only on the Research in Motion (RIM) BlackBerry platform and is mostly used for training. It features text, graphics, video, and audio, and will handle surveys, call requests, or e-mail requests. It administers tests, and tracks results and content usage.
- *eXact iTutor:* This software from Giunti Labs in Italy is the world's first wearable, wireless mobile learning platform. It is location-based and voice/gaze controlled for workplace delivery of crisis management instructions and JIT (just-in-time) training materials.
- *KMx:* This software from Knowledge Management Solutions, Inc. (KMSI), provides development and delivery of e-learning courseware, knowledge management and collaboration tools for mobile devices, including the Apple iPhone and Microsoft Windows CE devices with full conformance to the sharable content object reference model (SCORM) standard.

▶ *MLE-Moodle*: MLE-Moodle is a plug-in for Moodle, the popular open-source learning management system used around the world. It reconfigures Moodle to make it a Web-based mobile application accessible by any mobile phone with a Web browser.

▶ *Mobile Moodle for the iPhone:* The default template for the Moodle interface consists of a three-column layout that is very mobile friendly. However, it has some limitations for mobile environments, so different teams are working on developing specific applications to connect Moodle with various smartphones. One such group is a partnership between the Institute of Tropical Medicine Alexander von Humboldt (IMTAvH) in Lima, Peru, and the Institute of Tropical Medicine (ITM) in Antwerp, Belgium, who released their open source Mobile Moodle for iPhone application in 2010 (Fig 7.3).

▶ *MobLS:* This mobile learning management system from Emantras has electronic book features and is able to synchronize data and metrics with SCORM/AICC compliant native LMS systems. It provides high levels of security by encrypting the readable content, and it offers device ID specific rights management.

▶ *MOMO*: The MOMO (Mobile Moodle) project is another plug-in for the popular Moodle LMS. Mobile users install the MOMO client, a JAVA-based application, on their mobile phones (or any other JAVA and Internet capable device). Through this client, they can access courses wherever they are located.

▶ *Sakai:* This open source learning management system (or virtual learning environment for those in the United Kingdom) has a group of developers that is producing features that make this LMS mobile ready. For example, Brock University in Canada has a Sakai site that can be viewed in a layout that is optimized for mobile devices like the iPhone/iPod touch or other PDAs and phones with a Web browser (BlackBerries, Android, and Windows Mobile phones).

## Mobile Learning Content Management Systems

In the e-learning world there is also a category of software for managing online content called learning content management systems (LCMSs). Although they

**FIGURE 7.3 Sample screen shots from the Moodle for iPhone application. Used with permission.**

started out as separate concepts, many LCMSs and LMSs have come to look the same, as each group borrows features from the other. At least one vendor, Xyleme, is specifically marketing a mobile learning content management system. The Xyleme LCMS for Mobile Learning provides a set of publishing templates that enables training content to be delivered on demand to any Java-enabled mobile device including iPhones, BlackBerries, Windows mobile devices, and other smartphones or PDAs. It supports SCORM-compliant courseware, as well as mobile renditions of rich media. Flash, and video, and animations can be downloaded to any mobile device supporting these formats.

On the Internet, management of content for mobile learning tends to be simpler, with various content aggregation Web sites springing up to serve this growing market. For example, the cc.mLearnopedia Web site (http://cc. mlearnopedia.com) tracks posts about mobile learning from 16 different sources, with more likely to be added. The move to cloud computing where information resources are stored in large data centers to be accessed from anywhere in the world (with proper authorization) has meant that learners can choose the most relevant resources for their needs. This may lead to a reduction in demand for large-scale learning management systems and learning content management systems. These systems were developed for the "instructionist" model of training and may simply not be able to keep up with the rapid technological changes in the mobile learning field.

 ## Team Management

Although they may not use the actual term, groups of employees who are often on the move but who also work together on one or more shared projects are known as "mobile teams." Sometimes they are also called "virtual teams," "offsite teams," or "teleworkers."

Michael Schrage (1995) suggests that the concept of a team as an organizational structure with set roles may be outdated. He says, "The real basic structure of the workplace is the relationship. Each relationship is itself part of a larger network of relationships. These relationships can be measured along all kinds of dimensions—from political to professional expertise. The fact is that work gets done through these relationships." With mobile teams, good relationships are critical for success.

At Brandon Hall Research, where I have been a senior analyst for about four years, most staff members work from home a lot of the time, but they are also on the move, checking in and communicating via mobile phones if needed. The world of work has truly become portable, so an employee's location is not a critical factor in whether a person can work or not. This is the goal of mobile computing—that you can work from any location and still access all the information you need to carry out your tasks.

Part of the shift from Web 1.0 to Web 2.0 has been the change in emphasis from individual learning to team-based collaborative learning. This represents a fundamental shift in how learning occurs, as we move from a model of instructor-led teaching of individuals to one of learner-led finding, doing, and collaborating in small groups. In response, vendors around the world are developing mobile team management and project management software. Here is a sample of some of the mobile solutions available:

- *@Task*: This project management software offers WAP 2.0 access for all your mobile devices. It works on both Apple iPhone and Research in Motion BlackBerry.
- *HyperOffice*: This project management software works on desktops, laptops, and smartphones. It features include to-do lists, import/export tasks, notifications of updates, integration with Microsoft Outlook, shared project resources and interlinking of project files, contacts, schedules, and e-mail.
- *IBM Lotus Notes Traveler*: Use this well-known collaboration software on your desktop, and then take your e-mail, calendar, and contacts with you. Connect back to company information even when you are mobile.
- *Merlin iPhone*: This project management software runs on the iPhone and the iTouch and connects with Merlin Server software running on an Apple Macintosh computer. It is a free download from iTunes.
- *TASKey*: This mobile Web project management software has automatic Gantt charts, PDF Gantt reports, collaborative task maps, personal to-do lists, and much more. It tracks an unlimited number of projects and tasks.
- *Teamspace:* Teamspace is a groupware system for international Web-based collaboration and mobile teamwork. The idea with this software is to "create your own team and work together with colleagues all over the world."
- *Wrike*: With Wrike for BlackBerry, you enter tasks and projects and then manage them by mobile e-mail. You will receive e-mail notification if there are any changes in the details or status of a task made by your colleagues.

There are at least six dimensions that are relevant in tracking mobile learning teams. These are identity of the learner, the location and time that learning takes place, the facilities available to the learner, the activities undertaken that lead to learning, the characteristics of the learner, and the cultural community in which the learner is embedded. But team awareness and ease of contact among team members is another dimension (Ferscha et al., 2004). The following organizational systems are crucial for the successful support of effective mobile teams: an information and knowledge management system (team memory), an awareness system (team awareness), team interaction systems (meeting support), mobility systems (mobile infrastructure), and organizational innovation systems (team workplace innovation support). If you plan to manage a mobile team, these systems need to be in place (Ferscha, 2000).

## The Shift in Power with Mobile Learning

This chapter on the management of mobile learning and the use of mobile technologies for management gets to the heart of the recent changes in mobile learning as well as the near-future changes that are likely to occur. To have mobile learning work well, power has to shift from instructors and managers to the learners themselves. This means that employees will need to be more self-directed and learn because they need to know something, not because they are being forced to learn.

This change of focus from instructor-led to self-directed or do-it-yourself (DIY) learning works best in organizations where the management structure is collegial and participatory and where the structure of power is somewhat flattened. Organizations that are not prepared for such changes will find the implementation of mobile learning much more difficult. Sheryl Herle discusses these issues in more depth in Chapter 10. But first we turn to the development of a business strategy for mobile learning in the next chapter, and then to the design and production of mobile learning content in Chapter 9.

# Developing a Future-Oriented Mobile Learning Strategy

*By David Fell, MBA*

> " As the quantity of information available increases exponentially and the general pace of life accelerates, the ability to navigate, access, validate and share information will be a pivotal skill in an increasingly complex environment."
> —*Geddes, 2004*

Business processes and the competitive environment that businesses operate in today are more complex, interrelated, and fluid than ever before. Business leaders have been forced to move beyond traditional organizational structures in order to create alliances with suppliers and outsourcing vendors, and partnerships with customers, political groups, regulatory entities, and even competitors. This evolution has spawned the use of a new term, "co-opetition," which describes companies that sometimes cooperate to win business together and under different circumstances compete against each other to win new business.

Through these alliances, organizations are able to deal with the pressures of unprecedented change, globalization, rapidly changing technologies, and increasing complexity. The multifaceted nature of this competitive environment means that the information technology projects that are implemented in businesses today are also more complex than ever. In the midst of this complexity comes a clear and growing trend toward more employee mobility and access to the Internet via mobile devices. The strategic question faced by business leaders is not whether or not mobile technology will be used by employees, but whether or not we chose to leverage the mobile technology that our employees are increasingly using to engage them in learning. And if we do choose to engage them in mobile learning, how do we do this in a manner that effectively creates value for the corporation?

The field of mobile learning is still in its infancy. Because new capabilities and uses of mobile technologies are still being invented, companies will need to develop a future-oriented mobile learning strategy to anticipate the growth of these new capabilities. As electronic technologies continue to get smaller, we will see convergence of mobile technologies with numerous other emerging trends, such as artificial intelligence, cloud computing, nanotechnology, biotechnology, and ubiquitous computing. By its very nature this chapter is more speculative than the rest, but it is designed to assist business leaders in planning and anticipating ways in which mobile learning can add value to a business unit or corporation. The chapter starts with a review of the current market research and trends in the field of mobile learning and then moves through a traditional Porter's five forces and value chain analysis and concludes with a proposal for the development of a future-oriented mobile learning strategy—the mobile learning edge: nomadic strategy.

Mobile technology is not just a new delivery platform for learning; it also provides a new tool and context for business leaders to create, share, and evaluate knowledge as it is being experienced by our increasingly mobile workforce. Business leaders will need to develop a strategy to monitor developments in mobile technology as well as access the knowledge being created with mobile technology so that they can capitalize on this increasingly important raw material. Professor Claus Weyrich, of Siemens AG in Germany contends that, "Knowledge has become the most important raw material of our time: knowledge about technologies, knowledge about markets and consumers, knowledge about the complex relationships among the many variables in our environment, and knowledge about relevant future trends" (Pillkahn, 2008, p.5).

The concept of mobility applies not just to the technology, the people, and the process of learning on the move; it also applies to the mobility and flow of knowledge both inside and outside the corporation. The field of knowledge management has moved through many of the same technology adoption cycles as the field of learning technology, and the distinction between the two has often been somewhat artificially maintained to the detriment of both. Although this is an argument for another book (bridging the field of learning technology and knowledge management technology), it is important to at least float the idea up front that mobile learning has the potential to bridge both learning and knowledge management.

Earlier in this book Gary Woodill identifies several of the key elements of the mobile learning industry as it is currently constituted through a variety of the supplier types:

- *Content providers* develop custom original materials to run on mobile devices.
- *Content conversion providers* take current e-learning content and rework it for display on mobile devices.
- *Application providers* are software development companies that write applications (apps) specifically for the mobile learning industry.
- *Hardware providers* are the companies that design, manufacture, and sell the mobile devices that are used in this industry.
- *Service providers* offer a wide variety of services including project management, translation, consulting, and design.
- *Solution providers* try to package the entire value chain for mobile learning and manage it from beginning to end.

As the corporate mobile learning industry continues to develop and evolve, business leaders will need to create a framework for evaluating and assessing the value and the quality of these products and services. There is an eloquent argument made by Sheryl Herle in Chapter 10 about how to choose an appropriate vendor for implementing your mobile learning solution, and the same recommendation applies at the level of strategy development. Choose mobile learning technology vendors that have a vision of how their technology will evolve along with the market and how they will work with you on your evolving strategy. The mere existence of new technologies is not enough on its own to guarantee that the adoption of these services will add value to the corporation—business leaders need to figure out how to incorporate them into broader corporate learning strategies and how to use these new products and services for capturing and disseminating knowledge as it is developed by the corporation.

# Trends Analysis

Trend spotting has become a major growth industry, and the field of information technology has generated an inordinate share of interest in this emerging field. The information technology bubble from 1999–2001, which created a major boom and subsequent bust in the stock market, is one of the primary drivers of this interest in trend spotting and its mantras of get rich quick; lead with vaporware and deliver product later; gain an advantage over your competitors by adopting new technologies; and, increase productivity through technology automation. But as every consumer who purchased a BetaMax player knows, not every new technology trend leads to the anticipated or desired outcome. As with the adoption of VHS, it is not even the superior technology that wins.

The key issue in evaluating trends related to mobile learning in the business environment is to identify relevant trends and respond to them in a way that adds real value to the business. All three authors of this book have been strong and vocal advocates of the potential for new technologies to add value to businesses. We have also over time seen our fair share of spectacular technology implementation failures.

Ironically many of the businesses and business leaders that are most receptive to new technology are also the ones who have failed to find real value in the implementation of the new technology. As Pip Coburn noted in his helpful 2006 book *The Change Function*, new technologies are adopted only when the present crisis in your business is more painful than the "total perceived pain of adoption" of the proposed new technology. People simply don't want to change. Fortunately, the learning curve for people to use a mobile phone is relatively high, given that we all know how to use a regular phone. But some of the features of smartphones may never be used, except by a die-hard group of technology fanatics that likes trying every feature a technology has to offer. From our perspective part of the good news about the trend in mobile learning so far is that appears to support a rapid and iterative adoption process that is more aligned with the speed of decision making in the modern business context.

In a November 2008 report (Jones, 2008), "M-Learning Opportunities and Applications," analysts at Gartner Inc., the well-known technology consulting firm, posed this critically important question: "Why Is This a Good Time to Explore M-Learning? Educators have been experimenting with m-learning for some time, but several factors combine to make this a good time for corporations to explore its potential." By 2010, the factors cited by Gartner have become even more prevalent and clear in their potential to drive businesses to consider mobile learning:

- ► Costs are decreasing and capacity is increasing. As mobile technologies increase market share and ubiquity, the price of the devices continues to fall. There are currently netbooks on the market that have more computing power and storage than most desktop computers had 10 years ago, and these are being sold for less than $400. As new versions of mobile phone hardware and software are being developed almost continuously, the memory capacity and processing power of the devices are improving every day.
- ► The theory and practice of learning with mobile technology has moved beyond infancy. While m-learning can by no means be called a mature field in the way that e-learning has developed, there is an increasing amount of experience and research to back it up. Conferences such as mLearn and Handheld Learning have been held for about a decade and are starting to draw media attention and the attention of business leaders. These international conferences on m-learning have created a forum for business leaders to discuss the how, what, and why of mobile learning.
- ► As businesses look to cut costs and increase productivity, there is an ongoing increase in the number of virtual workers. Many large corporations are building new offices that do not have dedicated space for all employees but rather cubicles and boardrooms that can be booked by the day or week. As an increasing number of employees work from home-based offices, the volume of mobile technology increases in order to support their connection to the business. This trend has significant implications for the delivery of training, knowledge management, and learning. Organizations can't expect to change the nature and location of work without also planning for new ways to provide the supporting systems and processes that employees will require in order to be successful: training and orientation, human resources services, and even general connectivity to their fellow employees.
- ► The demographic trends favor mobile learning. As the baby boomers start to retire and leave the workforce in increasing numbers they are being replaced by a generation that has been raised on the Internet and the use of mobile phones, iPods, and BlackBerries. Traditional classroom-based

training and learning is rapidly becoming outdated as young people expect to gather and transmit information on their mobile devices.

▶ The speed of business decision making is constantly increasing. E-mail, BlackBerries, and mobile phones have created a business culture that went from the speed of fixed line phone calls, personal meetings, and surface mail to an expectation of 24/7 decision making and a trend that has been called "management by BlackBerry."

One thing that cannot be disputed in terms of the emegence of future trends is the growth of mobility devices and access related to the Internet itself. In the Pew Internet and American Life project report, "The Future of the Internet III,"released in December 2008, 77 percent of experts and 81 percent of total respondents agreed with the statement that:

> The mobile phone is the primary connection tool for most people in the world. In 2020, while "one laptop per child" and other initiatives to bring networked digital communications to everyone are successful on many levels, the mobile phone—now with significant computing power—is the primary Internet connection and the only one for a majority of the people across the world, providing information in a portable, well-connected form at a relatively low price. Telephony is offered under a set of universal standards and protocols accepted by most operators internationally, making for reasonably effortless movement from one part of the world to another. At this point, the "bottom" three-quarters of the world's population account for at least 50% of all people with Internet access—up from 30% in 2005 (Anderson and Rainie, 2008, p. 5).

In an age of increasing globalization and new sources of competition in domestic markets, business leaders need to think not only about the increasing mobility trends of their own workforce, but also about the mobility and device preferences of a global audience. What are the expectations for communication and information retrieval from our employees, current customers, potential customers, and competitors? How will information about our products and services be distributed into the global marketplace? When customers or employees are unhappy with our products, services, or company policies, how and where will they react?

The growth of mobile computing as a trend needs to also be evaluated independently from the devices or platforms that are facilitating its growth. Information mobility, knowledge flow, employee mobility, and product/service globalization are also ubiquitous trends that are having a significant impact on the field of training and knowledge management. Businesses need to make a critical strategic choice on this issue: Will we plan for ways to engage our employees and customers in the manner in which they increasingly expect to be engaged (via their mobile devices) or will we choose to forgo this approach? A final word on the significance of mobility trends in the training and learning context comes from the 2010 Horizon Report (Johnson et al., 2010), which suggests that the "mobility computing time-to-adoption horizon is one year or less."

## Technology Life Cycles

A number of industry analysts have been tracking the adoption rates, market development, and technology life cycle for mobile learning since early 2000, including: Brandon Hall Research; the MASIE Learning Consortium; Gartner Research; Bersin & Associates; Ambient Insight; the eLearning Guild, and others. In order to provide a context for the development of a mobile learning strategy, we examined a cross section of the analyst assessments related to mobile learning.

In the summer of 2008, Judy Brown and David Metcalf published their "Mobile Learning Update Report" on behalf of the MASIE Center and the Learning Consortium. The report highlighted feedback from a survey conducted at the MASIE Center on current mobile learning practices and future plans and desires. The data reflect the responses of over 200 members:

## Current State of Mobile Learning

- ▶ 24 percent of respondents currently deploy some mobile learning in their organizations.
- ▶ The most common transactions on a mobile device currently include placing and receiving organizational phone calls (98 percent), e-mails (91 percent), and text messages (83 percent).

- Many use mobile devices for writing/word processing (68 percent) and to deploy audio podcasts (63 percent).
- 73 percent of mobile learning today is not integrated with an LMS.
- 52 percent of respondents use in-house resources to develop mobile learning.
- 53 percent of mobile learning initiative funding comes from a training department.

 ## Planning for Future Mobile Learning

- 38 percent of organizations are not currently planning any mobile learning.
- 26 percent are currently building a business case for mobile learning.
- Popular future deployment plans for mobile devices include assessments/ surveys (77 percent), performance support (73 percent), and study aids (70 percent).
- Members showed a significant interest in using mobile devices to provide voice recognition (93 percent), display books (82 percent), display Flash (64 percent), and enter data (61 percent).
- A wide range of implementation challenges served as obstacles to implementing a mobile learning initiative. They include limited resources (11 percent), organizational acceptance (11 percent), and access to mobile devices (10 percent).

What is striking about the results of the MASIE Learning Consortium survey is the wide variety of activities that are included and incorporated into the category of mobile learning. Phone calls, e-mails, and text messages are not usually thought of as delivery support tools in the traditional framework of learning and development. However, phoning a colleague or text messaging a supervisor can be a very effective just-in-time approach to gathering information about a client or new service offering. When employees use a phone or text message to access this information, they are pursuing a course of self-directed learning that may appear to be self-evident to them, but has not likely been incorporated as a process or strategy into the overall plan for corporate learning and development.

## *Case Study*

## Improving Capability Development at Accenture with Mobile Learning

Accenture is a global management consulting, technology, services, and outsourcing company. Committed to delivering innovation, Accenture collaborates with its clients to help them become high-performance businesses and governments. Accenture has approximately 187,000 professionals in 52 countries and works with clients in nearly every major industry worldwide, including 91 of the Fortune Global 100, two-thirds of the Fortune Global 500, and government agencies around the world.

Accenture's *business need* centered on the recognition that key segments of its target audience for corporate compliance training are traditionally difficult to reach. These groups understand the importance of required training and want to take it, but their schedules seldom allow the 30 or 60 minutes in front of their computer needed to complete it. This *receptive audience,* therefore, welcomes any convenience that makes training easier to complete. These same groups are our most prevalent users of handheld devices—mostly BlackBerries and Windows mobile devices. Collectively they have *sufficient technology* and are technologically savvy.

The consequences of failure to complete required compliance training can be serious for the individual, who cannot rise above a certain performance rating and is not eligible for promotion unless required training is complete. The consequences can be equally serious for the organization, by decreasing the pool of employees available for promotion, not to mention the consequences, both legal and productive, of having employees in violation of compliance requirements.

## MOBILE SOLUTION

The overall objective for the mobile learning project was to provide an alternate, more convenient way for Accenture's professionals to complete required corporate training and thereby increase the speed and ease of uptake of professional development courses.

Using Accenture's myLearning learning management system (LMS), a prototype course was created, with 12 screens of content from the *Confidential! Protecting Assets and Information* required corporate course. The design included:

- Multiple-choice, select-all-that-apply, and fill-in-the-blank interactions
- End of the course quiz
- Scenarios/dialogues
- Graphics and simple animations

The reaction of the target audience to the prototype was overwhelmingly positive. Of the audience, 92 percent indicated that they would use their mobile device for taking required training. Most preferred training that could be completed in chunks of 10 minutes or less. Over half indicated that they wanted a solution that they could download on their device rather than one that would rely on a live connection, since a downloaded option would allow them to take the training on an airplane, in a subway, and in other locations where connectivity is a problem. Interestingly, some of the participants indicated that they used the prototype while sitting at their homes at the end of a long day. In other words, they used it during naturally occurring downtime.

The culture of consulting work is mobile, and the workforce was looking for a solution that fitted the consulting lifestyle. The nature of downtime is that it comes in 10–20 minute increments. Offering mobile learning solutions makes learning more prevalent inside the consulting culture when learning is not tied to the desk.

The next step was to create a mobile learning capability blueprint to define the goals for mobile learning, as a guide in the process of development and deployment, and establish metrics that would let Accenture know when goals were achieved.

Since the prototype phase, seven mobile courses have been built and deployed. These are still early days, yet the data collected so far suggest that satisfaction with the mobile courses and the learning environment is significantly higher than with desk-top computer based training (CBT) versions, and 95 percent indicate that they would recommend this learning approach to colleagues.

### Results

Course evaluations so far show that the mobile courses outperform the CBT courses in every area of satisfaction. The mobile courses rate an average of .2 higher than their CBT equivalents in total ratings. In satisfaction with the learning environment, the difference in satisfaction is even more pronounced, with the mobile courses rating an average of .32 points higher than their CBT equivalents.

Participant comments from course evaluations have been overwhelmingly positive. The vast majority of the participants are pleased with the convenience and the learning environment that the mobile platform offers.

The myLearning mobile initiative has also shown itself effective in meeting the business goals for the delivery platform. Evidence gathered so far indicates that the audience is both receptive to the delivery platform and grateful for the increased ease of use. Uptake and course completions have been tracked since the beginning of the pilot program. Course completions have been rising since the rollout of the full release in October 2009, evidence of the continuing success of the delivery platform and the enthusiasm of the target audience for taking mobile courses. The demand for the creation of more mobile courses has been very high among the target audience.

Evidence from course evaluations shows that the learning objectives for the content are being fulfilled by the mobile courses, as well as, if not better than, courses on other delivery platforms. Yet it is the mobile platform's ability to serve the hard-to-reach, on-the-go population of learners that abounds in the consulting industry that has shown its true value. The rising number of course completions and the continuing positive response of course participants demonstrate the effectiveness of the myLearning mobile initiative in reaching the target audience.

Because of the success of the mobile initiative and the positive reaction of participants, four additional mobile courses have been added, with more to come. These same courses have been launched for the Windows Mobile environment and in the near future they will also be available on iPhones. These three platforms constitute those used by the vast majority of the target audience.

In addition, the success in delivering mobile learning to Accenture's employees is now being leveraged to deliver mobile learning solutions for its clients.

The trend of using a wide variety of mobile technologies to gather information and learn new concepts reflects the evolving perspective of employees toward corporate learning. The traditional approach to organizational learning (and knowledge management) is one that is vested in the structure of the human resources department and utilizes a centralized knowledge and information dissemination strategy. Learning with mobile technology reflects a more decentralized knowledge acquisition strategy that starts with searching for what you need to know and using the most relevant tools that you have to acquire the information you need within the timelines that you need it. If you are a doctor treating a critically ill patient with an obscure disease that you have no experience with, the fastest way to learn what you need to know is to call an expert or someone who has had experience with that disease. This is a form of just-in-time learning using mobile technology. Organizations need to support their employees with multiple technologies to allow them to access information when they most need it from the sources that are most appropriate.

According to market research conducted by Ambient Insight LLC it is estimated that "despite the current financial crisis, the U.S. market for mobile learning products and services is growing at a five-year compounded annual growth rate (CAGR) of 21.7% and revenues reached $538 million in 2007." (Adkins, 2008, p. 5) This has translated into what they are calling *a perfect storm* that is driving user adoption of mobile learning (Fig. 8.1).

### "A Perfect Storm" Drives the Adoption of Mobile Learning

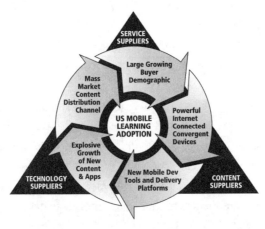

**FIGURE 8.1 A "perfect storm" drives the adoption of mobile learning. Courtesy of Ambient Insight. Used with permission.**

While many technology adoption cycles are driven by the introduction of a single new product or service offering (which is then copied and replicated by competitors), it is clear from the Ambient Insight analysis that the mobile learning adoption cycle is being driven by a diverse number of forces. Each new product or service offering into the mobile technology market space creates a new opportunity for other service and content providers to expand their offerings for mobile learning. This perfect storm is being supported financially through "private investment and venture capital firms that have injected a significant amount of capital into the market, enabling suppliers to accelerate development (and innovation) and get products into the pipeline faster" (Ibid, p. 9).

In support of this positive market perspective for mobile learning, Nick Jones (2008) suggests in the Gartner Research report, "M-Learning Opportunities and Applications," that "mobile handsets will be the dominant m-learning devices for some time, with more than 1.2 billion shipped in 2008 . . . smartphones are in the minority, comprising approximately 15 percent of all handsets shipped globally; enhanced phones make up a little more than 60 percent, and the remainder are basic phones." This trend is expected to rapidly change, with more and more smartphones being sold as they become more capable.

 ## Preparing Scenarios of Possible Futures

True innovation in mobile learning will not necessarily come from the strict application of the same business models that have served for either traditional face-to-face training or e-learning, but rather the new mobile learning business models will likely come from one of several possible sources:

- ▶ *The extension of existing business models for e-learning into the mobile learning ecosystem*: Watch for incremental growth in competition against existing vendors and service providers in the traditional e-learning market. There will likely be a focus on the conversion of existing types of content covered in other areas of this book into mobile content.
- ▶ *Fundamentally new business models:* Expect the creation of new "blue ocean" strategies (Kim and Mauborgne, 2005) that both create value and

decrease price. Mobility offers a great opportunity to decrease price through mass distribution; while just-in-time delivery and user-generated content offers an opportunity to add significant value to corporate learning strategies. Traditional corporate training requires long processes of analysis, development, and distribution. Mobile learning increases speed to distribution as well as reach and variety of development opportunities.

▶ *The translation of existing business models from other markets into the realm of mobile learning.* Franchise, syndication, mass production, mass customization, make your own applications, auction to highest bidder, uniqueness at highest price, fee for service consulting, advertising pay per click, subscription, community of experts, research services licensing, rental, lending library, sponsorship, membership, and so on are all possibilities.

▶ *The amalgamation of a unique combination of existing solutions from both inside and outside the mobile ecosystem.* For example, a partnership between Google and MIT to promote and extend MIT Open courseware to new markets or certifications would be an interesting development.

The evolution of these new generic business models will require the application of sound learning theory to mobile technology in order to create specific m-learning businesses. Some of the current and future m-learning business models include:

▶ *Just-in-time learning:* The volume of corporate information that is created with information technology is alarming, and employees cannot be expected to internalize the entire body of corporate knowledge. Instead, successful employees are rapidly moving toward a just-in-time learning and knowledge management strategy. This is particularly important in occupations that require decision making based on clients' past history or experience with the company. An account manager who is visiting clients at their work site can no longer expect to know everything about the client, but rather is expected to have access to everything that is relevant. Mobile technology provides a platform for just-in-time learning.

▶ *Contextual learning:* Museums, historical sites, and art galleries have already started to implement contextual learning for visitors. Rather than have a large group of people crowded around a single display, visitors can receive a guided tour with both audio and visual contextual information through their own mobile devices in a variety of media formats. Such guided tours can be personalized to the visitor's age, gender, culture, language, and previous visits to the museum. YouTube videos of historical reenactments can bring to life the static artifacts that are housed in a museum or an archeological site.

▶ *Pushed and situational assessments:* One of the many challenges with traditional corporate training has been the evaluation of long-term retention of knowledge and behavior change. Corporations spend huge amounts of money to train employees on products, services, and behaviors with very few effective ways to assess the long-term return on this investment. Mobile devices allow corporations to push assessments out to employees to evaluate how they react and respond in the real world long after the training is finished. Employees can also be asked to use their mobile devices to conduct situational assessments in order to provide visual feedback on the progress of a particular project and/or to demonstrate how they are actually responding in a real world situation.

▶ *Information storage and delivery:* Mobile technology permits employees to bring corporate reference material with them into the field. If we continue to see an increasingly mobile workforce, it is clear that these workers will need to have mobile access to the corporate body of knowledge.

▶ *Performance support for specific tasks:* Developers are creating new devices that can be used to automate or provide performance support to specific routine tasks. When parcel delivery companies show up at your door to deliver a contract or piece of equipment, there are no longer paper forms that need to be signed but rather digital signature devices that electronically track the delivery and payment for services.

▶ *Security and performance assessment reporting:* Mobile technology is being used in airports and locations where a high level of security is required to provide real time reporting. The information gathered on mobile devices is fed back into a central database and used as part of the security reporting process. In the context where live performance assessments are happening (particularly for front-line security personnel) mobile devices are used to provide real time performance assessment feedback for the maintenance of employee certifications and access to secure areas.

▶ *Inexpensive public service learning:* In many rural areas in developing countries, radios have historically been a delivery medium for public service and public education messages. Given the relatively lower cost of erecting cell towers compared to the traditional approach of terrestrial cabling, many developing nations have now leapfrogged developed countries with their mobile access infrastructure. It is now possible to use SMS (short message service) and voice messages to deliver these public service announcements.

▶ *Information feeds for quick updating:* For anyone who has received a news update or sports score via SMS or RSS (really simple syndication) on their mobile device, it is readily apparent that corporations could benefit from tapping into this easy process for providing corporate updates and sharing emergent knowledge.

▶ *Mobile creation of corporate knowledge and learning materials:* The cameras that are available on most mobile phones these days are more than sufficient for creating field-based learning materials and short video clips. Editing may be required to effectively translate this new content into acceptable learning material for redistribution, but the speed and portability offer a fantastic new content creation tool for learning developers to gather input from field staff.

## Strategies for Mobile Learning: The Next Five Years

In order to effectively develop possible strategies for mobile learning for the next five years, it is necessary to understand the strategic context and competitive environment into which mobile learning will evolve. A return to the first principles of strategic business analysis using Michael Porter's classic five forces framework (Porter, 2008) provides a clear overview of the market forces at play (Fig. 8.2). Porter's five forces are the threat of substitute products, the threat of established rivals, the threat of new entrants, the bargaining power of suppliers, and the bargaining power of customers.

The application of the five forces model provides an industry-level context for the mobile learning industry that business leaders can draw upon to develop their own specific organizational strategy for mobile learning. The five forces analysis suggests that while buyer and supplier power within the mobile learning industry is relatively balanced (at a medium level), there is a

## Porter's Five Forces Analysis of Mobile Learning

**Threat of New Entry: High**
- There is weak supplier concentration currently
- Switching costs will be low if employees already have mobile technology
- Depending on the services offered, the capital requirements will be minimal
- Access to distribution of mobile services will be relatively easy as distributors will be looking for new services to drive adoption

**Supplier Power: Medium**
- Supplier switching costs relative to firm switching costs will be low if the firms emerge from an existing e-Learning industry
- Degree of differentiation of inputs is mixed depending on the application of the technology
- Presence of substitute inputs is low
- Supplier concentration is weak
- Cost of inputs relative to selling price of the product is relatively low

**Competitive Rivalry: High**
- Rate of industry growth is greater than 20 percent
- Industry concentration is low
- Diversity of competitors is high
- Fixed cost allocation per value added will depend on type of service pricing model
- Economies of scale are possible

**Buyer Power: Medium**
- Low buyer concentration to firm concentration ratio
- Early adopters will have higher bargaining leverage
- Buyer volume will depend on the supplier business models
- Buyer switching costs relative to firm switching costs will be low if mobile devices are already in place
- Buyer information availability will be low in new market
- Availability of existing substitute products is relatively high
- Buyer price sensitivity will be high due to expectation of cost savings with mobile

**Threat of Substitution: High**
- Buyer propensity to substitute will be high if alternative options emerge
- Relative price performance of substitutes is unknown
- Perceived level of product differentiation will depend on quality and relevance of services that are offered

**FIGURE 8.2 Porter's five forces analysis applied to mobile learning.**

high degree of competitive rivalry and a high threat of substitution by new entrants into the mobile learning industry. This market context suggests a relatively volatile and rapid growth of the industry which warrants a cautious approach to strategy development and commitment of resources. At this point it is important not to lock into a proprietary technology or exclusive vendor relationship because it is too early on in the industry cycle. Look for open-architected technologies and content formats for delivery of mobile learning in a competitive market that is likely to change rapidly.

In moving from the broader mobile learning industry analysis to the specific business level options for developing a mobile learning strategy, another useful tool is Porter's value chain analysis (Porter, 1985). A value chain is a set of interdependent business activities that adds value to a product at each stage of its production and distribution. It consists of "primary activities" including inbound logistics, operations (production), outbound logistics, marketing and sales (demand), and services (maintenance). In addition, there are "support activities" such as administrative infrastructure management, human resource management, technology (R&D), and procurement. All these activities added together form a value chain for a given product. Wei and Lin (2008) at the University of West Florida used a version of Porter's value chain analysis developed by Terry Anderson (2004) and extended it to create an interesting concept called the value increasing m-learning model (VIML).

This model provides an excellent generic application of value chain analysis for the mobile learning industry. Business leaders should be able to take this template and apply the relevant information from their own company to analyze their own value chain, and identify "strategically relevant" mobile learning activities that could add value to their business. Conversely, an application of the value chain analysis to a specific company may indicate that mobile learning would not add value in the broader context of the company's competitive advantage, and this will save time and effort in developing a strategy and implementation model for a technology project that may ultimately fail.

## The Mobile Learning Edge: A Nomadic Strategy

One of the most important skills for a digital nomad is the ability to evaluate and respond to the shifting context that one finds oneself in at a given time. This ability is also required in the realm of learning because the opportunity to learn something new, or to create new knowledge, depends heavily upon the environmental context that one finds oneself in at a specific time. What do you need to know? When do you need to know it? How can you find the information or knowledge that you need? What tools do you have available to assist in your learning? Mobile technology can be a support tool for learning, but it can also be a philosophical approach to the possibility of learning anytime anywhere—knowing that you can find information when you need it. Mobile learning can be part of a larger process of training and development that corporations use to keep their employees up to date and equipped to perform their jobs:

▶ Nomads learn by exploring their environment and developing new approaches to fit the circumstances.

▶ Nomads don't learn by standing still; they learn by continuing to move forward into new situations and contexts.

▶ Nomads learn from many different sources.

▶ Nomads learn iteratively through trial and error with real expertise emerging after multiple iterations.

With this philosophical perspective on learning mobility and our overview of the trends and analysis of the mobile learning industry, it is not surprising that we are advocating for a mobile learning strategy that is flexible and iterative and that adds business value in an incremental way based on the ongoing development of the mobile technology life cycle. It is important to clarify at the outset that the nomadic strategy approach being proposed is not meant to become *the* overall enterprise strategy, but rather it is a specific strategy for successfully deploying mobile learning throughout the enterprise. We believe that adopting a nomadic strategy for mobile learning is a good fit for the current state of the industry and the technology, but it is not necessarily the best strategic approach for all technology projects or businesses. This book is not advocating a one-size-fits-all approach to mobile learning, but rather an approach that suggests that you identify ways to enhance the value creation proposition of the corporation using mobile learning—and if you don't find any, then you wait and reevaluate again in the future.

The concept of a nomadic approach to strategy is not entirely new to the field of corporate strategy research. In their 1998 book *Strategy Safari*, Henry Mintzberg et al. identify and evaluate 10 unique schools of corporate strategy thinking that emerged in the twentieth century. While none of these 10 schools of strategic thinking stands on its own as an overarching framework for best practices in enterprise strategy development, Mintzberg and his colleagues do suggest that the collective insight of the 10 schools can be integrated into a comprehensive strategy development process: "Strategy formation is judgmental designing, intuitive visioning, and emergent learning; it is about transformation as well as perpetuation; it must involve individual cognition and social interaction, cooperation as well as conflict; it has to include analyzing before and programming after as well as negotiating during; and all of this must be in response to what can be a demanding environment."

In our view the starting point for the strategy development process for a mobile learning nomadic strategy is with the "learning school." Given the complex environmental context that we have described in this book and the rapidly changing nature of the mobile technology industry, it is best to start with a strategic approach that allows you to learn over time from the experiences that you gain in implementing mobile learning. "The concept of emergent strategy . . . opens the door to strategic learning, because it acknowledges the organizations capacity to experiment. A single action can be taken, feedback can be received, and the process can continue until the organization converges on the pattern that becomes its strategy" (Ibid, pp. 189–190). Once the strategic patterns for the effective use of mobile technology start to converge within the industry, organizations can then formalize and expand on the best practices identified from their own experiences with mobile learning. This approach requires a willingness on the part of the organization to be open to finding the best approach rather than expecting to have the best approach in the first iteration. It also requires a commitment to ongoing and frank evaluation of the implementation of mobile technology with a clear focus on the highest priority of adding to the value creation process of the organization.

To be specific we are recommending that in adopting a nomadic approach to mobile learning strategy:

- Corporations develop strategies that support employee learning and development through the exploration of their environment and the development of new approaches to learning delivery using the mobile devices that they are familiar with. Corporations need to promote a sense of exploration with employees rather than simply passing on knowledge that has worked under previous circumstances.
- Corporations need to develop strategies that are flexible enough to promote forward momentum and incorporate the emergent advantages of new technologies and new situations and contexts.
- Corporations need to develop mobile learning strategies that draw on many different sources both inside and outside the corporation. Mobile learning strategies need to support decentralized learning and identify opportunities for employees to transfer this type of learning back into the corporation.
- Corporations need to create an iterative strategy development and implementation process for mobile learning that anticipates that there will be trial and error required and multiple iterations.

# Creating Mobile Learning Content and Experiences

Up to this point, I have presented the mobile learning ecosystem along with the many possible uses of mobile learning. But, unless you are a technophile or early adopter and have already experimented with mobile learning, you are probably interested in how you can create your own mobile learning applications, activities, and experiences.

To date, creating mobile learning content and experiences has not always been an easy task. This is because, at the present time, the environment in which one needs to design and develop mobile learning content is a complex mix of different forms of mobility, different technologies, a variety of types of learners who learn in different contexts, and trainers with many different approaches to instructional design. Moreover, content and experiences are somewhat restricted by the requirements of different mobile carriers and regulated by several levels of government. Add to that the huge number of possibilities for content and/or activities involving mobile devices, to say nothing of the many design processes that can be used to approach this task. Niall Winters (2007) agrees:

Designing mobile learning experiences is a complex task, requiring the assimilation and integration of deep knowledge from educators, researchers, practitioners, designers and software developers. While each party may have expertise in several of the associated knowledge domains, no single party has expertise in all of them.

There is also a technical side to creating mobile learning content and experiences; however, this book is *not* a technical introduction to programming mobile phones or a description of the intricacies of the many mobile phone networks and infrastructures. Rather, I provide training managers and business executives with an overview of the problems and processes involved in creating mobile learning content in order to help them manage the team of designers, developers, and project managers that are needed for any significant mobile learning content creation project or large-scale deployment of mobile learning devices.

As we see in Chapter 2, the mobile learning ecosystem consists of over 4 billion mobile phone subscriptions, using over distinct 5,000 mobile devices, with more than 30 different Web browsers, a multitude of input and output choices, a network infrastructure controlled by large carriers for mobile phones, and the changing Internet, with new concepts such as mashups and cloud computing. In order to produce effective learning content to work on mobile devices, a designer needs to take all the variables of this system into account. The mobile environment is *not* the Internet, where standards have been developed to allow you to build and render text and media-based web pages and send messages and media files around the world. Unlike the World Wide Web, there is a limited opportunity to change the system and little in the way of guidance to learn from examples of those who've gone before. In undertaking to create mobile learning content and experiences, you are truly a pioneer!

Marshall McLuhan wrote, "We look at the present through a rear view mirror. We march backwards into the future" (McLuhan and Fiore, 1967). This tendency is manifested in many different ways. Just over 100 years ago people spoke of "horseless carriages"; today we speak of "wireless devices." Our first versions of many technologies are populated by content that does not take the "affordances" of the new technologies into account. For example, about a decade ago, the first versions of mobile learning, what we might call "mobile learning 1.0," were usually the same as the e-learning programs of the time—

"courses" made up of many "pages" of text and graphics, but delivered on a very small screen. Given that e-learning courses were based on a classroom metaphor, the instructionist approach to teaching was used; the result was mini lectures, slide-based presentations, flash cards, and multiple-choice tests. While there is still a role for these techniques in the mobile learning toolbox, these methods are a throwback to old ways of thinking.

Once we realize that the old ways don't work very well and that there are new possibilities provided by mobile technologies, things start to change. For Mobile Learning 2.0, we have started looking for the *unique* new advantages of this emerging technology.

The reason I refer to both mobile learning *content* and mobile learning *experiences* is that these two words epitomize the two major ways of approaching the development of mobile learning materials. Mobile Learning 1.0 was all about content, the learning materials that instructors wanted to learners to read, listen to, or review. Mobile Learning 2.0 is more about creating learning experiences—activities that are engaging and challenging and that result in significant changes to knowledge and behavior, or about providing online resources that learners can find without the intervention of an instructor. In the near future, mobile learning designers will use a mix of all these approaches.

## The Mobile Learning Design Process

Central to the creation of engaging and effective learning content and experiences for mobile learning is the role of the designer. Designers are creative people who work with both the possibilities and the constraints of a particular environment to create a solution that works for a specific set of needs or problems. Designers need a wide range of experiences and knowledge in order to find the best combination of elements that goes into a solution. In other words, they have to know the characteristics and needs of the end users, the limitations and possibilities of the technologies they're working with, the best methods for facilitating the learning of others, and, in the corporate environment, the business objectives for which mobile learning is being offered as a solution.

**FIGURE 9.1 Stages in the design and development of mobile learning content and experiences.**

Perhaps the first question to ask is, "Why should this particular learning design be mobile?" That is, what need is being served by the use of mobile technologies? If there is not a good answer to this question, then you might want to reconsider whether developing a mobile learning solution is worth the effort involved. But if you find that there is a particular advantage to being mobile, then look at the end goal of what you're trying to achieve and "reverse engineer it." Sketch out the individual actions in the "clickstream" that the end user will need to perform in order to have your learning goal(s) realized.

A mobile learning design involves several different design disciplines that work through a set of development stages (Fig. 9.1). It is also aided by good project management. The suggested stages of design for mobile learning experiences and content are:

▶ Evaluate and plan for business needs for mobile learning.
▶ Understand targeted end users and their contexts.
▶ Know the limitations and affordances of the technologies involved.

▶ Define security requirements.

▶ Identify access and delivery constraints.

▶ Develop the mobile learning strategy.

▶ Design the interaction flow and graphic user interface for ease of navigation.

▶ Program a functional prototype or use authoring tools

▶ Build a learning application.

▶ Test and evaluate the mobile learning application using target mobile devices.

▶ Modify and retest if necessary.

Let's look at each of these stages in turn.

## Evaluate and Plan for Business Needs for Mobile Learning

In Chapter 8, David Fell outlines the steps required to formulate a business strategy for mobile learning. Any mobile learning project undertaken within an enterprise has to connect to the business needs (or even a particular crisis) that drives the adoption of this technology. In 2008, in a report that David and I cowrote for Brandon Hall Research (Woodill, Fell, and Woodill, 2008), we looked at the steps involved in planning for and evaluating learning management systems, and these steps can be adapted to any other learning technology, including mobile learning. The steps are:

▶ Develop a business case for investing in mobile learning.

▶ Consider alternatives to mobile learning—is this the best solution?

▶ Articulate vision and scope for the entire project, resulting in the development of a "project charter."

▶ Develop an implementation strategy and project management plan that includes a presentation of the business case, an assessment of the impact on the organization of implementing mobile learning, and a strategy for management change.

▶ Develop the communications and marketing plan for the project.

▶ Identify all stakeholders for this mobile learning project.

▶ Gather requirements, including the development of "use cases" for each business unit and group of stakeholders.

However, business pressures might dictate that you move more quickly than the time that this process requires. As my other colleague, Sheryl Herle, indicates in the next chapter, it may be best to simply get a pilot project going in order to observe the impact of mobile learning on employees. More and more, companies are turning to social scientists such as ethnographers and sociologists to carry out observation studies of how employees adapt to a given learning technology (Paay, 2008). This kind of rapid prototyping and observing reactions and use works best when costs can be kept relatively low.

## Understand Targeted End Users and Their Contexts

In designing for mobile learning, one of the first tasks is to recognize what form of mobility is involved. As discussed previously, mobile learning can mean learning from a mobile device even if one is in a fixed location such as a classroom; it can also mean learning accomplished by a person who is on the move and yet remains connected, via a mobile device, to relevant and useful information. Mobile learning can also refer to anyone who is moving through an environment and is connected to the information cloud via ubiquitous technologies such as digital signage, kiosks, RFID tags, bar codes, or always-on wearable computing devices. Identifying the type of mobility is first step that will shape the direction to take for the many design decisions that follow.

In order to design effective mobile learning, you must thoroughly understand the end users. This means defining and evaluating a variety of human factors including:

- *Locations and settings:* Where will the mobile learning activities take place? Under what conditions of lighting, noise, weather, obstacles, and social environment will the learner interact with his or her mobile device?
- *Movement and posture:* Will the learner be moving while learning? Will he or she be sitting, standing, or walking?
- *Devices and usages:* How will the learner operate the mobile device? Will he or she be using one hand, two hands or a stylus, finger, keyboard, numeric pad, or touch screen?
- *Workloads, distractions, and activities:* Is the carrying of a device for mobile learning critical to the person's functioning in the job? Does it

enhance productivity and effectiveness? Or, is it a distraction from what the person needs to do?

▶ *Users and personas:* What are the special characteristics of the users who will be undertaking mobile learning? What about accessibility for people with disabilities? Have you worked out a set of typical users (personas) for the deployment of mobile learning in your company?

The above human factors refer to the *usability* of the proposed solution. Usability can make the difference between quick adoption of a new technology and its rejection by intended users. Dugger (2003) suggests the following points for optimizing the usability of handheld devices:

▶ *Handhelds excel at perceived speed:* A mobile device must be quick to use.
▶ *Too many features frustrate customers:* Mobile technologies need to be quick to learn and easy to use.
▶ *A handheld device must be easy to carry and not require frequent recharging:* Loading lots of features can make a mobile device bigger and heavier, thus shortening battery life.
▶ *Handhelds must be wearable:* Mobile devices must be more than just portable. They must be so small and light that a person can carry one everywhere, in a pocket or a purse, without even thinking about it.
▶ *Handhelds are about the user:* What counts is the user experience, not a list of features.
▶ *Handhelds are used frequently but briefly:* People generally use mobile devices in frequent, short bursts. In fact, the usage patterns of handhelds are exactly the opposite those of PCs. Therefore, taking similar approaches to product design is a fundamental mistake.

Sometimes it is helpful to work out a set of "use case scenarios" before going too far along in the planning process for mobile learning. Use case scenarios work out just who will be using the mobile learning solution and how they will be using it. OnPoint Digital, a U.S.-based mobile learning solutions provider, describes several different typical use cases for mobile workers:

▶ *Road Warriors*—Connecting your outside sales professionals and field technical teams whose jobs keep them at the "front line" of your business.

▶ *Commuters & Business Travelers*—Making training/development available whenever and wherever your workers have the time and need.

▶ *Factory/Warehouse Employees*—Facilitating new ways to take ongoing and just-in-time training "out of the classroom and onto the shop floor" using portable, low cost, and easy to support mobile devices.

▶ *Partners, Contractors & Vendors*—Enabling consistent training and information delivery of your organization's policies, procedures and practices as well as facilitating data gathering from diverse sources.

▶ *New Hires & Matriculants*—Providing first round company overviews to applicants-in-process and new hires even connecting from home using their telephone or cell phone (OnPoint, 2008, p. 26).

The real purpose of understanding user needs is to take action that will improve the likelihood of employees adopting new learning technologies. For example, reducing cognitive load by making things simple will help with user acceptance of mobile learning as a viable solution. Using drop-down menus instead of typing makes it easier for the user to interact with a mobile phone. Whenever possible, designers should allow users to personalize the way their implementation of mobile learning works.

## Know the Limitations and Affordances of the Technologies Involved

In Chapter 2, I describe the many facets of the mobile learning ecosystem. A mobile learning designer should be familiar with the characteristics of the devices that will be used and the infrastructure on which mobile learning will be delivered. For example, in North America it is common knowledge that BlackBerries are the most popular smartphone for people in business. This is not the case outside of North America. In India, very basic phones from Nokia predominate. Abhijit Kadle (2009) says that in India "90 percent+ of phones do not support GPRS data connectivity or lack a HTML standard compliant browser." He adds,

While this may seem strange to someone from the West, it's well known in India that the bulk of the phones are cheap and basic—phones such as these do not feature operating systems capable of handling an installable or fully featured browser. These are the phones that are selling in millions and are the ones that provide most of the voice and SMS traffic on the network.

If you are designing mobile learning for India, you should take this information into account. It turns out that 90 percent of the phones in India will support a standard called the wireless application protocol (WAP), which doesn't need an Internet connection or Web browser to work, and which supports multiple scripts and languages—an important point in such a multilingual country.

In selecting the right technology mix, designers are confronted with myriad choices. One of the first issues to consider is whether to use a mobile version of a Web site to deliver learning content and experiences, or to develop a proprietary application for specific mobile phones. Brian Fling (2006) presents the different choices for mobile Web applications:

- *Small screen rendering (SSR):* Rely on browsers like Opera Mini or Blazer to reformat.
- *Programatically reformat:* Programatically strip HTML of superfluous elements.
- *Use handheld style sheets:* Define an alternate mobile style sheet for your code.
- *Create a mobile-specific site*—Create a unique Web site specific to mobile users.

However, Barbara Ballard (2007), a well-known mobile Web designer, is adamant that simply creating smaller pictures and text is *not* the way to go. "Mobilize, don't miniaturize," she says. "Miniaturizing treats the mobile environment and technology as a subset of the desktop environment. . . . Mobilizing precisely targets mobile user needs, making best possible use of technology." This, of course, is an ideal that may not work for countries or companies that still have basic phones and lack proper mobile infrastructure.

Certainly, we should be moving away from any page metaphor to a much smaller unit in our thinking. This is why some designers are referring to "learning snacks," "learning nuggets," or "chunks of learning"—small bits of information and media that travel easily to a mobile device. One approach is to design reusable "multimedia learning objects" that can be used by a variety of mobile phones (Bradley et al., 2009).

Most likely a mobile learning designer will be faced with a daunting diversity of devices. Each device type may have a different operating system, different Web browser, different input and output parameters, and different levels of computing power. And each will likely operate on the networks of different carriers. There are several approaches for dealing with this situation:

1.  Write proprietary applications using a cross-platform computer language such as Java. This will allow the application to run on any mobile device that supports the Java language.
2.  Limit the amount of computing power and memory consumption needed by the mobile device. This is a "thin client" model where most of the work for the application is done on a server, with the results sent to the mobile device. Use minimal display properties and separate the presentation layer from the data content.
3.  Use software agents to automate routine tasks, including adapting educational content to the specifications of the end user's operating system (Ally et al., 2005). Mobile content formatting can be done dynamically on the fly with the proper detection of the user's device type (Cartman and Ting, 2009).

As I've indicated, designing for mobile learning requires a grasp of many different disciplines. One of the most important disciplines is the psychology of teaching and learning, which needs to take place within the above parameters.

## Define Security Requirements

The simple fact mobile devices are highly portable means they will travel wherever their owners may roam day or night and are far more likely to be lost or stolen compared to a worker's laptop or desktop PC. Accordingly, enterprise IT groups are keen to find and implement ways to restrict access at both device and content levels to ensure the person attempting access to training content is, in fact, the registered owner of that device. A wide array of security features can be employed to restrict access to device-based mobile learning services ranging from simple username and password credentials and caller-ID identification verification methods to more sophisticated multi-tiered authentication schemas including challenge questions, serial number or electronic security number (ESN) verification and token-based single sign-on. Enterprise-class mobile learning platforms provide end-to-end support through content encryption (secured on server, secured in transit and secured on device) as well as remote wipe and disable capabilities.

## Identify Access and Delivery Constraints

Enterprise mobile learning initiatives often require ways to help identify and accommodate how and when mobile content is to be accessed and how it is delivered. Despite the fact our mobile devices and networks are getting better and faster with each new generation, many on-the-go workers may experience issues when the time comes for them to access and/or download their mobile assignments on their device. Given the on-device experience most mobile workers have is generally related to their use of standard voice communication services and message exchange (e.g., making calls and doing email), they likely have little comprehension that the video-based learning module they've just launched is literally 500 times larger than the average email they read or send. To make content access and delivery as easy and seamless as possible, mobile learning teams must identify ways to publish and distribute content to mobile workers as easily, efficiently and cost effectively as possible. A few of the proven methods include compression optimization strategies based on available bandwidth allocations, scheduled/off-hours content pushes, and content delivery prioritization based on network availability.

## Develop the Mobile Learning Strategy

Up to this point in the mobile learning design process, we have had to consider the business needs of the project, explore the characteristics of the end users and their contexts, and understand the technologies we will be working with and their constraints. In the traditional model of education and training, the next stage would be to develop an instructional design to convey the right information to the learners. However, because mobile learning is not mainly about instruction, I refer to this next stage as developing a "learning design" or "mobile learning strategy." We need a concept of how to facilitate learning using mobile technologies, and "mobile learning strategy" implies that it is both a creative task and a technical one and that it may or may not involve "instruction" as a component.

Ryu and Parsons (2009) contend that there are "three pillars of learning" a mobile learning designer has to take into account. These are individual learning, social learning, and contextual learning. With individual learning a person searches out new information to add to the knowledge he or she already has. Social learning involves two or more people who learn together and from each other. Contextual learning refers to the fact that we learn from our environment which contains a lot of information that triggers memories and evokes knowledge.

Learning also depends on the type of content that needs to be made available to the learner. Ryu and Parsons describe four types of mobile learning content:

- *Exposition:* Organizing content that is presented as textual information.
- *Exploration:* Telling stories or discussing representation as a narrative along which one can move.
- *Elaboration:* Sharing and discussing concepts to broaden one's knowledge base.
- *Exploitation:* Creating new experiences to lead to fresh insights and knowledge.

Robert Gadd (2010), chief mobile officer at OnPoint Digital, has divided mobile learning content into six levels, which vary from simple to complex. I have adapted his levels and added an additional level as follows:

- *Level 1—Messages:* One-way electronic messages in the form of short message service (SMS, also known as text messages) and electronic mail (e-mail).
- *Level 2—Interactive messaging:* Two-way messaging campaigns such as the collection of data from surveys and the administration of tests.
- *Level 3—Voice-based content and assessments:* Audio-based content such as narrated podcasts, audio broadcasts, and voice responses to mobile surveys. Telephone conversations between a learner and a mentor would also fall at this level.

- *Level 4—Reference materials and static content:* Material that is accessible to the mobile user on demand. Support for job aids and just-in-time learning.
- *Level 5—Learning content and courseware:* Interactive and lesson-based materials that have been assembled by an instructor. Similar to e-learning on a small screen.
- *Level 6—Rich media:* High-end audio and video productions playable on a smartphone or notebook computer.
- *Level 7—Interactive and immersive media:* The delivery of device-based learning games, virtual reality, augmented reality information, and augmented reality learning games via mobile devices (Fig. 9.2).

If you design and develop mobile learning, your learning strategy will probably fall into one of the above levels. The first three levels are suitable for almost any mobile phone including the most basic. The last four levels require that the learner use a smartphone or lightweight computing device such as a netbook or tablet computer.

The seven levels of learning content listed above are very general, but, as a designer, it is important to identify what level you are trying to achieve. Beyond that, you need to look at your learning objectives for the end users

**FIGURE 9.2 Augmented reality can include the mixing of a real image (photo or video) with a virtual image. Courtesy of Metaio Inc. Used with permission.**

whose learning you're trying to facilitate. This will determine the actual activities and information that you will produce for your mobile learning design.

Learning designers have many choices for how to facilitate learning. The specific techniques that you choose to implement in your mobile learning design depend on your learning theories (see Chapter 3), your experience at training or teaching, and the characteristics and needs of the learners you are trying to train.

Not all mobile learning applications require the use of rich media or immersive interactive environments. Anttila and Jung (2006) conducted a set of studies on the use of rich media for mobile applications. They say, "[a] number of themes consistently emerged in all the studies, especially the high-level motivations for media use. We called these *constant design drivers.*" Design drivers for the use of rich media include the following:

- One of the main reasons for media use is to escape boredom.
- Media are accessed as a short microbreak between other activities.
- Media are used for mood management for longer breaks or anticipated situations.
- Participants want to be aware of what is going on in their immediate surroundings.
- Mobile media device users are subject to unanticipated interruptions from the environment (e.g., phone ringing while listening to music).
- Participants have specific uses for specific media channels (e.g., the Internet for content acquisition and distribution; messaging for selected sharing).
- Participants want to keep up to date with their peer group and with what is going on in the rest of the world.
- Participants have different roles in their peer groups as facilitators, distributors, or consumers of shared media.
- Communication has a role as an enabler and is a by-product of media sharing.
- Familiarity with relevant cultural icons and ownership of media or devices are used as social capital.
- Participants want to pay only for media they want (e.g., buying only one song from an album).
- A mobile phone is the most likely device to be carried with the participant at all times.

## Design the Interaction Flow and Graphic User Interface for Ease of Navigation

Whatever concepts and techniques you choose, you need to sketch them out and flesh out the details with a storyboard. The storyboard should include an "interaction flow chart" that takes you in sequence from the beginning to the end of the mobile learning experience. It is also useful at this stage to start working with your graphic designer on the look and feel of your mobile learning content and the screen navigation. It is a good idea to develop a mockup or prototype using a tool like Microsoft PowerPoint to show the sequence that the learner will experience. Cartman and Ting (2009) advise:

> Creative . . . refers to both interaction and visual design. Interaction design is responsible for determining the user flow, constructing the interface, and projecting the flow of information. Visual design refers to the skin that is placed upon the interaction design. With mobile, the best visual design is clear and concise. Creative also considers how interaction will function on the various handset sizes.

For those who don't have a creative director who can do all the above, another approach is the use of *design patterns* or templates. A design pattern is defined as "a high-level specification for a method of solving a problem by design" (Pratt et al., 2009). As the mobile learning industry progresses, look for more design templates and rapid design tools to be made available by vendors.

So, where does one start with mobile learning design? Certainly it is helpful to read a few of the new books that have been published on mobile design and development. Three books I found helpful in terms of thinking about mobile learning design are:

- ▶ *Mobile Design and Development* by Brian Fling (O'Reilly, 2009)
- ▶ *Mobile Web Design* by Cameron Moll (Self-published, 2007)
- ▶ *Strategic Mobile Design* by Joseph Cartman and Richard Ting (New Riders, 2009)

Alternatively, you can download an electronic copy of the free *Mobile Web Developers Guide* written by Brian Fling in 2007 for mTLD Ltd., the official global registry for the *.mobi* top level Internet domain (Fig. 9.3). To

**FIGURE 9.3 A free *Mobile Web Developer's Guide* by Brian Fling is available. Courtesy of dotMobi (mTLD Top Level Domain, Ltd.), a wholly owned subsidiary of Afilias Limited.**

download your copy, go to http://mobiforge.com/starting/story/dotmobi-mobile-web-developers-guide.

To date, there have only been a handful of articles and book chapters specifically on the topic of mobile *learning design and development*. You will find most of them listed in the bibliography at the end of this book. Because of the growing popularity of mobile learning, you can expect more helpful books and articles to appear that will aid in the design of mobile learning.

## Program a Functional Prototype or Use Authoring Tools to Build a Learning Application

To achieve your learning design strategy, it may be necessary to have a computer programmer on your team. Certainly it's an advantage to have a technical person available to help you navigate through the maze of devices and infrastructure that you need to take into account. If programming is not necessary, then you may want to work with one of the many authoring tools for developing mobile learning. Alternatively, you may want to take digital materials that are already developed and convert them into mobile learning content. Let's review these three choices in more detail.

First, most *proprietary* content needs to be programmed by one or more skilled software developers.

Programmers who work with mobile learning need to be familiar with a number of programming languages, computer protocols, and development environments. Here are the major application development environments, content creation and authoring tools, and assessment and survey tools used in producing mobile learning content and experiences:

## Application Development Environments

*Java*—specifically Java Micro Edition (Java ME) is the predominant programming platform for mobile phones. It is used in the Research in Motion BlackBerry, the Google Android operating system, and is also available for select Nokia Symbian mobile phones. Each device manufacturer either provides or recommends an Integrated Development Environment (IDE) to assist programmers in constructing, managing and testing their application code for each development platform. For example, IBM's open source Eclipse IDE is popular with most Java programmers.

*Objective C*—this is the computer language used to program for the Apple iPhone, iPod touch and iPad tablet mobile devices. In addition to knowing this language, programmers need to download Apple's Xcode software development kit (SDK).

*C++*—a computer language used in some Nokia Symbian mobile phones.

*.Net/C#*—a development framework and computer language used in devices using Microsoft Windows Mobile operating environments.

*Flash* ——Adobe's well-known development environment works on many mobile phones although Apple has moved to prevent Flash-based content delivery to their mobile devices. Most major device manufacturers have joined Adobe's *Open Screen Project* consortium to demonstrate their support for Flash-based content playback on mobile devices. This group includes Microsoft, Google and Research in Motion (RIM) with the delivery of Adobe Flash Player 10.1 which began to ship summer 2010.

## Other Mobile Development Environments Include:

*GO*—Google's new programming language for mobile development

*BREW*—this is a proprietary language and development platform from Qualcomm, designed to work with their mobile phones.

*VoiceXML*—this is the World Wide Web Committee's (W3C) standard XML format for interactive voice dialogues between a human and a computer. Used for voice applications.

*WAP*—WAP stands for "Wireless Application Protocol" and was the standard early on in the development of mobile phones. It still works for many basic phones that are on the market.

*WML*—WML stands for "Wireless Markup Language" and works within the WAP environment to produce HTML-like effects on the display of many mobile phones.

*XHTML-MP*—the letters of this acronym stand for "Extensible Hypertext Markup Language: Mobile Profile." It is the main protocol used for programming for mobile web applications. It is used in conjunction with "Cascading Style Sheets" (CSS) which define the look and feel of each screen on a mobile phone.

## Commercially Available Content Creation & Authoring Tools for Mobile Learning

In addition to programming a mobile application from scratch, a number of authoring utilities, tools and platforms are commercially available from a variety of companies that provide varied levels of support for mobile content creation; the value of each of these available offerings is highly dependent on who is using them and for what particular purpose. Let's segregate the marketplace into the three different categories of (1) m-Learning Utilities, (2) m-Learning Authoring Tools and (3) m-Learning Platforms to help classify the value created and the markets served through all of these available offerings.

## Mobile Learning Utilities

> *m-Learning Utilities*—m-Learning utilities represent the entry-level offerings in the marketplace and are easy-to-learn products that are ideal for early experimentation and proof-of-concept efforts for new mobile learning practioners and teams.  Most m-Learning tools and utilities are generally low cost or even freeware and take only a few hours to learn and master. Popular m-Learning utilities include:

- Acrobat—Adobe Systems Incorporated. (USA)
- Impatica for PowerPoint—Impatica, Inc. (Canada)
- Various Apps—Kallisto Productions Inc. (USA)
- MLEX—Mobile Learning Experiment. (Open Source)
- Mob5—Creuna. (Denmark)
- MOBL21—Emantras. (India)
- Moveable Type—Six Apart Community. (Open Source)
- Multimedia Fusion 2——ClickTeam. (France)
- PowerPoint—Microsoft Corporation. (USA)
- Veodia. (USA)
- Winksite. (USA)
- Wirenode. (Czech Republic)

## Mobile Learning Authoring Tools

Mobile learning authoring tools are specialized applications that assist content authors in the design, testing and publication of mobile friendly content for their mobile learning audience. While this class of content authoring tool helps to simplify and streamline the effort to generate content, most authoring tools can only generate content for a limited number of mobile devices and delivery modalities. Authoring tools are generally inexpensive and take several hours to a few days to learn and master. Key mobile learning authoring tools include:

- ▶ Captivate, Creative Suite & Dreamweaver—Adobe Systems, Inc. (USA)
- ▶ Presenter & Engage—Articulate Global Inc. (USA)
- ▶ Camtasia Studio—TechSmith Corporation (USA)
- ▶ Desire2Learn 2Go—Desire2Learn (Canada)
- ▶ DominKnow Mobile—DominKnow, Inc. (Canada)
- ▶ Drona—Deltecs Infotech (India)
- ▶ Float Learning—Float Learning (USA)
- ▶ Lectora Publisher—Travantis (USA)
- ▶ iQpakk—MentorMate (USA)
- ▶ MyLearning Authoring Tool—Tribal/CTAD (UK)
- ▶ Push Mobile Media—Push Mobile Media (USA)
- ▶ Toolbook—SumTotal (USA)
- ▶ UpsideLMS Mobile—Upside Learning (India)
- ▶ Vcommunicator Authoring Suite—Vcom3D (USA)
- ▶ vMobiLearn—Vistacast LLC (USA)
- ▶ WebBuilder—ReadyGo (USA)

## Mobile Learning Platforms/Solution Providers

Mobile Learning platforms are highly sophisticated end-to-end solutions from full support vendors and service providers. All platform-based offerings include extensive support for content creation, delivery, tracking and reporting as well as provide extended features for content security and cross-platform integration. Platform-based offerings are generally available directly from the developer/ vendor as well as resellers and strategic partners and, as enterprise-grade offerings, carry a premium price for premium support and extensive feature sets and operational functionality. Platform-level offerings are distinct from mobile learning authoring tools in that they may be used to package and deploy mobile learning content created using other third party applications and utilities. The leading mobile learning platform providers include:

- ▶ CellCast Solution—OnPoint Digital (USA)

- CertpointVLS Mobile—Certpoint Systems (USA)
- Chalk Pushcast—Chalk Media (Research in Motion - Canada)
- eXact Mobile—Giunti Labs (Italy)
- Hot Lava Mobile—Outstart (USA)
- Moving Knowledge Engine—Moving Knowledge (USA)
- Rubicon—Intuition Publishing (UK)

Of course, content created in each of these systems will usually only work within a particular operating system, unless it is generic Web-based content. One solution for this problem is offered by vendors of "conversion tools" that take content in one format and then convert or "transcode" that content into multiple formats that work on a variety of mobile device platforms. Converting content to mobile formats is much more involved than simply taking existing materials and making them smaller for mobile screens. It involves analyzing existing content and making recommendations on how best to convert it to a design that is compatible with mobile learning. Select content may also need to be converted into several "lowest common denominator" formats and frame rates to decrease overall file size to facilitate easier over-the-air content delivery. In most cases this means a rethinking of instructional design for mobile delivery. After content has been converted, it needs to be tested for quality control. Examples of companies offering conversion tools for mobile content include:

- *Adobe Captivate* converts Flash files to video in order to play content on smartphones that do not support Flash.
- *Comnos* supports a large range of conversions of images, audio, and video to mobile formats.
- *NetFront* converts standard web pages for display on mobile devices.
- *OnPoint Digital* provides a suite of tools for conversion of mobile content into fourteen different smartphone formats spanning video, audio, text and slide-based deliverables.

## Assessment & Survey Tools

A different set of authoring tools is needed for producing polls, surveys and quizzes for mobile devices. The main contenders are:

▶ Poll Everywhere—Poll Everywhere

▶ ResponseWare (BlackBerry and iPhone)—Turning Technologies

▶ iQuiz Maker (iPod)—iQuizMaker

▶ MiLK (Mobile Learning Toolkit)—ACID

▶ Mobile Study—MobileStudy.org

▶ PocketExam—Bizon

▶ PodQuiz-hyperMix Maker

▶ Perception—QuestionMark

▶ Quizzler Pro—Pocket Mobility

▶ SMS Quiz Author—Tribal/CTAD

▶ StudyCell—StudyCell

Whatever programming route that you take, you will need to produce functional prototypes of your application for testing and evaluation on the various devices on which it will run.

## Test and Evaluate Your Mobile Learning Application on Target Mobile Devices

By now you probably realize how complex it is to design and develop sophisticated mobile learning applications. Before releasing your application to the market, you'll need to thoroughly test it and evaluate how it works on all targeted mobile devices. Fortunately, there are a number of tools available that can help you with this task. Robert Gadd (2010b) writes:

> If you want to ensure the best possible experience for every class of mobile learner, you'll need to build a collection of working mobile devices, simulators/emulators and testing tools to span the potential reach of your target audience. Leave "no stone unturned" by testing the full end-to-end experience from distribution/delivery to installation/loading to access/playback to reporting/analysis.

If possible, use real operational handsets to do all testing. The handsets should be replicas of the handsets that the learners who try your application will use. Failing that, there are emulators and simulators from manufacturers that can be downloaded for free. While not as good as the real thing, they are often very useful for initial testing and demonstrations. Of course, if you find that things don't work as planned, you will need to modify your application, and retest.

## *Case Study*

# Nike Provides Just-in-Time Product Information Using the iTouch

Nike's Sports Knowledge Underground (SKU) is a Web-based solution built in-house that delivers Nike product education and fundamental selling skills to over 80,000 retail sales associates (non-Nike employees) selling Nike product around the globe. The overall objective of the solution is to positively affect the dialogue about Nike products at what is called the "moment of truth" or the point of sale. The more relevant and rich the information that Nike can provide for retail partners, the more confident and comfortable they are when talking about Nike products with their customers.

The recent slowdown in the economy was particularly tough on the retail industry and had many financial consequences. Almost all retailers significantly cut or eliminated payroll hours that would normally be used to train their sales associates. In addition, to reduce overall labor costs, most retailers hired more part-time sales associates during the holiday season to cover their sales floors, instead of using more expensive and experienced full-time associates. Unfortunately for customers and manufacturers like Nike, the retail partners put these part-timers on the sales floor with limited or no product training.

For most Nike retail partners, the current Web-based solution is accessed from a dedicated computer in the back room. But with reduced or eliminated payroll hours available to train sales floor associates, an alternative delivery vehicle was needed that would allow the sales associates to stay on the selling floor and not have to go to the back room to learn about Nike products. Although Nike has a great tool proven to drive sales, the retail partners weren't allowing their sales floor associates to come off the selling floor for any kind of training, regardless of brand or manufacturer.

 ## MOBILE SOLUTION

Nike's solution was called SKU Mobile. Because the retail industry is challenged with extremely high turnover of sales floor personnel and the typical age range is from 18 to 24 years of age, everything about the way in which Nike built the SKU solution was catered specifically to its external retail audience (i.e., the

24/7 access, integration with retailer's systems of HR records, very short learning modules or movies, printable tech sheets, and a fully customized curriculum).

Knowing that the floor staff would be very familiar with Apple's iPod Touch and would immediately embrace it, Nike decided to use it for product training. The iPod Touch provides the screen resolution, clarity, and horizontal orientation that Nike needed for its product movies. Because retail sales floor associates in the sports apparel industry are not allowed to have cell phones on the sales floor, the iPod Touch was an obvious choice over the iPhone (although the SKU Mobile app works on either device).

The mobile devices were placed in a nice rubber case that was attached to a lanyard. The lanyard was long enough that the retail sales associate could comfortably view the content while the iTouch was attached to the lanyard, or they could detach the device from the lanyard to share with a customer. They were assigned the device for a period of time, the device was assigned to the footwear wall, or the associates checked out the device with management. Initial security concerns were unfounded as not a single device was lost during the entire pilot.

The pilot program was conducted from October to January with two of Nike's largest retail partners in the United States (one mall-based and one a "big box" store) and with some Nike-owned retail locations in the United States. In addition, Nike's technical reps were included in the program. Because of the overwhelmingly strong response and feedback from the program, the project team was given the green light to build a second generation app. Phase 2 of the iPod Touch pilot of SKU Mobile was launched at the end of March 2010.

Using the mobile device, a retail sales associate can access information on any of Nike's product categories (footwear, apparel, and equipment) with a touch of a finger or a finger stroke. In addition, the interface allows quick and easy access to a brief consumer profile or the product, access to key features and benefits of the product in the form of a more detailed tech sheet, and access to a short video on the product. The reference mode allows quick and easy access to instant sharing of information with a customer or a quick answer a customer's question without having to log in. When there are no customers in the store, the training mode allows the sales associates to complete their assigned curriculum, take the quizzes, and get credit for completions.

## Results

The weekly feedback about SKU Mobile was overwhelmingly positive from all participants. They saw it as a very effective training tool and as a quick and handy reference tool when working with customers on the sales floor.

Here are some of the findings:

▶ 7 out of 10 associates preferred using the iPod Touch in their Nike SKU product training.

▶ Almost 7 out of 10 associates experienced an increase in personal sales.

▶ 6 out of 10 associates experienced an improvement in their confidence in selling Nike products.

▶ Almost 1 out of every 4 (22 percent) of the sales floor associates experienced an immediate sale after using the SKU Mobile app.

▶ On average, we saw a 6 percent higher completion rate per week for stores that participated in the Nike SKU Mobile iPod Touch pilot compared to those that did not. (Those numbers would have been significantly higher and will be significantly higher once we have multiple devices in each store.).

▶ In our first week of the pilot alone, the staff of one of our retail partner participants completed over 1,000 modules through the use of SKU Mobile.

Mobile learning allowed Nike to provide an extremely powerful, useful, and effective tool to its retail partners in their most financially challenging time and in their most crucial business period (the holiday season). It provided a much more flexible delivery solution for the retailers—a solution that met many of their challenges (limited or no payroll hours to take someone off the sales floor, high turnover, more part-timers with less overall Nike product knowledge and limited selling knowledge, and so on). In addition, mobile learning allowed Nike to provide a truly on-demand and just-in-time training and reference solution. The program absolutely affected the dialogue about Nike products at the moment of truth or point of sale, and did so without taking a single retail sales associate off the sales floor.

Finally, there are mobile site checkers that will test your Web site to see if it is mobile friendly. Two such site checkers are validator.w3.org and ready.mobi.

## Final Thoughts on Developing Mobile Learning Applications

As I said at the beginning of the chapter, you are truly a pioneer if you are developing mobile learning applications. This statement is not meant to discourage you, but to make you realize that it is not a simple undertaking. One of the decisions you will need to make is whether or not to develop your mobile learning application within your company or to use a custom developer. If you are selecting a custom developer, it is important to evaluate whether it understands how different the mobile learning environment is from the e-learning environment. Many vendors of e-learning services are now turning to mobile learning development as a "natural extension" of their previous work. It is not. Look for a developer who understands the difference between e-learning and mobile learning.

Inevitably, someone (usually in management) will ask the question: How much is it all going to cost? A Forrester Research report in 2009 set the price of a no-frills mobile application at a minimum of US$20,000, and estimated that a more sophisticated app could cost as much as US$150,000 (Lomas, 2010). Of course, it's difficult to give an exact figure for the cost of development of any computer application without knowing specifications and the production values expected. As mobile learning becomes more prevalent, new do-it-yourself tools will arrive to lower the price, custom developers will become more experienced with their techniques, and a pool of experienced programmers and designers will be available for you to hire. At the same time, this technology keeps developing very quickly so that it is necessary for you to check for the latest information. One such source is the support Web site for this book, at http://mobilelearningedge.com. While you are there, please drop me a note with questions or information.

# Implementing and Managing an Enterprise Mobile Learning Offering

*By Sheryl Herle, B.Ed.*

In addition to the concepts presented by my colleagues around the notion of being a learning "nomad," I hope the term "pioneer" is one that finds its way into your lexicon and attitude as you embark on deploying mobile learning within your enterprise. The first quote is for those learning leaders who are, or who soon will be, leading the charge in advocating for enterprise-wide deployment of m-learning. Expect bumpy roads as you chart a course for mobile learning across unbroken ground, but rest assured that the journey is not impossible. It's not that you have to become a mobile technology expert in order to embark on implementation of mobile learning. Mobile learning isn't any trickier than moving a culture to e-learning. It's actually easier, because, in many ways, we have a great deal of previous experience to rely on—we've adopted the Web, we've handed out laptops, and we've successfully turned binders full of paper-based classroom

> "The way of the pioneer is always rough."
> —*Harvey S. Firestone, founder of the Firestone Tire & Rubber Co., 1868–1938*
>
> "Once an organization loses its spirit of pioneering and rests on its early work, its progress stops."
> —*Thomas J. Watson, Jr., president of IBM from 1952–1971*

content into engaging e-learning. Then again, remember how difficult some of those early e-learning strategy conversations were in the late 1990s when we were embarking on a giant mindset shift from classroom "training" to self-paced learning?

The second quote is for sharing with those colleagues who will challenge your rationale, continue to dismiss the idea of mobile learning altogether, poke holes in your business case, and inevitably ask, "Why do we need mobile learning when people already have access to e-learning?" In the face of this paradigm resistance, continue to innovate and progress.

There is no doubt that we are in the early pioneering days of mobile learning. There has been steady growth in the publication of mobile learning literature over the past two years, but the majority of the thought leadership being shared in blogs and journals is commentary on mobile network and device evolution, content conversion, instructional design strategies, and LMS integration capabilities. At this stage of mobile technology adoption, the majority of the learning industry is still focused at a project level—experimenting, learning, and achieving early success with one-off content deployments. As I write this at the turn of 2010, there aren't more than a couple of scholarly articles and paid research reports that discuss the notion of enterprise implementation and management of mobile learning. The earliest m-learning adopters are only now in the midst of expanding mobile learning from local level initiatives and projects to an enterprise offering and seeking to formulate an overarching governance framework for workforce mobility. It will be some time before we see more literature being produced on the notion of best practices in implementing and managing enterprise mobile learning.

It is this expansion to an enterprise level that fascinates me in my work on learning governance with clients across a variety of industries. In exploring why most organizations still hesitate to fully embrace mobile learning, learning leaders articulate their perception of barriers using different terms, but each of them essentially points to the following three main obstacles to moving forward with mobile learning:

1. Lack of expertise in mobile instructional design and conceptualizing how corporate learning can take place both formally and informally via mobile devices.
2. Lack of awareness of the full scope of costs, benefits, and risks at the enterprise level. This plays out in the struggle to formulate accurate

and compelling business cases to move forward with mobile learning. Executive stakeholders continually push (and rightly so) for further articulation of a more comprehensive strategy and business case before considering or approving m-learning initiatives. What these leaders are essentially seeking is to see an enterprise-level strategy in order to understand how one-off projects fit within a larger context of enterprise issues and complexities.

3. Conflicting accountabilities, interests, and procedures among content stakeholders (learning creators and business budget holders) and IT implementers.

The earlier portions of this book serve to provide a wealth of information on mobile learning benefits and ideas on mobile instructional design, so, with this chapter, we concentrate on understanding some of the enterprise cost and risk considerations associated with mobile learning deployments. Also, we'll take a look at the need for innovative new thought paradigms around enterprise-level program implementation when embarking on mobile learning deployment.

## The Struggle to Make the Business Case for Mobile Learning

While mobile learning is a compelling new frontier for many companies and our gut instinct is to push for deployment knowing that workforce mobility is the norm of the future, a solid business case to embark on enterprise mobile learning is still a rare find. Even if a project team might appear to cost out an attractive ROI and break-even time frame for delivering a particular mobile learning program, a comprehensive picture of true enterprise costs are seldom included or accurately estimated. Project teams think of the costs of mobile learning as the project costs only—the costs of analysis, design, delivery, implementation, and evaluation of that particular project alone. However, as we will explore, the enterprise implications of moving to a mobile learning culture carry far greater costs, which are often overlooked. A few of these overlooked but substantial costs are borne from necessary enterprise-level governance tasks such as:

▶ Creating enterprise policies related to mobile adoption.
▶ Redesigning enterprise processes and organizational structures to accommodate adoption of mobile learning.
▶ Devising new financial models with mobile utilities, devices, and content being budgeted for at the enterprise level, changing the way functional units get projects approved and deployed.

In addition to having to think globally about cost considerations when we're drafting our business case, we need to recognize the increased challenge of proving cost efficiencies when mobile is not a replacement learning platform but rather, an *additional* learning platform in almost every organization. What I mean by this is that mobile learning costs are an additional enterprise cost, layered on top of existing desktop costs; e-learning costs; user support costs, learning management system administration costs; instructional design costs; classroom training costs; and facility, telephony, and equipment costs. New resources need to be added to the organization in order to strategize, build, launch, and support mobile learning rather than simply redirecting current resources to new delivery channels. In this sense, at this early stage of adoption, mobile learning learning is an exponential cost within the enterprise—content$^2$, servers$^2$, devices$^2$, user support$^2$, data costs$^2$, and so on.

I have yet to encounter an organization that is planning to halt all classroom training in favor of transitioning to mobile learning or an organization where mobile content deployment is replacing all e-learning. The catch-22 is that until mobile learning capability is fully deployed throughout the enterprise, in order to maintain learner reach, we cannot begin to retire currently used means of learning delivery and drive out their associated costs. Like print delivery in the early days of Web adoption, we couldn't divest ourselves of all print distribution until the full enterprise was able to access the material through the corporate portal. The same holds true for e-learning today. There are still a number of workplaces that offer classroom or self-paced print materials to account for those employees not able to access or use e-learning offerings. In time, we will see older technologies and training methods being retired, and enterprise costs will be driven out as mobile productivity increases. But for now, mobile is an additional investment in most learning departments which makes constructing a business case that much more of a challenge.

Given the sheer magnitude of mobile implementation costs, when one factors in the ancillary costs of culture change and the costs to administer and support mobile use within an organization, it will be a very rare occurrence when any organization can articulate sufficient business requirements to make a compelling business case to deploy mobile devices and content *for the sake of learning alone*. In other words, learning leaders must partner with other business stakeholders to define a joint business imperative for mobile adoption. If you think back to early e-learning days, the same imperative held true. An organization never would have deployed personal computers to all workers just for the sake of adopting e-learning. The computers and infrastructure came first, and only then did it make sense for learning to leverage that investment.

This is not to say that there isn't a business case for m-learning. It's just that we have to recognize the inherent challenge to build a business case for it. This challenge to build a business case extends beyond just making the numbers work. Organizations are also inherently challenged by the traditional IT business analysis processes typically used to arrive at a business case. Organizations need to revisit today's business planning paradigms with a critical mindset and seek to adopt new business analysis and planning processes that are as innovative as the tools we're trying to deploy.

## Revisiting the Process of Business Requirements Definition

In times of rapid technological change, the typical IT discipline of beginning a project with hours of business analysis documentation is not practical. I say this as a contrarian but also having been a traditional business analyst myself in the late 1990s and then being on the business side and trying to lead innovation in enterprise Web adoption (not to mention countless frustrations I have experienced with clients since the early 2000s in trying to implement e-learning, and now mobile learning and social collaboration tools).

The typical process by which we arrive at a business case with IT projects is to begin by defining user requirements, then add up the total costs to supply a solution to meet the requirements, and finally, work on the business case to prove that what we are requesting is a wise investment given the ancillary business benefits that can be realized. Sounds like a simple and rational process, but with IT players wearing stringent business requirements thinking caps, the adoption of innovative technologies is often thwarted. In a recent discussion with a large group of IT decision makers, I was very pleased to see a senior IT leader address the notion of perhaps loosening up on the need for stringent business requirements and business casing when intangible user benefits are evident and demand is high. The example he cited was that if we operated only from the premise of proving business requirements, it would be difficult to make a case for outfitting employees with pencils in an organization where PCs are ubiquitous and paperless is the desired strategy. How true! Imagine the burden of proof that would also exist in trying to demonstrate business requirements for standard mobile functionality such as text messaging, IM, or pinging from peer-to-peer when peer groups all reside in the same building and already have land line phones and e-mail via PC workstations. Various forms of quick messaging are long-proven technologies, and we all know that rapid messaging on a mobile unit does serve a function that is completely different from phoning someone or staying tied to your desk to send and receive an e-mail, but it would be very difficult to quantify a true business ROI for this functionality.

Let's consider for a minute the historical rationale behind the practice of defining user requirements in order to better to start to understand the culture clash we are experiencing today in trying to implement innovative technologies in mature business organizations. The process of defining user requirements harkens back to the days of laborious coding by software engineers on mainframe systems where there was no such thing as quick and easy system configuration or even content authoring tools. Every system tweak and word change was custom, costly, and time consuming. Therefore, the specifications coming from the business team had to be crystal clear, and there had to be weighty merit for the request if the work was to proceed. This practice of having to demonstrate absolute business "requirements" versus "wish lists" still exists as an IT project norm today.

However, with mobile learning and other innovative technologies such as social collaboration, where the technology itself is actually changing the way humans interact, learn, and work, we cannot effectively state a business requirement or predict the next use case fast enough to keep up with the innovation we are experiencing. The result of trying to apply traditional business requirements processes when implementing a dynamically innovating technology is pure frustration — frustration on the business's part in working with IT, dedicating endless months in meetings to articulate and document requirements and being pressed to make the case for why currently existing processes, tools, and methods won't satisfy the business need. At the same time, there is also frustration on IT's part with the business stakeholders wanting to circumvent and shortcut traditional business analysis processes when, through the IT member's lens, the same business stakeholders seem to be spinning on strategy and unable to clearly define true requirements.

Remember that a fundamental focus of most enterprise IT department these days is not necessarily to empower the organization with new and innovative tools with which to experiment, but rather to control risk (security, reputation, and financial), eliminate functional redundancy, reduce business operating costs, and increase satisfaction with IT support. Adding mobile devices to the enterprise poses challenges in all these areas. IT partners will be doing their jobs well only when they question all aspects of why mobile is necessary and "exactly" how you expect the devices to be used.

On the other hand, business leaders are rewarded for staying one step ahead of the competition in seeking out productive and innovative ways to fuel a workforce. Likewise, they are doing their jobs well when they push to move beyond comfortable technologies and processes in search of leading edge solutions. It is this clash of mindsets, interests, and accountabilities that presents one of the major hurdles to adopting m-learning (as well as other innovative and quickly morphing technologies).

However, no learning leader will be successful entering his or her next meeting with the IT department and stating that they must stop all business requirements work! These practices are just too entrenched and organizational mindsets just aren't that pliable to be changed overnight. The key is to have some flexibility in the stringency of the definition of business requirements.

Finding a happy middle ground in defining a process that works both for IT and business/content stakeholders is a key to implementation success. When purchasing and implementing publicly available software platforms and applications, it is equally important to ensure that you don't over purchase functionality that will never be used. Therefore, creating your business requirements shopping list still serves a purpose, but, in these times of rapid innovation, there is a greater risk of underpurchasing functionality. You will want to adapt your business requirements process to leave room for both anticipated and unanticipated innovation. Bring your purchasing decisions up to the level of focusing on finding the right partner who can keep pace with the functionality being demanded by users as innovation occurs rather than seeking out spec by spec functionality that is an absolute must have. This middle ground is harder to arrive at within traditional organizations with long-standing practices, and it is generally these organizations that struggle more than young, entrepreneurial workplaces that have less formal process controls and, therefore, an easier time adapting procedures to use what works.

As noted, developing a business case for mobile learning will be a bit of a Herculean challenge, and the traditional starting point of defining user requirements isn't a productive exercise, so where does an eager learning leader start on the journey to mobile learning implementation?

Fear not! Learning leaders have a tremendous opportunity before them to shape and influence a brilliant enterprise-sized mobile strategy. But, the pioneering path to be taken requires a fresh approach simply because mobile learning is still so new and its frontiers are yet undiscovered.

 ## Develop a Vision of Your Overall Mobile Culture

If your organization is ready for mobile adoption or has mobile deployed in pockets of the organization, the first discussion to embark upon is the notion of governance and control. You should not being concerned with defining what employees *will do* with the devices; you will never be able to keep pace with anticipating new uses as whole new technologies and applications emerge in the mobile world each month. Instead, focus on what you aren't ready for employees to be able to do with mobile devices. As you can see, this is the converse of articulating business requirements, but it is the only way to strike a balance between allowing rapid innovation and wildfire adoption, and having key controls in place.

Thus, an effective starting point for planning for mobile adoption—for both business and learning purposes—is to create an aligned enterprise vision for your mobile culture for the entire enterprise, with cross functional engagement at the most senior levels. The good news is that "the genie is not going back in the bottle" in terms of the explosion of ubiquitous mobile technologies in the workplace. There are plenty of business stakeholders to partner with to create a strong case for multipurpose mobile adoption within the workforce.

Clearly the best business stakeholders to align with are those who stand to gain the most from migrating to mobile functionality. Outside sales reps and mobile service agents who often beg for mobile access to corporate knowledge are the most common starting points in terms of an audience for mobile learning. However, if you restrict input to sales/service and the learning team who supports these functions, you still run a high risk of creating a project silo. To create a true enterprise solution, alignment needs to take place with key members of HR, business strategy/marketing, and sales customer and service, with a view to multipurpose uses of one mobile platform and a comprehensive enterprise view to both organizational potential and risks. The focus of this group is to define *what* the mobile culture should look like. Determining *how* (IT and operations) and costing out options (finance) will come later in the journey.

With your primary audience in mind and business partners at your side, you are now ready to begin the process of articulating your company's overall mobile learning culture. Think of questions such as these:

- ► What if a salesperson could find the answer to the client's question within 3 minutes in the middle of a sales presentation?
- ► What if employees could have a forum to ask anything and get 10 colleagues offering support within the hour?
- ► What if disgruntled employee No. 13579 posted an offensive comment on the corporate knowledge network?

The temptation to partition out audiences and define scenarios by audience will become evident within the first meeting, but try to resist doing that or you are back on the path to defining user requirements. Simply think "employees" when constructing your scenarios and resist naming those employee groups/ departments at this stage.

After opening the vision of mobile possibility to its widest extent, seek to understand if there is any contributing member who does not believe mobile deployment would have a substantially positive impact on the organization. Now resist the urge to drop resisters from the team. Instead, turn the discussion to exploring the risk scenarios inherent in mobile adoption. Here is where we can offer a full spectrum of issues that need to be considered based on some of the prevailing best practices in mobility device management.

# Controlling versus Enabling

At the core, the decisions your organization needs to make center around two elements—control and enablement of your workforce. Once your organization settles on a clear set of enterprise principles for controlling mobile use versus enabling participation in a mobile world, you can align learning projects, pilots, and R&D efforts to these principles and experience much greater success than trying to start from a project objective. Organizations don't generally like to explicitly admit to creating control mechanisms to guide workforce behavior, but all organizations have a system of controls in place in the form of policies, processes, approval hierarchies, reviews, audits, and the like. Therefore, a much needed discussion is one that centers on the state of desired cultural control.

First, does the organization want and need to control the devices used by employees, or is the organization open to allowing employees to use personal devices for work purposes? Personal mobile devices are everywhere and can't be excluded from the workplace through any reasonable means. Banning employee devices from the workplace would create anarchy and a great deal of resistance. So, does the organization have a desire to capitalize on those existing devices and make content and functionality available for access by a vast array of personal devices, or would it rather invest in deploying company-provided devices?

Before deciding, carefully consider:

▶ How the organization will apply information access and security controls to the workplace network.
▶ How the organization will control appropriate content on an employee's device. In worst case scenarios, consider the legal risks of losing intellectual property or having employees violate content laws by being in possession of illegal content or even adding illegal content to the organizational infrastructure.
▶ How the organization will provide user support when employees can choose any device and any carrier and data plan they desire.
▶ How the organization will control or encourage use of device-embedded functionality (like GPSs, cameras, MP3 capability, etc.) or popular consumer applications.

▶ How the organization will deal with employees who violate policies or misuse or abuse mobile privileges.

## Case Study

## OnPoint Digital Solves Issues of Security and Control for a Mobile Sales Force

A global, diversified health care company was seeking more efficient ways to provide just-in-time information to its outbound sales teams on a variety of subjects including medical devices, pharmaceuticals, and biotechnology products. Sales management believed that an enterprise mobile learning solution could further leverage the company's existing investment in BlackBerry wireless handhelds—already used for business communications—to deliver and track up-to-date rich media content to sales representatives based on their unique product portfolios. Sales reps could use their smartphones to brush up on new products while sitting in their car or in a clinic waiting room before making their client presentations.

Because of the highly proprietary nature of the videos, podcasts, and written materials the company wished to distribute, issues of security and control were of paramount concern. The company's IT management mandated that all deployed content (1) needed to be delivered in an encrypted manner, (2) could not be removed from the device or forwarded to other parties, and (3) if the device was ever lost or stolen, that it could be remotely wiped to ensure information integrity. And though enterprise-scale mobile learning platforms do provide for these heightened levels of security and control, the nature of the content itself introduced some new challenges that needed to be overcome.

Existing IT security practices and policies already included the requirement of device passwords and mandated encrypted content storage, but up until this project, all company-issued BlackBerry devices were used only for voice and e-mail communications. The challenge was that these older BlackBerry devices could not easily handle playback of the encrypted content, thus negatively affecting the overall user experience. The devices worked fine for voice calling and e-mails but felt clunky and slow whenever the rich media files were downloading or being decrypted for on-device viewing. And like any other present day organization, the company was seeking ways to improve efficiencies while decreasing operational expenses, so a planned "technology refresh" of its older BlackBerry devices was postponed until prevailing market conditions had improved.

# MOBILE SOLUTION

To overcome these challenges, administrators worked with OnPoint to identify and implement an easy and failsafe way to transcode (or compress) all available media files into multiple formats optimized for playback on the company's newer devices as well as the legacy devices, without sacrificing image quality. In fact, each media file (video or audio) was transcoded into five different formats thus ensuring the most efficient delivery and playback experience for every user based on the currently issued device model; newer devices automatically received the high-quality file formats, and older devices automatically received smaller video files that downloaded faster and launched with minimal delay. The CellCast Solution platform also helped to define and automate all the procedures needed to prepare, package, schedule, deliver, and track all mobile-enabled content to mobile workers and facilitated remote device control and security.

## Results

An additional (and previously intangible) benefit resulted from the sales reps' interaction with their clients when rep actually used their phone to help show or explain something. There was an increased level of interest from the health-care providers, doctors, and clinicians themselves to access the same content (or at least a marketing-approved version of the content) on their own supported smartphone devices. As a direct result, the transcoding profiles have been expanded to produce a total of 11 different file formats to ensure the ideal viewing experience for all internal and external participants.

Wherever possible, look to replicate your current organizational policies in a mobile world rather than strike new norms or policies around mobile use. For example, look to lessons learned from deploying PCs and laptops. If your company does not allow personal laptops being connected to the workplace network for a variety of risk control reasons or you don't allow for random software installations, you probably don't want to opt for employees using personal mobile devices as part of your enterprise mobile strategy. It is also important to note that you cannot effectively choose a medium level of control, with some portion of your workforce using personal devices and another portion using company supplied devices. In order for enterprise governance to be effective, base principles for deployment and employee policies and supports should be consistent across the enterprise.

Unlike the current mobile play in K–12 and higher education institutions where use of personal devices is the only option, and despite the prevalence of employee-owned mobile devices in the workplace, you will find that the majority of large North American corporations have opted to supply employees with mobile devices. Companies are generally choosing to supply the devices for all the same legal, financial, and technical reasons companies supply and restrict hardware and software today—it simply allows for greater risk control and more cost-effective application development and user support.

However, there are other companies (more midsized companies with less stringent IT controls in place) that are encouraging employees to obtain their own devices and choosing to control use through a combination of caps on expense reimbursement and through employee commitments to abide by applicable HR and IT policies that explicitly state acceptable terms of use. Recently, I learned of a very large Canadian company that has taken yet another approach after nearly a decade of BlackBerry use: it has issued a new policy expressly requiring employees to obtain a personal device for personal communication and not to use employer-supplied e-mail accounts or mobile devices in any way for personal communication.

Regardless of the device deployment strategy chosen, you can be sure that personal devices will still be prevalent in the workplace as employees participate in a mobile life that they wish to keep separate from their employer. Banning personal devices from employees' pockets, briefcases, and purses is not a rational option, so it is a best practice to ensure that company policy addresses the use of personal devices in the workplace.

Deciding on whether a device is company-provided or not may seem like a simple decision, and you are likely wondering how this relates to mobile learning. But, consider how many mobile learning business cases have been drafted on the premise of being cost-effective since employees already have mobile devices in their pockets. But what if your mobile computing environment requires special mobile computers that all need to conform to the same specifications?

Once your organization takes a stand on device deployment, deciding on other mechanisms of control can follow. For example:

▶ Who gets mobile devices? What are the criteria for "needing" a device? Is the decision based on role-specific duties that are performed with a mobile device, or are devices deployed differently by geographic region, level within the organization, or other factors altogether? Whatever the rationale, ensure that your company has a very clear set of written standards or criteria for device entitlement.

▶ In deciding who gets devices, also consider the legal impacts that can be associated with deploying mobile technology. This is especially a concern around employee interpretations and manager expectations of hours of work. Do you have a specific policy that outlines use of the mobile devices after hours? What seems like a harmless mobile deployment can soon turn into messy union negotiations or legal actions regarding lack of compensation for overtime. On this issue of controlling work hours and hours of access to m-learning content or any other corporate applications, companies have traditionally been forced to rely on HR policy to spell out acceptable behaviors around respecting employees' personal time. However, technical controls can also be implemented here. Take for example the time restriction functionality offered by OnPoint Digital's CellCast technology that allows an administrator to restrict a learner's access time—by individual employee or for a whole department or geographic location where local labor laws may prompt the restriction (Fig. 10.1).

▶ How do you control employee data and voice costs on devices?

▶ When deciding how the company determines an appropriate time frame for device upgrades or how the company controls for lost, stolen, or damaged devices and recouping devices from departing employees, look to current practices around laptops and PCs. Do the same terms apply to mobile devices?

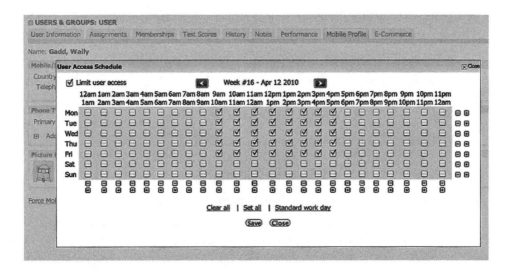

**FIGURE 10.1 Software can be used by administrators to control the time of day during which mobile phones belonging to a company can be used. Courtesy of OnPoint Digital.**

▶ How do you control for personal use of the device? For example, is it acceptable for employees to use the camera on their device to take personal photos? Can they send or receive personal data? Make personal long-distance calls?

▶ What will you encourage employees to access with the device? What data will you block or discourage employees from using? Given the rapid pace at which new mobile applications are introduced, you will want to make decisions based on general principles rather than commenting specifically on particular applications. Formulate employee policies that apply to a broad range of functionality, content, and content sources. In other words, don't get into the details of creating acceptable use policies for a specific site such as Facebook but rather create a set of principles related to user-generated content and participation in public social networking forums of any kind.

As you can see, deploying mobile learning is not simple or inexpensive once you explore the full range of related cultural impacts mobile deployment can have. However, with clear enterprise guidelines and policies and processes in place, learning leaders can concentrate on learning strategies and content creation, focusing the learning department's efforts on seeking innovative ways to capitalize on the convenience and novelty of mobility in learning.

# Build a Comprehensive Enterprise Mobility Governance Framework

Typically, the first interest in mobile learning is sparked through vendor demos or discovery of a unique mobile project being showcased at a Webinar or at a conference. In other words, interest, exploration, and thinking about mobile learning almost always begins at the project level. It is natural for organizational "intrapreneurs" and early adopters to get excited about new opportunities for innovation, improvement, and optimization, and immediately seek to bring innovative technology into practice within the organization by finding a project to pilot.

However, I propose that a project level genesis to mobile learning actually diminishes an organization's ability to take mobile learning to the enterprise level. The reason for this is that humans naturally become guided (and in this case restricted) by prevailing project level thinking, functionally siloed project sponsorships, and stakeholders and well-meaning project teams that apply traditional project management practices.

I am certainly not suggesting that you abandon planning and simply hand out devices with open access to a user-generated content platform and see what happens. Those organizations that rely solely on a grassroots project implementation strategy will be those that struggle the most with enterprise barriers and unexpected challenges in managing enterprise mobile learning.

To elaborate, let me share a nameless, but typical, organizational saga.

The sales leader of a large corporate organization meets with a vendor who demonstrates a sales training program just instituted at a competitive organization. The technology is just emerging, but this vendor has brilliant programmers who have surmounted data integration challenges and managed to deploy content to the sales force in a manner never before experienced. The learner and manager feedback is terrific, and the productivity gains are quickly apparent. On top of it all, the cost to deploy this program is actually lower than pulling the reps in for face-to-face training sessions across the country, and the entire learning program can be deployed consistently within a matter of weeks instead of months.

After the meeting, the vice president of sales books time with the vice president of learning to discuss this vendor's offering and puts in his order for one completely outsourced training program—to be delivered next quarter.

The learning team engages the outside vendor and struggles at first with learning the ins and outs of the new technology, but, ultimately, the vendor delivers, and the program is a great success.

Shortly after launch, the marketing department takes a great interest in the sales training that was delivered and wants to extend the program to another distribution arm as well as add some new functionality and content. This time the project goes a little more smoothly, and both the learning team and the vendor are delighted to deliver a week ahead of schedule, even when it meant having to get approvals for new user support processes for the entire sales distribution workforce.

By now, members of the learning team are feeling pretty confident about their ability to start to produce more content in-house for delivery through this vendor platform so they invest in more software and a few days of in-class training for three instructional designers. The pace of content production for these designers is certainly slower than that of the vendor, but the cost savings justify the time delay. The learning team is able to produce and deploy four more learning programs by the end of the fiscal year, despite the fact that it loses one instructional designer to a competitor and has to train a new recruit.

As part of the organization's IT planning process for the new fiscal year, the IT department informs the learning group that the technology platform it has been delivering content on is overloaded. Added to that, IT refuses to support the platform any longer as the technology is not compatible with the direction the rest of the IT infrastructure is going in. The learning department is forced to upgrade to a new platform and go through an extended request for proposal (RFP) process to select a new technology vendor. The new plat-form that is chosen is very impressive in terms of functionality. The cost to deploy the new platform is over $500,000 and will be phased in over the next 12 months. This slows content production capability tremendously, but the learning team needs to buy time to have the first vendor convert content any-way. So although business units have already expressed their needs for more content, the business units will have to hold their training efforts off for at least one more fiscal quarter.

The vendor quote for content conversion now comes in at an increase of 25 percent over the original quote because the vendor realized that there were some issues with technical compatibility that weren't discussed earlier. But, given the benefits that the new platform provides in tracking learning deployments and simplifying project-by-project administration, the organization does not sway from the technology conversion project and gets approval for a cost overrun of 25 percent.

Meanwhile, the call center leadership comes forward with a whole new strategy for customer service and can't wait for the corporate learning platform to be deployed in the next fiscal year. After much discussion, countless late nights for the project SWAT team and review of the completed project risk assessment, the decision is made to approve the business case for the call center to move forward with a different outside vendor application that can meet the timeline requirements and satisfy 80 percent of its functional needs.

Six months into the conversion of the corporate learning platform and some early success with the new call center learning application, executive stakeholders start to raise concerns about the need for one unified learner support center and a one-stop shop for user authentication into the various distinct programs. Migrating the distinct applications to a one-user support group poses a logistical and staffing challenge and, single sign-on is nearly impossible given the diverse data structures and lack of a unique user identifier across programs and departments. On top of that, the sales department now refuses to contribute any more of its budget to learning infrastructure to continue to support the learning content conversion given that the revised third quarter/fourth quarter sales targets won't allow any time for training until the next fiscal year.

The learning leader is now operating beyond his area of expertise and organizes a lunch with the CIO in hopes of gaining support for a large-scale project review to gather the full scope of user requirements, review all application technology and migration options and to produce a three-year technology road map which spells out a plan to streamline and simplify the current myriad of learning technology at a more effective cost.

By now, I am sure you understand the point of this story. In fact, the story may sound very much like the average e-learning journey many organizations have taken over the last five to ten years as we pioneered along, learning more about the PC as an effective medium for delivering learning experiences, using ever-evolving content development tools, watching LMS technology appear and mature, and only now coming to realize the extent of governance required to keep various departments aligned on standard learning technology platforms. My story clearly emphasizes the overall enterprise struggles versus the learning successes that many organizations achieved, but the point is to highlight the chain of interdependent decisions that are made every day at the project level within organizations and how these project-level decisions result in a complex, expensive, and inefficient system of disparate projects to manage at the enterprise level. While there is always a justifiable rationale for approving short-term project-level strategies in order to live within organizational constraints, meet urgent business objectives, and simply keep business moving at an acceptable pace, learning leaders are uniquely poised to avoid project-level traps with mobile learning because we have a great deal of rich experience with the implementation of e-learning. Look to your organization's own unique learning experiences from implementing e-learning and be sure to apply these learnings to your mobile program planning.

The highest impact lessons I have taken from enterprise e-learning are those with the most complexity and largest costs attributed to them. To that end, I share the following four key lessons to be kept top of mind when considering mobile learning implementations:

- ▶ *Learning content is medium dependent:* In the same way that classroom content is not directly transferable to e-learning without redesign, no classroom or e-learning content is directly transferable to mobile learning without redesign or, at minimum, tweaking and chunking into more "snack-sized" modules that users can complete on the go. Beware of making a business case for mobile learning on the premise of reusing content without including a substantial budget for instructional review and redesign.
- ▶ *Centralized content governance is necessary for an optimal user experience:* With good enterprise design standards in place, digital learning content can be efficiently produced through a network of vendors and internal resources, but central administration of content testing and publishing is still the ideal to achieve effective learner consistency and user support, content security, and management of intellectual property. If your organization lacks enterprise design standards for e-learning and you have multiple groups producing and hosting e-learning, you will want to invest some time in creating alignment, consistency, and

efficiencies before expanding your content governance workload with mobile learning.

▶ *One enterprise learning management system (LMS) is more effective than multiple content hosting platforms and learner data repositories:* Whether your enterprise is defined by a global collection of workplaces or one site, housing content on multiple platforms creates access and usability hurdles for learners, substantially increases the cost to deploy and manage content, and doesn't allow for content reuse or easy learning reporting. The price and scale of one LMS platform might seem daunting, but in the long run, managing one platform is less expensive than managing multiple platforms. Avoid the trap of project-level decisions that will have you buying a variety of incompatible vendor solutions in order to meet short-term business objectives and then paying three to four times the cost of the initial investment to try to rationalize systems to one platform within a few years. It may seem very attractive to squeak smaller mobile projects through departmental budgets and host content on an interim, vendor-provided platform, but what this results in for the enterprise is redundant functionality, multiplied administration and support costs, and difficulty (if not impossibility) in creating a comprehensive learner transcript as employees change roles and organizations continually shift in structure. Again, start with and stay aligned with an enterprise view with your mobile learning efforts.

▶ *A highly structured approach to learning vendor management is critical to realizing cost efficiencies, protecting intellectual capital, and achieving a flexible, scalable learning function:* Reaching out to the vendor community to help propel your mobile learning program is the fastest, most effective way to jump into mobile learning, in the same way that it is far faster to learn how to swim with a good coach teaching you rather than trying to learn on your own. We have seen companies struggle with the build/buy balancing act in e-learning for the better part of a decade. Those companies that are truly successful at implementing e-learning at a rapid pace, (with a rational average cost per learner) have struck the right balance and know what is best outsourced and when to assign precious internal resources to the task. Beyond this, these best-practice organizations have also created very structured procurement management programs, policies, processes, and formal contracts to guide all procurement interactions within a very competitive and crowded vendor community.

The mobile learning vendor community is still rather small, but the majority of learning content vendors is already offering mobile content creation services. It won't be long before the market is flooded with mobile learning players. Sorting through the offerings of those players and selecting trusted partners to work with is not a task to tackle superficially. Be sure that you work closely with your corporate procurement leaders and IT partners to establish clear ground rules for interacting with, selecting, and contracting with mobile learning vendors.

In conclusion, I hope you now understand the rationale for sending you back to read the whole book in sequence before peeking at this chapter for the secrets to a quick mobile learning implementation. I am sure that the word "pioneer" is apt to stick with you, given the depth of understanding you now possess of the challenges that lie ahead in crafting and implementing an enterprise mobile learning program. In providing a wide breadth of considerations and surfacing some common pitfalls of which you need to be mindful, you should now have a clearer mental road map of the journey you will take from your initial enterprise mobile culture definition through to experiencing success with multiple mobile content deployment initiatives.

The greatest hope is that you can also now see how far the learning industry has come with e-learning in the space of just one decade and that you can thrive on repeating that cycle of innovation with mobile technologies. Our industry is fully equipped with the wisdom of very applicable best practices gained from pioneering through e-learning into the mobile age. So, although we may have no ability to predict the next mobile learning use case or define our business requirements beyond yesterday, we do know we can continue to adeptly evolve the corporate learning function at the present warp speed of business.

# Appendix
# Resources for Mobile Learning

This appendix is designed to help you move forward with mobile learning. It lists the main associations, blogs, conferences, portals, and publications that support this emerging field. This resource list will be updated regularly in the support Web site for the book at http://mobilelearningedge.com.

 ## Associations

The International Association for Mobile Learning (IAMLearn) is an international group organized to promote excellence in research, development, and application of mobile and contextual learning. The current president is Professor Mike Sharples of the United Kingdom, one of the most published people in the field of mobile learning. Annual conference. Individual membership is approximately $70. http://mlearning.noe-kaleidoscope.org

 # Blogs

Blogs are a great source of information on the latest developments in mobile learning. Leading blogs on mobile learning in business include:

Cell Phones in Learning
http://www.cellphonesinlearning.com

Golden Swamp
http://www.goldenswamp.com

Ignatia Webs
http://ignatiawebs.blogspot.com

Learning in Hand
http://learninginhand.com

mLearning Blog
http://mlearningblog.com

mLearning Is Good
http://mobileben.wordpress.com

mLearning Trends
http://mlearningtrends.blogspot.com

mLearning World
http://mlearningworld.blogspot.com

mLearning: beyond the digital divide
http://mlearn.edublogs.org

mLearnopedia Blog
http://mlearnopedia.blogspot.com

MobilED
http://mobiled.uiah.fi

MobileDot
http://mobiledot.blogspot.com

MobileLearningEdge (support blog for this book)
http://mobilelearningedge.com

moblearn
http://moblearn.blogspot.com

MoCoZone
http://mocozone.blogspot.com

The Mobile Learner
http://themobilelearner.wordpress.com

Mobile Learning Foresight
http://mamk.research-update.info

Mobile Learning News
http://mlearning.noe-kaleidoscope.org/ne

Mobile Libraries
http://mobile-libraries.blogspot.com

Mobile, Work-Based and Lifelong Learning
http://www.christoph.pimmer.info

Ubiquitous Thoughts
http://ubiquitousthoughts.wordpress.com

uLearning Blog
http://ulearning.edublogs.org

Workplace Learning Today
http://www.brandon-hall.com/workplacelearningtoday

# Conferences

Handheld Learning Conference
http://www.handheldlearning.co.uk

Interactive Mobile and Computer Aided Learning Conference
http://www.imcl-conference.org

mLearn Conference—IAMLearn
http://mlearning.noe-kaleidoscope.org

mLearnCon—eLearning Guild
http://www.elearningguild.com

Mobile Learning Conference—IADIS
http://www.mlearning-conf.org

 # Portals and Web Sites

mLearnopedia
http://cc.mlearnopedia.com

 # Publications

Mobile learning articles are found in many different journals. The following journals are specifically dedicated to mobile learning:

*International Journal of Mobile and Blended Learning*
*Mobile Technologies and Learning*
*International Journal of Mobile Learning and Organisation*

# Bibliography

The following bibliography represents many of the books and articles written on mobile learning in the past decade, especially those on mobile learning for adults. Many of the articles and conference papers can be easily found by entering the title into a search engine, or by going to the master mobile learning bibliography on the support Web site for this book, at http://mobilelearningedge.com. The bibliography also contains all the references mentioned in this book. The bibliography on the Web site will be kept up to date with new materials on mobile learning as I find them.

Adkins, Sam (2008). *The U.S. Market for Mobile Learning Products and Services: 2008–2013 Forecast and Analysis*. Ambient Insight Research Report.

Agar, Jon (2005). *Constant Touch: A Global History of the Mobile Phone*. Thriplow, UK: Icon Books.

Ahmad, Nabeel (2008). "What Use Do Multi-touch Mobile Devices Have in Workplace Learning?" *International Journal of Advanced Corporate Learning*, vol. 1, no 1.

Alessi, S., and Trollip, S. (2001). *Multimedia for Learning: Methods and Development*. Boston: Allyn and Bacon.

Alexander, Bryan (2004). "Going Nomadic: Mobile Learning in Higher Education." *EDUCAUSE Review*, vol. 39, no. 5, September/October 2004.

Alexander, Bryan (2010). "Using Smartphones to Track Attendance," *Liberal Education Tomorrow*, June 1.

Ally, M., Lin, F., McGreal, R., Woo, B., and Li, Q. (2005). An Intelligent Agent for Adapting and Delivering Electronic Course Materials to Mobile Learners. *Proceedings of MLearn 2005 Conference*, Capetown, South Africa.

Ally, Mohamed (ed.) (2009). *Mobile Learning: Transforming the Delivery of Education and Training*. Edmonton, Canada: Athabasca University Press.

Ananthaswamy, Anil (2009). "Mobile Messaging Network Counsels Cape Town Drug Users," *New Scientist*, issue 2722, August 22.

Anastopoulou, S., Barber, C., et al. (2002). Object Manipulation in Educational Multimodal Systems for Contextual Learning. *Proceedings of the European Workshop on Mobile and Contextual Learning*, The University of Birmingham, England.

Anastopoulou, S., Sharples, M., Ainsworth, S. and Crook, C. (2009). "Personal Inquiry: Linking the Vultures of Home and School with Technology Mediated Science Inquiry." In Pachler, N. and Selpold, J. (eds.), *Mobile Learning Cultures across Education, Work and Leisure. Book of Abstracts*, 3rd WLE Mobile Learning Symposium, London, March 27, 55–57.

Andersen, Verner (2004). A Mobile First Aid Training System for Training Doctors in Stabilizing Casualties On Site. In Attewell, Jill, and Savill-Smith, Carol (eds.), *Mobile Learning Anytime Everywhere*: a book of papers from MLEARN 2004 (pp. 217–220).

Anderson, J., and Rainie, L. (2008). *The Future of the Internet III*. Pew Internet and American Life Project Report.

Ankeeny, Jason (2009). Mobile Posse's MobiCRM debuts via MetroPCS. *Fierce Mobile Content*, November 10.

Anttila, A., and Jung, Y. (2006). Discovering Design Drivers for Mobile Media Solutions. Paper presented at the Computer-Human Interaction Conference (CHI 06), Montreal, Canada.

Arnedillo-Sánchez, I., Sharples, M., and Vavoula, G. (Eds.), (2007). Beyond Mobile Learning Workshop. The CSCL Alpine Rendez-Vous, Kaleidoscope, Mobile Learning SIG.

Arnold, Jennifer Taylor (2007). "Learning on the Fly: Choose the Right Tools to Deliver Learning Content to Employees Anytime, Anywhere," *HR Technology*, September.

Attewell, J., and Webster, T. (2004). "Engaging and Supporting Mobile Learners." In Attewell, J., and. Savill-Smith, C. (eds.), *Mobile Learning Anytime,*

*Everywhere: A Book of Papers from MLEARN 2004*. London, United Kingdom: Learning and Skills Development Agency.

Attewell, Jill (2005). Mobile Technologies and Learning: A Technology Update and m-Learning Project Summary. Report, Learning and Skills Development Agency.

Ballard, Barbara (2007). *Designing the Mobile User Experience*. New York: John Wiley.

Begg, Andy (2000). Enactivism: a personal interpretation. Paper presented at a seminar at Stirling University, August 22.

Belanich, J., Orvis, K. and Sibley, D. (2003). Maximizing Training Effectiveness using PC-Based Games. In A. Rossett (Ed.), *Proceedings of World Conference on E-Learning in Corporate, Government, Healthcare, and Higher Education 2003*, 1515–1518.

Bell, G., and Gemmell, J. (2009). *Total Recall: How the E-Memory Revolution Will Change Everything*. New York: Dutton Adult.

Bellina, L., and Missoni, E. (2009). "Mobile Cell-Phones (M-phones) in Telemicroscopy: Increasing Connectivity of Isolated Laboratories," *Diagnostic Pathology*, vol. 4, no. 19.

Bradley, C., Haynes, R., Cook, J., Boyle, T., and Smith, C. (2009). "Design and Development of Multimedia Learning Objects for Mobile Phones. In Ally, Mohamed (ed.), *Mobile Learning: Transforming the Delivery of Education and Training* (pp. 157–182). Edmonton, Canada: Athabasca University Press.

Brown, J. and Metcalf, D. (2008). *Mobile Learning Update*. Saratoga Springs, NY: The MASIE Center and the Learning Consortium.

Brown, J. S., and Duguid, P. (1991). "Organizational Learning and Communities of Practice: Toward a Unified View of Working, Learning, and Innovation," *Organizational Science*, vol. 2, no. 1, pp. 40–57.

Bruner, Jerome (1966). *Toward a Theory of Instruction*. Cambridge, MA: Belknap Press.

Burke, Kay (1999). *How to Assess Authentic Learning*. Arlington Heights, IL.: Skylight.

Byrne, P., and Tangney, B. (2006). Animation on Mobile Phones. Paper presented at the IADIS Mobile Learning 2006 Conference.

Cartman, J., and Ting, R. (2009). *Strategic Mobile Design: Creating Engaging Experiences*. Berkeley, CA: New Riders.

Chan, Selena (2006). m-Learning for Workplace Apprentices: A Report on Trials Undertaken to Establish Learning Portfolios. Paper presented at M-Learn 2006 Conference.

Chan, S., and Ford, N. (2007). mLearning and the Workplace Learner: Integrating mLearning ePortfolios with Moodle. *Proceedings of the MoLTA Conference.* February.

Chang, B., Wang, H., and Lin, Y. (2009). "Enhancement of Mobile Learning Using Wireless Sensor Network," *Learning Technology,* vol. 11, nos. 1 and 2, January–April.

Chayko, Mary (2008). *Portable Communities: The Social Dynamics of Online and Mobile Connectedness.* Albany, NY: SUNY Press.

Chen, S., and Michael, D. (2005). Proof of Learning: Assessment in Serious Games. *Gamasutra,* October 19.

Clark, Andy (2008). Supersizing the Mind: Embodiment, action, and cognitive extension. Oxford: Oxford University Press.

Clark, Lyn (2009). New research to bring assessment into digital age. Australian Flexible Learning Framework, December. 3.

Coburn, Pip (2006). *The Change Function: Why Some Technologies Take Off and Others Crash and Burn.* New York: Portfolio.

Cook, J., Bradley, C., Lance, J., Smith, C., and Haynes, R. (2007). Generating Learning Contexts with Mobile Devices. In Pachler, N. (ed.), *Mobile Learning: Towards a Research Agenda. Occasional Papers in Work-based Learning 1* ,pp. 55–73. London: WLE Centre.

Cook, J., Pachler, N., and Bradley, C. (2008a). Appropriation of Mobile Phones for Learning. Paper given at mLearn 2008. Telford, United Kingdom.

Cook, J., Pachler, N., and Bradley, C. (2008b). "Bridging the Gap? Mobile Phones at the Interface between Informal and Formal Learning," *Journal of the Research Centre for Educational Technology.* Special Issue on Learning While Mobile, vol. 4, no. 1, pp. 3–18.

Cook, John (2008). Phases of Mobile Learning. Online presentation slides, London Mobile Learning Group.

Crofts, S., Dilley, J., Fox, M., Retsema, A., and Williams, B. (2005). "Podcasting: A New Technology in Search of Viable Business Models," *First Monday,* vol. 10, no. 9, September.

Cross, Jay (2006). *Informal Learning: Rediscovering the Pathways that Inspire Innovation and Performance.* San Francisco: Pfeiffer.

Davis, B., Sumara, D., and Luce-Kapler, R. (2000). *Engaging Minds: Learning and Teaching in a Complex World.* Mahwah, NJ: Lawrence Erlbaum.

Dede, C. (1996). "The Evolution of Distance Education: Emerging Technologies and Distributed Learning," *American Journal of Distance Education,* vol. 10, no. 2, pp. 4–36.

de Lorenzo, Rob (2009). 10 eBook/Audiobook Resources for Mobile Learning. *The Mobile Learner*, April 25.

Dugger, Mark (2003). *Zen of Palm: Designing Products for Palm OS*. Sunnyvale, CA: Palmsource, Inc.

*Economist* magazine (2006). "Getting the Internet on Track," *Economist Technology Quarterly*, September 21.

*Economist* magazine (2008). "The New Nomadism," Special report. April 10.

Edwards, R. (2005). "Knowledge Sharing for the Mobile Workforce," *Chief Learning Officer*, May.

Eisenberg, Anne (2009). "Far from a Lab? Turn Cellphone into a Microscope," *New York Times*, November 7.

Ferscha, A. (2000). Workspace Awareness in Mobile Virtual Teams. *Proceedings of the IEEE 9th International Workshop on Enabling Technologies: Infrastructure for Collaborative Enterprises* (WETICE'00), Gaithersburg, MD, March, pp. 272–277.

Ferscha, A., Holzmann, C., and Oppl, S. (2004). Team Awareness in Personalized Learning Environments. Online paper. Johannes Kepler University of Linz, Austria.

Finke, M., Tazari, S., and Balfanz, D. (2004). MUMMY: Mobile Knowledge Management. 2nd public report. November.

Firestone, Harvey (1868–1938). Quote from http://www.quotedaddy.com

Fling, Brian (2006). Designing for Mobile: Bringing Design Down to Size. Online presentation, Blue Flavor.

Fling, Brian (2007). *Mobile Web Developers Guide*. Online manual. mTLD, Inc.

Fling, Brian (2009). *Mobile Design and Development*. Sebastopol, CA: O'Reilly.

Freire, Paulo (1970). *Pedagogy of the Oppressed*. New York: Continuum.

Frohberg, Dirk (2006). Mobile Learning Is Coming of Age: What We Have and What We Still Miss. Paper presented at DeLFI 2006 Conference.

Gadd, Robert (2010). "mLearning Content Types—Overview and Intro," *mLearning Trends*, January 19.

Gadd, R., and Guest, K. (2009). CellCast Solution Guide. OnPoint Digital White Paper.

Gaggl, Leo (2009). "m-Learn: Mobile Evidence Gathering Using GoogleDocs," *Digital Nomad*. February 18.

Gangar, Kunal (2009). "Toshiba Creates Translation Tool for Mobile Phones," *TechTicker*, December 28.

Garrison, R., and Anderson, T. (2003). *E-Learning in the 21st Century: A Framework for Research and Practice*. London: RoutledgeFalmer.

Geddes, S. J. (2004). "Mobile Learning in the 21st Century: Benefit for Learners," *Knowledge Tree e-Journal*, no.6.

Gorlick, Adam (2009). Media Multitaskers Pay Mental Price, Stanford Study Shows. *Stanford Report*, August 24.

Gragtmans, Paul (2010). Personal communication. E-mail.

Greenemeier, Larry (2009). "Medical Monitoring Networks Get Personal," *Scientific American*, Online, September 18.

Greenspun, P. (2005). Mobile phone as home computer. Online paper, MIT.

Gronstedt, Anders (2007). "The Changing Face of Workplace Learning," *Learning Circuits*, January.

Guy, Retta (ed.) (2009). *The Evolution of Mobile Teaching and Learning*. Santa Rosa, CA: Informing Science Press.

Hahn, Jim (2008). "Mobile Learning for the Twenty-first Century Librarian." *Reference Services Review*, 36(3), 272–288.

Hall, Mary (2008). "Getting to Know the Feral Learner." In Visser, J. and Visser-Valfrey, M. (Eds.) *Learners in a Changing Learning Landscape: Reflections from a Dialogue on New Roles and Expectations*. Berlin: Springer, 109–134.

Hambley, L., O'Neill, T., and Kline, T. (2007). "Virtual Team Leadership: The Effects of Leadership Style and Communication Medium on Team Interaction Styles and Outcomes," *Organizational Behavior and Human Decision Processes*, vol. 103, no. 1, pp. 1–20.

Heiphetz, A., and Woodill, G. (2010). *Training and Collaboration with Virtual Worlds*. New York: McGraw-Hill.

Hoeg, Rich (2007). Jump Drive Learning.. or.. Wiki on a Stick. *NorthStarNerd. org*, August 6.

Holzmann, C., and Hader, A. (2010). Towards Tabletop Interaction with Everyday Artifacts via Pressure Imaging. *Proceedings of the 4th International Conference on Tangible, Embedded and Embodied Interaction* (TEI 2010). Cambridge, MA,: ACM Press. January.

Hoppe, G., and Breitner, M. (2004). Sustainable Business Models for E-Learning. IWI Discussion Paper Series 7, January 7.

Horng, C., Horng, G., and Sun, C. (2007). "Mobile Learning Combined with RFID for Technical and Vocational Education and Training," *Mobimedia'07*, Month 8, 2007, Nafpaktos, Aitolokarnania, Greece.

Huss, Mikael (2009). "Mobile Phone Diagnosis," *Follow the Data*, November 14.

IBM (2005). The Mobile Working Experience: A European Perspective. White Paper. Somers, NY: IBM Global Services.

Inman, Mason (2009). "Barcodes Could Reveal Your Food's Credentials," *New Scientist*, no. 2712, June 16.

International Medical Solutions (2009). New Mobile Patient Communicator Gives Patients an Interactive Education Tool and Boosts Nurse Productivity. Press release.

Jarche, Harold (2007). "The Future of Learning is DIY." *Life in Perpetual Beta*, Feb. 26.

Järvelä, S., Volet, S., and Järvenoja, H. (2005). Motivation in Collaborative Learning: New Concepts and Methods for Studying Social Processes of Motivation. A paper presented at the Earli 2005 conference, August 22–27, 2005, Nicosia, Cyprus.

Johnson, Johna (2008). "The Business Case for Mobile Collaboration." *Network World*, March 6.

Johnson, L., Levine, A., and Smith, R. (2009). *The 2009 Horizon Report*. Austin, TX: The New Media Consortium.

Johnson, L., Levine, A., Smith, R., and Stone, S. (2010). *The 2010 Horizon Report*. Austin, TX: The New Media Consortium.

Jolicoeur, Pierre (1999). "Restricted Attentional Capacity between Sensory Modalities," *Psychonomic Bulletin & Review*, vol. 6, pp. 87–92.

Jones, Nick (2008). M-Learning Opportunities and Applications. Gartner Report.

Jones, Nick (2009a). All Your Mobile Delusions Are Wrong. *Gartner Blog Network*, May 16.

Jones, Nick (2009b). The Three Screen Delusion. *Gartner Blog Network*, August 22.

Jones, Nick (2009c). Future Mobile Collaboration. *Gartner Blog Network*, September 15.

Jordans, Frank (2009). *World's Poor Drive Growth in Global Cell Phone Use*. Associated Press news release, March 2.

Jovanov, E., Milenkovic, A., Otto, C., and de Groen, P. (2005). "A Wireless Body Area Network of Intelligent motion Sensors for Computer Assisted Physical Rehabilitation," *Journal of Neuroengineering Rehabilitation*, vol. 2, no. 6.

Kadle, Abhijit (2009). Mobile Learning—Three Reasons for the Return of WAP. *Upside Learning Solutions Blog*, December 4.

Kaplan-Leiserson, Eva (2005). Trend: Podcasting in Academic and Corporate Learning. *Learning Circuits*, June 2005.

Keegan, Desmond (2005). Mobile Learning: The Next Generation of Learning. Report, Distance Education International.

Kim, W.C., and Mauborgne, R. (2005). *Blue Ocean Strategy: How to Create Uncontested Market Space and Make Competition Irrelevant.* Boston: Harvard University Press.

Kirkpatrick, Donald (1994). *Evaluating training programs: the four levels.* San Francisco: Berrett-Koehler.

Klopfer, Eric (2008). *Augmented Learning: Research and Design of Mobile Educational Games.* Cambridge, MA: MIT Press.

Knowles, M. (1984a). *The Adult Learner: A Neglected Species* (3rd ed.). Houston, TX: Gulf Publishing.

Knowles, M. (1984b). *Andragogy in Action.* San Francisco: Jossey-Bass.

Koschmann, T., Kelson, A. C., Feltovich, P. J., and Barrows, H. S. (1996). "Computer-Supported Problem-Based Learning: A Principled Approach to the Use of Computers in Collaborative Learning." In T.D. Koschmann (ed.), *CSCL: Theory and Practice of an Emerging Paradigm.* Hillsdale, NJ: Lawrence Erlbaum, pp. 83–124.

Kukukska-Hulme, A., and Pettit, J. (2009). "Practitioners as Innovators: Emergent Practice in Personal Mobile Teaching, Learning, Work, and Leisure." In Ally, Mohamed (ed.), *Mobile Learning: Transforming the Delivery of Education and Training,* pp. 135–155. Edmonton, Canada: Athabasca University Press.

Kukulska-Hulme, A., Sharples, M., Milrad, M., Arnedillo-Sánchez, I., and Vavoula, G. (2009). "Innovation in Mobile Learning: A European Perspective," *International Journal of Mobile and Blended Learning,* vol 1, no. 1, pp. 13–35.

Kukulska-Hulme, A., and Traxler, J. (eds.) (2005). *Mobile Learning: A Handbook for Educators and Trainers.* London: Routledge.

Kukukska-Hulme, A., and Wible, D. (2008). Context at the Crossroads of Language Learning and Mobile Learning. Paper presented at the ICCE 2008 Conference.

Kukulska-Hulme, Agnes (2002). *Cognitive, Ergonomic and Affective Aspects for PDA Use for Learning. Proceedings of the European Workshop on Mobile and Contextual Learning.* The University of Birmingham, England.

Kukulska-Hulme, Agnes (2005a). "Introduction." In Kukulska-Hulme, A., and Traxler, J. (eds.), *Mobile Learning: A Handbook for Educators and Trainers.* London: Routledge.

Kukulska-Hulme, Agnes (2005b). Current Uses of Wireless and Mobile Learning: Landscape Study in Wireless and Mobile Learning in the Post-16 Sector. Online paper.

Kukulska-Hulme, Agnes (2007). "Mobile Usability in Educational Contexts: What Have We Learnt?" *International Review of Research in Open and Distance Learning*, vol. 8, no. 2, pp. 1–16.

Kukulska-Hulme, Agnes (2009a). "Mobility in Mobile Learning: Have We Only Scratched the Surface?" In Pachler, N., and Selpold, J. (eds.), *Mobile Learning Cultures Across Education, Work and Leisure*, pp. 151–154. Book of Abstracts, 3rd WLE Mobile Learning Symposium, London, March 27.

Kukulska-Hulme, Agnes (2009b). "Will Mobile Learning Change Language Learning?" *ReCALL*, vol. 21, pp. 157–165.

Lakoff, G., and Johnson, M. (1980). *Metaphors We Live By*. Chicago: University of Chicago Press.

Laurillard, Diana (2002). Rethinking University Teaching. *A Conversational Framework for the Effective Use of Learning Technologies*. London: Routledge.

Little, Bob (2007). MyKnowledgeMap Drives UK's Biggest Mobile Learning Project. Press release. York, United Kingdom.

Liu, E. (2004). Peer and Self Assessment for Mobile Learning. In Cantoni, L., and McLoughlin, C. (eds.), *Proceedings of World Conference on Educational Multimedia, Hypermedia and Telecommunications 2004*, pp. 4370–4372.

Lomas, Natasha (2010). Want to Build a Mobile App? How to Convince the CFO. Silicon.com feature, February 11.

Marwaha, Alka (2009). Texting Disease Away. BBC News (Online), Tuesday, June 2.

McGreal, R., Tin, T., Cheung, B., and Schafer, S. (2005). The Athabasca University Digital Reading Room: Library Resources for Mobile Students. *Proceedings of the MLearn 2005*. Qawra, Malta: IADIS.

McLean, Neil (2003). The M-Learning Paradigm: An Overview. A Report for the Royal Academy of Engineering and the Vodafone Group Foundation.

McLuhan, Marshall (1951). *The Mechanical Bride: Folklore of Industrial Man*. New York: Vanguard Press.

McLuhan, Marshall (1962). *The Gutenberg Galaxy*. Toronto: University of Toronto Press.

McLuhan, Marshall (1964). *Understanding Media: The Extensions of Man*. New York: McGraw-Hill.

McLuhan, Marshall (1966). Art as Anti-Environment. *Art News*, May.

McLuhan, Marshall and Fiore, Quentin (1967). *The Medium Is the Massage: an inventory of effects*. New York: Bantam Books.

McLuhan, Marshall and Fiore, Quentin (1968). *War and Peace in the Global Village*. New York: Bantam Books.

Metcalf, D., Hamilton, A., and Graffeo, C. (2009). *Proceedings of mlearn 2009: 8th World Conference on Mobile and Contextual Learning*. The University of Central Florida.

Metcalf, D., Milrad, M., and Sousa Pires, J. (2006). Renaissance mLearning: A Renewed Mobile Strategy. *Proceedings of MLearn* 2006, Banff, Canada, October.

Metcalf, David (2002). "Stolen Moments for Learning: mLearning," *eLearning Developer's Journal,* March 2002.

Metcalf, David (2006*). mLearning: Mobile Learning and Performance in the Palm of Your Hand*. Amherst, MA: HRD Press.

Mintzberg, H., Ahlstrand, B., and Lampel, J. (1998). *Strategy Safari: A Guided Tour through the Wilds of Strategic Management*. New York: Free Press.

Moll, Cameron (2006). Mobile Web Design. Online presentation.

Moll, Cameron (2007). *Mobile Web Design: A Web Standards Approach for Delivering Content to Mobile Devices*. Salt Lake City, UT: Cameron Moll.

Morville, Peter (2005). *Ambient Findability: What We Find Changes Who We Become*. Sebastopol, CA: O'Reilly.

Mosher, B. and Gottfredson, C. (2009). M-Learning vs. M-Support — Mobile "Support": Is it the Next Generation of M-Learning. *Performer Support: Learning @ the Moment of Need,* February 6.

Mullins, Justin (2010). "How Crowdsourcing Is Helping Haiti," *New Scientist,* no. 2745, January 27.

Naismith, L., Lonsdale, P., Vavoula, G., and Sharples, M. (2004). *Literature Review in Mobile Technologies and Learning*. Bristol: NESTA FutureLab.

Naismith, L., Sharples, M., and Ting, J. (2005). "Evaluation of CAERUS: A Context Aware Mobile Guide. Mobile Technology: The Future of Learning in Your Hands," *mLearn 2005 Book of Abstracts*, 4th World Conference on mLearning.

Nantel, Richard (2001). *How To Determine Your Readiness for Mobile e-Learning*. Sunnyvale, CA: Brandon Hall Research.

Nightingale, Katherine (2009). "Mobile Phone Diagnosis Approaches Field Trials" *SciDev Net,* April 15.

Ninh, H., Tanaka, Y., Nakamoto, T. and Hamada, K. (2007). A Bad-Smell Network Using Gas Detector Tubes and Mobile Phone Cameras. *Sensors and Actuators B: Chemical.* 125(1), July 16, 138–143.

O'Malley, C., Vavoula, G., Glew, J. P., Taylor, J., Sharples, M., Lefrere, P., Lonsdale, P., Naismith, L., and Waycott, J. (2003). WP 4 - *Guidelines for Learning/Teaching/Tutoring in a Mobile Environment.* MOBIlearn Project Report, June 10.

O'Malley, C., Vavoula, G., Glew, J.P., Taylor, J., Sharples, M., Lefrere, P., Lonsdale, P., Naismith, L., and Waycott, J. (2005). WP 4 - *Pedagogical Methodologies and Paradigms: Guidelines for Learning/Teaching/Tutoring in a Mobile Environment.* MOBIlearn Project Report, March 29.

Omar, A., Liu, L., and Koong, K. (2008). "From Disaster Recovery to Mobile Learning: A Case Study," *International Journal of Mobile Learning and Organisation*, vol. 2, no. 1, pp. 4–17.

OnPoint Digital (2008). *CellCast Solutions Guide.* White Paper.

Ophir, E, Nass, C. I., and Wagner, A. D. (2009). Cognitive Control in Media Multitaskers, *Proceedings of the National Academies of Science*, vol. 106, pp. 15583–15587.

O'Reilly, Tim (2008). "Voice in Google Mobile App: a Tipping Point for the Web?" *O'Reilly Radar*, November 18.

Paay, Jeni (2008). "From Ethnography to Interface Design." In Lumsden, Joanna (ed.), *Handbook of Research on User Interface Design and Evaluation for Mobile Technology.* Hershey, PA: Information Science Reference.

Pachler, N., Bachmir, B., and Cook, J. (2010). *Mobile Learning: Structures, Agency and Practices.* Berlin: Springer.

Pachler, N., and Selpold, J. (eds.) (2009). *Mobile Learning Cultures across Education, Work and Leisure.* Book of Abstracts, 3rd WLE Mobile Learning Symposium, London, March 27.

Pachler, Norbert (2007). *Mobile Learning towards a Research Agenda.* Institute of Education, University of London, June 2007.

Pachler, Norbert (2009). "The London Mobile Learning Group Socio-Cultural Ecological Approach to Mobile Learning: An Overview." In Pachler, N., and Selpold, J. (eds.), *Mobile Learning Cultures Across Education, Work and Leisure* Book of Abstracts, 3rd WLE Mobile Learning Symposium, London, March 27, pp. 97–99.

Pentland, Alex (2008). *Honest Signals: How They Shape Our World.* Cambridge, MA: MIT Press.

Perry, David (2003). *Handheld Computers (PDAs) in Schools.* Becta research report, UK.

Peters, Kristine (2007). "m-Learning: Positioning Educators for a Mobile, Connected future," *International Review of Research in Open and Distance Learning,* vol. 8, no. 2, June.

Pillkahn, Ulf (2008). *Using Trends and Scenarios as Tools for Strategy Development: Shaping the Future of Your Enterprise.* Erlangen, Germany: Publicis.

Pimmer, C., and Grohbiel, U. (2008). "Mobile Learning in Corporate Settings: Results from an Expert Survey." *Proceedings of the mLearn2008 Conference.* October 7–10, 2008. Ironbridge Gorge, Shropshire, United Kingdome. pp. 248–255.

Pimmer, Christoph (2009). "Work-Based Mobile Learning in the Health Sector—Concept of a Mobile Learning System Exemplified by Educational Scenarios of Junior Doctors." In Pachler, N., and Selpold, J. (eds.), *Mobile Learning Cultures across Education, Work and Leisure.* Book of Abstracts, 3rd WLE Mobile Learning Symposium, London, March 27, pp. 69–73.

Porter, Michael (1985) *Competitive Advantage: Creating and Sustaining Superior Performance.* New York: Free Press.

Porter, Michael (2008). "The Five Competitive Forces that Shape Strategy", *Harvard Business Review*, January, p.86.

Pratt, D., Winters, N., Cerulli, M., and Leemkuil, H. (2009). "A Patterns Approach to Connecting the Design and Deployment of Mathematical Games and Simulations." In Balacheff, N., Ludvigsen, S., de Jong, T., Lazonder, A., and Barnes, S. (eds.) *Technology-Enhanced Learning.* Berlin: Springer, pp. 215–232.

Prensky, Marc (2005). "What Can You Learn from a Cell Phone? Almost Anything!" *Innovate*, vol. 1, no. 5, June/July 2005.

Quinn, Clark (2000). "mLearning: Mobile, Wireless, In-Your-Pocket Learning," *LineZine*, Fall.

Quinn, Clark (2007). Don't Dream It, Do It: m-Learning by Design. In Wexler, S. (ed.), Guild Research 360° Report on Mobile Learning.

Quinn, Clark (2008). "M-Learning Devices: Performance to Go," *Learning Circuits.*

Quinn-Votaw, Kathleen (2009). Social Media – Add Power to Recruiting. *BuzzSense Media*, November 29.

Rainie, Lee (2006). "Digital 'Natives' Invade the Workplace." Online article, Pew Research Center.

Rideout, V., Foehr, U., and Roberts, D. (2010). Generation M2: Media in the Lives of 8- to 18-Year-Olds. Kaiser Family Foundation Report.

Riener, A., Aly, M., and Ferscha, A. (2009). Heart on the Road: HRV Analysis for Monitoring a Driver's Affective State. First International Conference on Automotive User Interfaces and Interactive Vehicular Applications (AutomotiveUI 2009), September 21–22, Essen, Germany.

Ritzer, George (2007). *The McDonaldization of Society*, 5th ed. Newbury Park, CA: Pine Forge Press.

Rodriguez, Diego (2007). Quoted in McConnon, Aili (2007), "The Name of the Game Is Work," *BusinessWeek* (online), August 13.

Rosenberg, Jonathan (2008). Our Googley Advice to Students: Major in Learning. The Official Google Blog, July 15.

Rosselle, M., Leclet, D., and Talon, B. (2009). "Using USB Keys to Promote Mobile Learning," *International Journal of Interactive Mobile Technologies*, vol. 3, special issue, pp. 32–36.

Ryu, H., and Parsons, D. (eds.) (2009). *Innovative Mobile Learning: Techniques and Technologies*. Hershey, PA: Information Science Reference.

Savill-Smith, C., and Douch, R. (2009). "The Use of Mobile Learning to Break Down Barriers between Education and Work in Further Education." In Pachler, N., and Selpold, J. (eds.), *Mobile Learning Cultures Across Education, Work and Leisure*. Book of Abstracts, 3rd WLE Mobile Learning Symposium, London, March 27, pp. 75–77.

Schrage, Michael (1995). *No More Teams! Mastering the Dynamics of Creative Collaboration*. New York: Currency Doubleday.

Secker, Jane (2008). *Social Software, Libraries and Distance Learners*. Literature review. University of London, Centre for Distance Education.

Sharples, M. (2000). "The Design of Personal Mobile Technologies for Lifelong Learning," *Computers and Education*, vol. 34, pp. 177–193.

Sharples, M., and Beale, R. (2003). "A Technical Review of Mobile Computational Devices," *Journal of Computer Assisted Learning*, vol. 19, no. 3, pp. 392–395.

Sharples, M., Chan, T., Rudman, P., and Bull, S. (2004). "Evaluation of a Mobile Learning Organiser and Concept Mapping Tools." In Attewell, J., and Savill-Smith, C. (eds.), *Learning with Mobile Devices*. London: Learning and Skills Development Agency.

Sharples, M., Corlett, D., and Westmancott, O. (2002). "The Design and Implementation of a Mobile Learning Resource," *Personal and Ubiquitous Computing*, vol. 6, no. 3, pp. 220–234.

Sharples, M., Taylor, J., and Vavoula, G. (2007). "A Theory of Learning for the Mobile Age." In Andrews, R., and Haythornthwaite, C. (eds.), *The Sage Handbook of Elearning Research* London: Sage, pp. 221–47.

Sharples, Mike (2003). "Disruptive Devices: Mobile Technology for Conversational Learning," *International Journal of Continuing Engineering Education and Lifelong Learning*, vol. 12, no. 5/6, pp. 504–520.

Sharples, Mike (2005). Learning as Conversation: Transforming Education in the Mobile Age. Paper presented at Conference on Seeing, Understanding, Learning in the Mobile Age, Budapest, Hungary, April.

Sharples, Mike (ed.) (2007a). *Big Issues in Mobile Learning: Report of a Workshop by the Kaleidoscope Network of Excellence Mobile Learning Initiative*. Nottingham, UK: University of Nottingham, Learning Sciences Research Institute.

Sharples, Mike (2007b). A Short History of Mobile Learning . . . and Some Issues to Consider. Online presentation. mLearn, Doctoral Consortium.

Siebert, S., Mills, V., and Tuff, C. (2009). "Pedagogy of Work-Based Learning: The Role of the Learning Group," *Journal of Workplace Learning*, vol. 21, no. 6, pp. 443–454.

Siemens, George (2004). "Connectivism: A Learning Theory for the Digital Age," *elearnspace*, Dec. 12, (updated April 5, 2005).

Smith, Stuart (2009). Mobile Learning: Is It Worth It? *3 Sheep Blog*, July 3.

Stahl, Gerry (2006). *Group Cognition: Computer Support for Building Collaborative Knowledge*. Cambridge, MA: MIT Press.

St. Arnaud, Bill (2010a) iPhone slowing down the Internet – desperate need for 5G R&E networks. *Bill St. Arnaud Blog*, April 20.

St. Arnaud, Bill (2010b) Enabling innovation with next generation 5G Internet + clouds-technical details. *Bill St. Arnaud Blog*, April 25.

Sugden, D., and Soon, L. (2007). Engaging Students through SMS Messaging. Updated presentation from the Ferl 2003 Conference workshop.

Sweeny, Alastair (2009). *BlackBerry Planet: The Story of Research in Motion and the Little Device that Took the World by Storm*. Mississauga, Ontario, Canada: John Wiley & Sons.

*Telegraph* (2009). "Royal Navy Uses PlayStations to Train Sailors." Telegraph. co.uk, Nov. 27.

Tenno, Helge (2009a). Mobile Abilities Map. Online slide presentation. *180/360/720*, October 25.

Tenno, Helge (2009b) Post-Digital Marketing. Online slide presentation. *180/360/720*, July.

Tétard, F., Patokorpi, E., and Carlsson, J. (2008). A Conceptual Framework for Mobile Learning. Research Report 3/2008, Institute for Advanced Management Systems Research.

Tétard, F. and Patokorpi, E. (2008). A Theoretical Framework for Mobile Learning and E-Inclusion in Finland. *ICIS 2008 Proceedings*. Paper 52.

Traxler, J., and Kukulska-Hulme, A. (2005). Evaluating Mobile Learning: Reflections on Current Practice. *Proceedings of MLEARN 2005*, Cape Town.

Traxler, John (2002). Evaluating m-Learning. Proceedings of the European Workshop on Mobile and Contextual Learning, The University of Birmingham, England.

Traxler, John (2003a). Evaluation Issues. *Proceedings of 2003 Conference on Mobile Learning: Reaching the parts the others don't reach*. University of Wolverhampton, United Kingdom.

Traxler, John (2003b). Mlearning—Evaluating the Effectiveness and the Cost. *Proceedings of MLEARN 2003: Learning with Mobile Devices*. London,: Learning and Skills Development Agency, pp. 183–188.

Traxler, John (2004). Mobile Learning—Content and Delivery. Online presentation. Telford, United Kingdom: Learning Lab.

Traxler, John (2009a). "Current State of Mobile Learning." In Mohamed Ally (ed.) *Mobile Learning: Transforming the Delivery of Education and Training.* Edmonton, Canada: Athabasca University Press, pp. 9–24.

Traxler, John (2009b). "Learning in a Mobile Age," *International Journal of Mobile and Blended Learning*, vol. 1, no, 1, pp. 1–12.

Traxler, John (2009c). "The Evolution of Mobile Learning." In Guy, Retta (ed.), *The Evolution of Mobile Teaching and Learning.* Santa Rosa, CA: Informing Science Press, pp. 1–14.

Tretiakov, A. and Kinshuk (2005). *Creating a Pervasive Testing Environment by Using SMS Messaging.* Paper presented at the IEEE International Workshop on Wireless and Mobile Technologies in Education, Tokushima, Japan, Nov. 28–30.

Tselios, N., Katsanos, C., and Avouris, N (2007a). Beyond User Centered Design: A Web Design Approach Based on Information Foraging Theory, Proceedings of Workshop Are New Methods Needed in User-Centered System Design?, INTERACT 2007, Rio de Janeiro, Brazil, September.

Tselios, N., Katsanos, C., Kahrimanis, G., and Avouris, N. (2007b). "Design and Evaluation of Web-Based Learning Environments Using Information

Foraging Models." In Pahl, C. (ed.), *Architecture Solutions for E-Learning Systems*. Idea Group Publishers.

Tucker, T., and Winchester, W. (2009). Mobile Learning for Just-in-Time Applications. Paper presented at the ACMSE '09 Conference, Clemson, SC, , March 19–21.

Turkle, Sherry (2009). Interview. PBS Web site, for program *Frontline: Digital Nation—Life on the Virtual Frontier*.

Vavoula, G. N. (2005). D4.4: A Study of Mobile Learning Practices. MOBIlearn project report.

Vavoula, G. N., Kukulska-Hulme, A., and Pachler, N. (eds.) (2007). *Research Methods in Informal and Mobile Learning*. WLE Centre, London.

Vavoula, G. N., Lefrere, P., O'Malley, C., Sharples, M., and Taylor, J. (2003). Producing Guidelines for Learning, Teaching and Tutoring in a Mobile Environment. Paper presented at the WMTE 2003 Conference, Taiwan.

Vavoula, G. N., and Sharples, M. (2002). "KLeOS: A Personal, Mobile, Knowledge and Learning Organisation System." In Milrad, M., Hoppe, U., and Kinshuk (eds.), *Proceedings of the IEEE International Workshop on Mobile and Wireless Technologies in Education* (WMTE2002), August 29–30 Vaxjo, Sweden, pp. 152–156.

Vavoula, G. N., and Sharples, M. (2007). "Future Technology Workshop: A Collaborative Method for the Design of New Learning Technologies and Activities," *International Journal of Computer-Supported Collaborative Learning*, vol. 2, no. 4, pp. 393–419.

Veeramani, R., and Bradley, S. (2008). Insight Regarding Undergraduate Preference for Lecture Capture. Research Report, University of Wisconsin-Madison E-Business Institute.

von Koschembahr, Christopher (2005). Mobile Learning: The Next Evolution of Education. *Chief Learning Officer*, February.

Vygotsky, L. S. (1978). *Mind in Society: Development of Higher Psychological Processes*. Boston: Harvard University Press.

Wali, Esra (2007). Are They Doing What They Think They're Doing? Tracking and Triangulating Students' Learning Activities and Self Reports. *Proceedings, Research Methods in Informal and Mobile Learning Conference*. Work-based and Learning for Education professionals centre (WLE), Institute of Education, London.

Wally, B., Ferscha, A., and Lenger, M. (2009). Presence Sensing Billboards. *Proceedings of the 2nd International Workshop on Pervasive*

*Advertising* (in Conjunction with Informatik 2009), Lübeck, Germany, September.

Wang, Yuan-Kai. (2004). Context Awareness and Adaption in Mobile Learning. *Proceedings of the 2nd IEEE International Workshop on Wireless and Mobile Technologies in Education* (WMTE '04).

Watson, Thomas J, Jr. (1914–1993). Quote from http://www.brainyquote.com.

Wei, J., and Lin, B. (2008). Development of a Value Increasing Model for Mobile Learning. *Proceedings of the Decision Sciences Institute Conference*, Baltimore, Nov. 22–25.

Weyrich, Claus (2008). "The Future is Partly Made of Clay." Foreword to Pillkahn, Ulf, *Using Trends and Scenarios as Tools for Strategy Development: Shaping the Future of Your Enterprise*. Erlangen, Germany: Publicis, 5–6.

Winters, Niall (2007). "Design Patterns for Mobile Learning." In Arnedillo-Sanchez, I., Sharples, M., and Vavoula, G. (eds.), *Proceedings of the Beyond Mobile Learning Workshop*. Dublin: Trinity College Dublin Press.

Wintrup, J., Foskett, R., and James, L. (2009). "Work-Based Learning and Student Agency: Developing Strategic Learners." In Pachler, N., and Selpold, J. (eds.), *Mobile Learning Cultures across Education, Work and Leisure* Book of Abstracts, 3rd WLE Mobile Learning Symposium, London, March 27, pp. 31–33.

Wood, A., and Woodill, G. (2008). *Learning Technologies for Healthcare Education and Training*. Sunnyvale, CA: Brandon Hall Research.

Wood, J., Price, G., et al. (2002). Mobile Devices for Breast Care: A Personalised Education Information Profiling System (PEIPS). *Proceedings of the European Workshop on Mobile and Contextual Learning*, The University of Birmingham, England.

Wood, J., Keen, A., Basu, N., and Robertshaw, S. (2003). The Development of Mobile Applications for Patient Education. *Proceedings of Designing for User Experiences* (DUX), San Francisco.

Woodill, G., Fell, D., and Woodill, C. (2008). *Planning and Evaluating Business Needs for an Enterprise Learning Management System*. Sunnyvale, CA: Brandon Hall Research.

Woodill, G., and Oliveira, C. (2006). "Mashups, SOAP, and Services: Welcome to Web Hybrid e-Learning Applications," *Learning Solutions Magazine*, May 15.

Woodill, Gary (2008). *Mobile Learning Comes of Age: How and Why Organizations Are Moving to Learning on Mobile Devices.* Sunnyvale, CA: Brandon Hall Research.

Woodill, Gary (2009). Hacking My Heart. *Brandon Hall Analyst Blog*, April 6.

Zeleny, Milan (2007). "The Mobile Society: Effects of Global Sourcing and Network Organisation," *International Journal of Mobile Learning and Organisation*, vol. 1, no. 1, pp. 30–40.

Zurita, G., and Nussbaum, M. (2002). Evaluating m-Learning. *Proceedings of the European Workshop on Mobile and Contextual Learning*, The University of Birmingham, England.

Zurita, G., and Nussbaum, M. (2004). "Computer Supported Collaborative Learning Using Wirelessly Interconnected Handheld Computers," *Computers and Education*, vol. 42, no. 3, pp. 289–314.

Zurita, G., Nussbaum, M., and Sharples, M. (2003). Encouraging Face-to-Face Collaborative Learning through the Use of Hand-Held Computers in the Classroom. *Proceedings of Mobile HCI 2003*. Udine, Italy: Springer-Verlag pp. 193–208.

# Index

Note: Boldface numbers indicate illustrations.

# About The Author

**G**ary Woodill is an independent emerging technologies analyst, who works for a variety of clients in researching and planning for their use of new tools for learning. He has been involved with computers in education since 1974, when he was introduced to the PLATO system for computer-assisted instruction in his master's studies in educational psychology. He helped develop educational materials for a Canadian videotext system in the late 1970s, and in 1985 started a course for teachers on computers in education at Ryerson University in Toronto. In 1984 Woodill received a doctorate in applied psychology from the Ontario Institute for Studies in Education (OISE) at the University of Toronto, and in 1993 he cofounded an educational multimedia company that developed educational CD-ROMs for children. In 1998 he designed an adaptable learning management system and has developed more than sixty online courses for various corporate clients. Woodill is coauthor of *Training and Collaboration with Virtual Worlds* (McGraw-Hill, 2010) and is the author of numerous articles and research reports on emerging learning technologies. He lives with his wife in Gore's Landing, Ontario.